Jan 2018

PRAISE FOR IAIN SINCLAIR

'Sinclair's prose is exquisite.'   Will Self

'Sentence for sentence, there is no more interesting writer at work in English.'   John Lanchester

'Anyone who cares about English prose cares about Iain Sinclair, a demented magus of the sentence. He is a sublime archaeologist of the present.'   James Wood

'Sinclair is a poet of the marginal, the interstitial, the forgotten and the occulted… I'm very glad Hackney has him to record its grubby, glorious weirdness.'   Hari Kunzru

'Sinclair's prose is vertiginous and polychromatic… a master of the literary collage.'   Peter Ackroyd

'The wildfire in Sinclair's writing has been focused… to a roaring blue lance of acetylene, bending hard language into thrilling new shapes with its heat and dazzle.'   Alan Moore

'A peerless London literary wanderer and street-level cultural archaeologist… delirious, often hilarious urban palimpsest where pin-sharp observation, cultural hauntings and offbeat memoir fuse in sentences that catch your breath like a lurid toxic sunset over Hackney Marshes.'
Independent

'No one has ever written quite like Iain Sinclair. He will, without doubt, prove the indelible diarist of our age – our post-punk Samuel Pepys.'   *Observer*

'Erudite, ingenious, exhilarating, involving, unpredictable, enchanting.'
Spectator

'He is incapable of writing a dull paragraph.'   *Scotland on Sunday*

'Sinclair walks every inch of his wonderful novels and psycho-geographies, pacing out huge word-courses like an architect laying out a city on an empty plain.'   JG Ballard

'Dazzling word-wizardry, unsettling and illuminating... so accomplished a stylist that he can (and indeed frequently does) write his way out of a lay-by.'   *Independent on Sunday*

'On Sinclair's territory there's nobody to touch him.'   *Sunday Times*

'The truest, most knowledgeable living writer on London.'
Evening Standard

'Sharp, astute... Sinclair is a London visionary and a crackling prose writer, he sees and maps esoteric connections.'   *Daily Telegraph*

'Sinclair breathes wondrous life into monstrous man-made landscapes.'
Times Literary Supplement

'His writing is so good it's invisible. Nothing escapes Sinclair's eye.'
Time

'If you are drawn to English that doesn't just sing, but sings the blues and does scat and rocks the joint, try Sinclair. His sentences deliver a rush like no one else's.   *Washington Post*

'[Sinclair's] is a style both measured and sumptuously wild – a beautiful, obsessive and individual style.'   *New York Times Book Review*

'A prose stylist almost without peer.'   *San Francisco Chronicle*

'One of Sinclair's greatest skills has always been his ability to take diverse if not chaotic source material and refashion it in a way that sometimes seems downright alchemical. Once Sinclair starts making connections he finds them everywhere... hard-edged, inventive, often wildly extravagant.'   *Los Angeles Times*

THE
LAST
LONDON

Also by Iain Sinclair

THE
LAST
LONDON

True Fictions from an Unreal City

IAIN SINCLAIR

ONEWORLD

A Oneworld Book

First published by Oneworld Publications, 2017

ISBN 978-1-78607-174-3
eISBN 978-1-78607-175-0

Printed and bound in Great Britain by Clays Ltd, St Ives plc

Oneworld Publications
10 Bloomsbury Street
London WC1B 3SR

Stay up to date with the latest books,
special offers, and exclusive content from
Oneworld with our monthly newsletter

Sign up on our website
oneworld-publications.com

FSC
www.fsc.org
MIX
Paper from
responsible sources
FSC® C018072

For the Five

Contents

'But sometimes the street spills over me, too much to absorb, and I have to stop thinking and keep walking.'

    – Don DeLillo

'I went againe to the ruins; for it was no longer a Citty.'

    – John Evelyn

LOSING

DANCERS ON THE BEACH

'We're right on the crest of a slump,' said the football manager, in the soft west-country burr that was his career-defining gimmick. He made it sound like a boast. '*Royt* on the crest of a slump.'

The sea did its thing. For three days, while we recovered from the walk, and there was no let up in the stream of bad news, the counter-narrative outcomes, posthumous predictions, debates and discussions under bright lights, the reflex demands for increased surveillance, tighter border controls, I kept my back to the wall, and stayed where I was on the cold concrete ledge, waiting and watching. The sea didn't care. The horizon was smoke with armed patrol boats. The mildly satirical stencil by Banksy, flattering bankers with a gentle dig, the kind of English wall movie stars like to collect, was protected by a Perspex screen put up by the council within hours of the cartoon's appearance. 'Heritage,' they said. 'Regeneration confirmed.' In the world at large, those two-dimensional outlines, the inarticulate blobs, were taking over the comic strips.

I started the countdown, a game with myself: that same evening the Banksy was being described on local TV news, just before the weather slot, as 'iconic'. A tribute to the edginess of a resort that would soon be called 'the next Hoxton'. St Leonards-on-Sea or *Shore-ditch*. They took the unstoppable tipping of sand in the hour-glass, Hackney to Hastings, as a statement of optimistic intent: artists settling, mobbing like gulls at the tideline, after being expelled from their London warehouses and railway arches. The only way I could hear the word iconic without grimacing was to immediately substitute *moronic*. Then it worked. Then it made perfect sense.

The relentless winter tide, having peevishly stacked a dune of shingle and sharp brown pebbles over the lower promenade, right up to the alcoves where rough-sleepers nested, had withdrawn, a few hundred yards closer to France. There was now a wet strip of sand, a beach on which an estranged couple were trying to dance to the hiss of a soundbox, while beating off the excited attentions of a large black dog, determined – with a freshly evacuated colon – to leave dirty paw prints on the male's tight canary suit.

This unforgiving yellow silk, the colour of a particularly malevolent processed-cheese slice, was well on the far side of brave: the lumpen samba-spoiler was professionally groomed, but porcine. His stiffly ridged hair-helmet was icecream-whipped. Under a generous rendering of face powder, the man couldn't sweat. A dad-dancer confident of approval ratings for his multi-talentless cavortings: that English adoration of the amateur presenting failure or disgrace as a badge of forgiveable sincerity. Never apologise, eat your worms and scorpions in the jungle. Embrace shame.

The dancer has a rictus grin of triumph at every semaphored gesture held, one nano-second too long, for the applause of the absent audience. (Audiences are thoroughly schooled in mass hysteria. The media is gaseous Babble, lurching between horror-porn and tears. 'So how do you *feel*?') He didn't glide, he punched. He thrust his bulging thighs at imaginary clefts. He simulated simulation. He self-pleasured. Always just that half-beat behind the tinny ya-ya-ya of the tribute mariachi combo.

I thought, at first, when I saw the couple silhouetted against the skeletal ruin of the burnt-out pier that it was a promotional video of some kind. An internet punt intended to boost the town by rehearsed spontaneity, weirdness going viral. I thought, as they clasped, that two men were really dancing; one of them a bouncer, still in gear, and the other in leisurewear or sleepsuit: tights, hooded trackie. Not so. The other was a woman. And the woman had the moves. She drilled the man. Then, bruised by his punchbag vigour, stepped back, to let him go it alone, as she clapped. She retreated, laid out a mat, and went through some deconditioning yoga poses.

Left to himself, and the endlessly looping track, the dancer's jerks and pelvic spasms were obscene. As were his triumphant smiles. They reminded me of popular prints from paintings by Jack Vettriano, slick products crafted from photographs: zombie dancers on the shore accompanied by *Downton Abbey* servants with umbrellas. Vettriano's interiors, where clothed males groped hired models in authentic suspenders, were bought by discriminating collectors, such as Sir Alex Ferguson and Jack Nicholson.

Planks of decking timber, salvaged from the petrol-bombed pier, were crafted into long dining tables and benches of the refectory kind favoured by pop-up Hackney bars and underground cafés. With a sales pitch combining artisan knots, rusty nails and virtuous recycling, and a splinter of sentiment for the good old days, the rescued pier furniture now dressed a thriving street of down-from-London shops. Camden Passage on Sea. Brighton Lanes and Russian-patronised kinos.

As the diarist John Evelyn remarked, after another conflagration, the Great Fire of 1666: 'London was, but is no more.' The city of words, referencing other words, etymologies of respect, was done. The metropolitan virtues and vices of former times had migrated, with the property boom, the rent hikes and fire sales of public housing, to the coast: a strategic destruction of the local. Seaside post offices were shut, jobs lost, counter services removed to a shopping-mall branch of WH Smith. With the brigandry given a positive spin as forcing obese geriatrics to take exercise by hobbling a mile or more into town. There were no trains on which to rely, but legions of disgruntled drivers, guards and travellers. Blue-and-white tape decorated the latest hit-and-run death sites. Self-medicators were followed around the shelves of pharmacies where they employ more security guards than nightclubs or supermarkets. Raging afternoon drinkers ram-raided budget vodka bottles from Asian minimarts before another evening breaking up benches for warmth. Awayday beggars tried their luck on a reserved pitch outside the Co-op's automatic doors. The asylum seekers, who once stared at the sea, and attempted conversation with independent female swimmers, were banished again, shipped further inland. Vast, empty churches rubbed

5

along on marriages of convenience between African men and ladies from Eastern Europe to whom they had not previously been introduced. This was London as it used to be, a broken democracy of warring clans; humans making the best of the mess in which they had landed themselves. Damaged content for the next bulletin.

Back in 1909, Ford Madox Ford, in an essay on 'The Future in London', predicted all of this: that London, our stretched city, would encompass Oxford, Cambridge and the south-coast settlements, a sixty-mile sweep from Threadneedle Street. Proving his theory with action, Ford relocated to Winchelsea. He said: 'It has to got to come. All south-eastern England is just London.'

I had walked here – and I would soon walk on, I'm not sure where – because my sense was that London, my home for fifty years, was being centrifugally challenged to the point of obliteration; of being unable to say just where, and why, it began and ended. I gave some credence to the notion certain scholars floated that London came into existence as a colonising strategy by the Romans: lay on baths, brothels, market places, and they will come. The scattered tribes and brutish hut dwellers would be unable to resist the buzz of the polis, the walled city, the hub. Its noise and movement. Its exotic goods and people. It worked for me. And there was material too, in slowly unpicking my ignorance and decoding the marks and signs, to provide the labour of a lifetime. Books that experimented with so many forms of failure, appropriate to different eras, until everything changed: the actual gave way to the virtual.

Roberto Bolaño writes somewhere about being in Berlin – there are riot police, fires still burning in the street – and finding German avenues dissolving into Blanes, into his place of Spanish exile, a seaside resort. It is not a translation, a trip, but a superimposition with no blurred edges. One city is another city; all the places of a fugitive life and career are a single cancerous cell. London is like that now, more a part of other expanded conurbations than of England: the real aliens are in Sunderland, Hull, Stoke-on-Trent. As the publication of books, what would once have been called a literary career, became little more than the excuse for presentations and themed 'Edgelands' readings in universities, galleries, shops and hospitals that looked just the same, generically neutral, faintly paranoid, with background hum of white noise, so my grip on the city that provoked and sustained my fictions faded. London was everywhere, but it had lost its soul.

Transposing the Hackney circuit that I walked every morning to Berlin, Paris, Liège, Seattle, Vancouver, Guadalajara, I never felt that I had moved far beyond the gravity of London. In Madrid, the same sleeping bag was positioned outside the same McDonald's burger franchise. And I'd swear that the same man was inside it. Across the ridges of a shuttered property, a failed nailbar, was the same Boris Johnson graffito. In Barcelona, I noticed a cycle-repair shop beside a hipster café, beside the plaque for the dead Roberto Bolaño. Local differences are minimal. In the traditional Barcelona restaurant favoured for after-Edgelands-conference meals were signed photographs of Orson Welles, Ava Gardner and Gary Lineker. In Madrid, it was Orson Welles, Ava Gardner and Gareth Bale.

On the road to the airport, which Ballard told me was the same in every capital, I noticed a hoarding for BEEFEATER – like a CGI vision of our own post-Olympic metropolis. THIS IS MY LONDON, it said. Brilliant blue canal. Regent Street. Buck House. Big Ben and Elizabeth Tower. Airbrushed Hogarth for a Hackney Wick gallerist's gin-rinse, not total submersion in madness and despair. THIS IS LONDON for a character with Mohican hair-prong, red leather dog collar and cool-guy-mascara. Fun city. Rich city. Fusion city. The man was David Muñoz, a Michelin-star cook, who flits between Madrid and London, working in Asian restaurants. He is married to a television presenter. Ballard could have made him up. MADRID CHEF TO BRING SHOCKING FOOD TO LONDON OUTPOST. That's what London is, an outpost.

And there was one other thing: in every city I visited, if I had time to identify the most promising and hidden-away bookshop, the owner would, quite shyly, ask after Martin Stone. Martin was someone I knew, many years ago, when I was beginning to publish London fiction. He was held in universal esteem and something approaching awe. It seemed that he existed outside time, being a contemporary of Arthur Machen, Martin Amis and Djuna Barnes. Books came to him for validation and received his pencilled price with a neat bracket for the edition and date. He was a Croydon boy everywhere, a once and future legend.

In Palermo, I witnessed London's future in the shape of monumental cruise liners parked along the harbour. And in Barcelona, the same floating tourist cities, brilliantly lit all through the night, devouring energy, taking full advantage of the Catalan capital's post-Olympic development status. The electively stateless passengers, gold-card consumers of international attractions, come ashore to shop, do the relevant museums, drink, nibble tapas (just like London), and take digital photographs of themselves against postcard backdrops. Our cities are becoming electrified iceberg liners, islands from which the underclass can be excluded; liners serviced by zero-hour contracted serfs. In time, the floating cities will be the only safe places in which to patrol the world's oceans. Sealife: perpetual tourism. With cinemas, gyms, theatres, private hospitals and cycle lanes.

Behind me an ambulance screamed on the coast road. The concrete hulk of a 1930s building modelled on the *Queen Mary* was as close as the south coast of England, home to London's dispersed economic migrants, would ever come to the cruise-liner lifestyle. I knew that I would have to book passage on a boat going nowhere when I started to see the carriages of the London Overground service as a schematic map. For several years, after the trauma of 2012, I had been walking in ever-increasing circles around the linked-up Overground railway; a workable metaphor for futility. Then, one morning, I really looked at the train. Three bands of colour: the paprika-orange of the shingle shore, a blue band for the sea, and the white of the Regency houses and chalk cliffs. Even the transport systems were telling me to get out.

The thuggish dancer in the tight yellow suit, now darkened around the armpits, threw his right arm high in the air. *Yes!* His partner had gone, carrying off the soundbox. This was where we were now. It was time to start work.

HMS *HAGGERSTON PARK*

'No one ever glances at people sitting on benches.'
Georges Simenon

He sits, slumps. Slithers. And settles. His back to the red bricks. Curvature of spine. No spine. A Vegetative Buddha on a hard bench. In a cloister. In a modest London park. I notice him, planted in his very particular space, soon after the park opens its gates, and he is there again on my return, late in the afternoon, before this high-walled oasis closes for the night. He is furniture, a fixture. A muddy root dragged from the earth. And left without nutrients. Exposed to sight.

The man has not moved, not once in all those hours. Perhaps his head has tilted a degree or so to starboard, a couple of inches closer to the heaving chest. He's hooded, dark-wrapped in the fur tatters of an overwintered Antarctic parka. He is evidence, an escapee from a recently discovered Edwardian photograph. A solid ghost from the sustaining darkness of a box camera rescued from melting ice.

How long does it take to become a ghost? To become part of the city in which you are lost?

A green prophylactic sheath, so green that it is almost black, shrouds this man's unthinkable nakedness. Listen. A hissing puncture of breath eddies a track through the daisy–dusted grass. His heart-beat slows to the point of stopping altogether, being absorbed into the pulse of place. And ours in surreptitiously watching him. The Vegetative Buddha anchors the city, the bow of the spine hooked to his ribbed bench. I am fascinated by his physical presence, the discipline of staying just where he is through the waste of daylight:

9

no food, no drink, no cigarettes. No digital devices. He is definitively off-line, definitively present. He challenges everything I think I know, the sorry accumulation of facts and broken histories required to facilitate my continued passage through familiar locations. My daily confirmation of self by witnessing the same structures, the same people in the same places. The man is wedged and supported by pillows of reeking ballast, carrier bags for protection not storage. Slogan visible: EVERY LITTLE HELPS.

Some of us walk, some wait. They sit or stand, unmoving, meat statues. This Haggerston Park slump was more disturbing: there was no escape mechanism, no ladder of language. The man on the bench was kept alive by the southwards drift of London towards the weather of money: hipster Shoreditch, the City and the river, the dream of a shining future in which we are all supposed to share. And to suffer for, in dust and dirt. Poverty and welcome death.

Within the opened parenthesis of this special enclosure – the former gas works, the filled-in canal basin undefiled by excesses of boosterism and regeneration – early walkers, joggers and canine accompanists stay resolutely inside their bubbles of entitlement. They swerve to avoid collisions, nodding acknowledgement only when it is strictly necessary. The sitting man is an invisible, a kind of human shrub; a dim, light-absorbing shape curtained by wisteria. They don't see him, he isn't there. And his own sight, the intensely local reach of his attention, redacts their nuisance contrails. They are unwelcome zephyrs. He drinks the agitated straw of their fretful momentum. And sneezes. Twice. And then once more.

Haggerston Park joggers are a different stripe to the gang who have colonised the towpath of the Regent's Canal. Those stylishly aerodynamic models, Silicon Roundabout athletes in their considered colours (green, lately, to complement the duckweed), take breakfast meetings as they run. They are aware of how they seem and how they want to seem. They advance, elbows out, barging aside mere pedestrians. Their pretty ears are plugged with devices. They are prepared to lease the view to invading TV crews lining up yet another gritty composition that takes in railway bridge, gasholder, and the ivy-choked and intermittently squatted gothic hutch alongside Empress Coaches. Fit young women haul accessorised dogs that are killing themselves to keep up. These wretched creatures are not allowed to shit: ever, anywhere. The canal is a double-banked street of narrow-boats with tricky names. Some of the boat people unclip slim-wheeled bicycles to join the peloton.

In Haggerston Park, a circuit of wood chippings, sodden in season, has been laid out against the high brick walls, past the gate where James Mason staggered and died in the Belfast snow of Carol Reed's 1947 film of *Odd Man Out*. But the track is too obvious an intervention and the body-image gladiators avoid it. But my man, the Buddha of the benches, is quite impervious to the passing figures that thump or stagger through his fixed frame. He is in a deeper trance: damaged, post-operative, on licence, somewhere close to persistent vegetative abdication of sensibility.

There used to be a Vietnamese couple, or Cambodian perhaps, man and wife, connected to the Shoreditch restaurants or the Community Centre in Whiston Road. They marched, briskly, in silence, no nod or wink when their paths crossed: he clockwise, she counterclockwise, around the plastic football pitches. They disappeared right after the 2012 Olympic moment.

The Romanian (or Armenian or Kurdish) women – my shameful ignorance of the Babel languages of the city hurts – are sociable and determined, faithful attenders at their early exercise klatch. I first noticed them as a group of five or six; strong, dark, contained; shaped after the fashion of Russian dolls. They conversed as they made their circuits, which extended incrementally, with no visible upgrade in pace, around the entire park; the southern section with the woodland walk, and then the enclosed northern portion invigilated by the unrecognised Buddha on his bench.

Two white women, blondes, they might be mother and daughter, approached each other, down the whole length of the straight path visible to the slumped figure with his back to the wall. If he had lifted his head from his chest. If he felt the need to register this trivial intervention. The passing scene. How buoyant, how fresh and bright the women were, that morning. How pleased, even surprised, to come across one another, as they travelled in opposite directions, in this place. The older, slightly heavier one was waving and laughing. Or so I thought, until they crossed without a flicker of recognition, and I saw that the 'mother' was yapping into her fist-phone. That the 'daughter' was counting her paces, achieving the required footfall for her exercise regime.

The park's defining quality was its partial enclosure: the high wall behind the sitting man's cloister, and the green wall to the south, beyond the toilet block, and the open fence on to the fitful stream of Queensbridge Road to his right. There was living history here, undispersed by improvers and salaried exploiters. An atmosphere that drew in London solitaries, along with fair-weather rug sprawlers, amateur and professional dog walkers, knots of uniformed Academy kids, and browsers of a certain dispensation testing the rose-scented and lavender-drenched air. No barbecues, no silver-torpedo whippets and shredded condom balloons. There were few published prohibitions but Haggerston Park never attracted the flash-mob hordes, the convention of chattering charcoal burners overspilling from Broadway Market into London Fields with no reference to the back story of resting geese, traumatised sheep and cattle taking a last munch before the tramp to Smithfield and slaughter. The road at the edge of the park is aspirational. An approved cycle track – they count the numbers – negotiating a spanking property cliff, growing floor by floor in the night, covertly, wrapped in flapping sheets like a Christo. And a City Farm. Cockcrow drowned by drills and sirens. The heartbreaking resignation of donkeys. Therapeutic animals on contaminated land.

The park of the Vegetative Buddha is an island, a refuge. He is Crusoe, electively shipwrecked on a daily basis, vanishing at nightfall, before returning to the precise position, marked out by stains of cold sweat and leaking body liquors, that is his and his alone. His ears are stopped to excited languages from every quarter of the globe. London is a magnificent plurality, an iteration of potentialities: new lives, new beginnings. The bared ice dentures of the City skyline on the southern horizon glint with invitation. There is no patch of ground on this earth beyond the reach of that insatiable bite. There is no corrupt fortune, no spurious liquidity of kleptocrats and arms-dealers that cannot be sweetened within a couple of miles of this park. But within the close folds, within the posthumous dream of the man on the bench, London is a treasure trove of particulars. The new-builds and transformed children's hospitals, the betrayed schools and bathhouses, speak of uniformity; gleaming surfaces, secure access, present debt and future profit. London as a suburb of everywhere: Mexico City, Istanbul, Athens. The same malls. The same managed alienation. The Babel of misunderstood tongues. In *Soft City*, back in 1974, Jonathan Raban admitted his confusion. 'Turned to a dizzied tourist myself, forgetful and jet-shocked, I have to hunt my head for the language spoken here.' We are transformed, as Raban anticipated, into dumb tourists in our own midden. 'But this is where you live; it's your city,' he said. 'London, or New York, or wherever – and its language is the language you've always known, the language from which being you, being me, are inseparable.'

The bench in the Haggerston cloister is steerage class, attracting new citizens and those who hope to achieve that status. They sit in the shadows, glugging on Red Bull, waiting for who knows what. Then departing for other benches, other parks, buses on which they will be challenged, properties where, if they arrive at the right hour, they might be allowed inside. Offered soup and a bed. Our hooded man, thick legged, heavy bodied, a deadweight, does not stir.

The low ceiling of the cloister can be touched by an upright six-foot man. Above the ceiling, masked in a profusion of wisteria, is the bridge of the ship, an observation platform favoured by unsanctioned teenage lovers. Most frequently Asian. And sometimes rough-sleeping Polish builders in body bags.

The frame of the view that the man on the bench continues to ignore is confirmed by two columns like stacks of carefully positioned brick doughnuts. Thin columns strangled by the gnarled trunk of the wisteria. There are flagstones in front of him, four lines, slabs with bumps and bubucles, open pores. The cracks between the slabs are dirt-encrusted, mortised with cigarette butts. Then a neat border of grey bricks, a cambered path, more bricks, furled cypresses in pots, and the carpet of grass on which twenty-three dogs, leads tangled, are trying to revert to a pack. The man on the bench absorbs it all, fixes the agitation with rigorous disinterest. Around him and beyond him, the conversations of dog people. The groaning of the last-breath jogger. The synchronised march of economic migrants. The back strut of the hard bench, offering support to his boneless mass, touched a nerve at the base of the spine, tapping the stored sunshine in the bricks, the breathless shifts and shimmers of the leaves and plants. The susurration of the drooping willow tent. Undisturbed in the shallows of Haggerston Park, our Vegetative Buddha is part of a climate of managed despair. He is outside time. And beyond language. His silence provokes our talk. His stillness our motion. He is learning to fade from his own consciousness and thus from the reach of a city that has no use for him.

Within the restless nightmare of the man on the bench, in which I am now trespassing, while trying to take no conspicuous notice, old stories flicker. From 1832, after the cutting of the canal system, and the swinish rush of exploiters responding to a revised geography, the Imperial Gas Light and Coke Company took over this ground, old market gardens and brick kilns, for their operations. A substantial part of the northern portion of the present park became a basin for coal-carrying barges. There were feeder ponds. Through the eyes of the Vegetative Buddha I saw water instead of grass. One morning, after a night of storms and heavy rain, immediately after the Brexit decision, the ill-considered quitting of Europe, gesture politics of the most stupid kind, Haggerston Park became a lake, herring gulls floating in strategic occupation.

Where did that name come from, Haggerston? Norseman's Hergotstane. Or Agostane: as John Rocque's map of 1746 has it. Hackerstone dissolving into stoned hackers. The walkers, rushing, striding out, chasing, are addicts, convinced that there is an improved and edited version of the world to be transfused through the pulsing tablet in the hand. They are wedded to these digital phylacteries, carried everywhere to announce an irrational faith in dangerously corrupted information systems.

On 29th July 1992, a helicopter landed in the park, breaking the code of silence. There were other noises from busy roads, Whiston and Queensbridge and Hackney. From dogs. And crows. And chickens. There was visual noise too, from spray cans, upbeat slogans, fences shielding music festivals. Red helicopters ferried road victims to the Royal London Hospital. Police helicopters from High Beach, on the edge of Epping Forest, hovered at twilight, reminding malcontents and post-code affiliations that they were under 24-hour observation. But the intrusion on that July day was unexpected. From the shining pod emerged a weird anthropomorphic couple, genetically modified rodents, honeymooners perhaps, Mickey and Minnie Mouse. Attended by their plutocrat Hollywood patron, Michael Jackson. He was trembling and waving, like one of the undead in aviator shades, on his way to another recorded charitable visitation at the Queen Elizabeth Hospital for Children in Hackney Road.

From the skies again, 15th March 1945: god's fire. A V2 rocket from Peenemünde achieved a direct hit on a Haggerston gasholder. Earth shuddering. Epoch defining. Oral histories recalled, as bright as ever, in old age. In that retina-tearing flash was an archive of deleted sepia landmarks: the Nag's Head pub, Tuilerie Street of the tile-makers, coal barges supplying the cylindrical iron retort in which London's gas was manufactured.

Wilderness, not to be tolerated – rubble, convolvulus, sycamore – was sanctioned as parkland in 1956 and opened to the public in 1958. The design by Rupert Lyell Thorpe, an old naval hand and jobbing London County Council architect, was shipshape, invoking the concrete boat buildings of the Thirties, beached avatars of the Queen Mary, like Marine Court in St Leonards-on-Sea. HMS *Haggerston Park*: a realised vision. A cruise ship with brick superstructure and meadowed deck was moored beside the canal, as part of an armada of imperial nostalgia, before casting off to conquer the unknown – in company with the weathervane galleon waiting for a fair wind above the decommissioned Haggerston Baths in Whiston Road.

The Vegetative Buddha's sightline, between the twin cypress trees, across the pond of grass, led to a giant compass in the form of a sundial. The flagpole, to starboard, by the raised bandstand area, was once a mast, dressed with a long spar, a main yard. Curved brick windbreaks suggested lifeboats. The gardeners and maintainers of the park respected the metaphor. They spoke of introducing a retired canal barge, planted with black grass, as a *memento mori* for the water traffic diverted when Haggerston Basin was filled in. Poplars would be set in a circle around the site of the bombed gasholder and trained to mimic its shape. Once you understand how nothing is lost and how tactful design carries industrial residues into an era of compulsory recreation, the odder details of the park make perfect sense.

The Haggerston enclosure sustains and informs those who choose to come here, to work, to exercise or sit. They are inoculated by its mythology. The microclimate is a heady drench, a bliss drug. I swallow it every morning. I pass this way, cheered by the constant presence of the man on the bench, in the late afternoon. Give me a lever of attention and one fixed point and I'll move the world. My silent oracle, the beached philosopher in his metaphorical barrel, oversees all the mysterious features laid out around the fringes of the verdant deck. A shallow declivity, produced by some finger-sized meteor fragment, made into a shrine by twelve slender birch trees. A sacred circle of eight stone blocks like an amputated henge. Willow skirts in which new children hide. Heaped woodchip trenches going into scrub woods like a First War invocation. Sheep and donkeys grazing together alongside intimations of vanished streets and tight terraces; a spectral vortex of bootmakers, cabinet fakers and mantua wholesalers. The smell of cabbages, pubs and coal heaps.

For us, and for the investors in the new flats with their new names, secure entrances, bicycle balconies, this older London is out of reach: a choice download, a tarot of approved images and sounds. Those who notice the man on the bench are hobbled by sentiment: that our city is a sentient being, an organism alive and alert in all of its parts. And capable, generation after generation, of renewing itself by recovering and recording the myths that matter. By tempering greed. By justified riot and the delirium of the mob soliciting reaction. Forcing the grim machinery of state to declare itself in new technologies of repression, a subtler category of taser and thumbscrew. London, after so many abortions and rebirths, is an exhausted womb. But something different is surely emerging. It always does.

The man on the bench – in my fabricated version of him, my ignorance of the actual circumstances that brought him here – is immobilised by that knowledge. He is liquid-coshed, brain-clubbed, wedged in the shadows. HMS *Haggerston Park*, the spatial integrity of its shape confirmed by his disinterested affection, sails on. What was he telling me? Was there any significance in the position he took up, every morning, turning right through the gate? I never saw him arrive. I never saw him leave. I was nudged into following his line of his witness, through the park and over Hackney Road, towards the City and the Thames.

I didn't get far, Yorkton Street. That old nun, another walker, the one who stormed up Queensbridge Road, arms swinging as if on ski poles, the figure in black I used to encounter in quieter times on the canal path heading towards Victoria Park, she came from here: the convent of St Saviour's Priory, one of the Sisters of St Margaret. By her pace, the miles she covered, stooped over, eyes glinting, I took these Sisters for a pedestrian order. Beating the bounds on a daily pilgrimage of grace. Good works delivered in person, like it or not. I never knew what to do with her challenging smile, her withheld benediction. Should I drop to my knees or indulge in some pantomime of respect for a fellow tramp?

The Yorkton corridor, with its car park where six-handed dog walkers met and exchanged leads, was a staging post in the Vegetative Buddha's reconfiguration of *Pilgrim's Progress*. On the right, marking the edge of the frame, the redbrick wall of the Arts and Crafts convent features a relief crucifixion, three sculpted figures. A gaunt harp-ribbed Christ with darkly carbonised features. Two women, one bareheaded, one covered – the Marys, Virgin Mother and Magdalene – at the base of the cross. The tree of execution rests on a skull, a mound of Golgotha rubble. This tableau, unnoticed by cyclists and joggers, is a stolid echo of Albrecht Altdorfer's *Crucifixion* of 1514–16. The stone cross seems to be an extension of, and in alignment with, the ship's mast in Haggerston Park: confirmation of the benched man's *Via Dolorosa*. Jesus nailed to the yardarm like a heretic Billy Budd, a warning to others. With no hope of resurrection.

Unravelling riddles, treating street names and street furniture, marks on walls, aerosol revisions to hoardings, found fragments, objects or lists or letters, sodden playing cards, as pages torn from a lost book, identifies London as a detective story. A story with unlimited chapters and no resolution. The point being to find the inspiration for the next journey, a new beginning. Another shot at redemption.

The Society of St Margaret was founded by John Mason Neale with the aim of providing prayer and charity for the marginalised, the invisibles of the city. The Dunloe Centre, occupying part of the Priory building, offers 'Destitution Services'. Notices in English and Polish highlight a weekly 'drop-in' for the homeless. The 'Refugee Council' declares an interest. Perhaps the man on the bench comes from here? We impose connections in a futile attempt to find meaning in a maelstrom of possibilities. 'Come and enjoy an afternoon of prayers and quiet reflection', says a notice on the door of the Priory. But not now: 'No service this week. Sisters holiday.' Where do they go? The solitary walkers of a certain age tapping out the bounds of their obscure ministry.

When Haggerston Park was a mere proposal, the latest 'green lung' promoted against post-war blight, a garden seeded from demolished terraces, the Reverend HA Wilson of St Augustine's church, across the road from the Priory, opposed the scheme. He felt very strongly that the neighbourhood needed housing, not a park arranged like a boat. Sixty years later, the church has no vicar or social mission. Shoreditch beards wheel their bicycles to the door, in order to service their start-ups in a building dedicated to new digital theologies. The church loomed on the edge of the park, adapting to use as a performance space, a bar, a restaurant, a gallery, while the Children's Hospital on the other side of Goldsmith's Row was boarded up, in video limbo, waiting on the right development package.

I heard that a group of eight stained-glass windows designed by Margaret Rope had been commissioned for St Augustine's church. They were completed and installed between 1931 and 1947. The Gentle Author, who blogs on 'Spitalfields Life', a diary of place and persons, hymns the windows as 'sublime works… depicting both saints of legend and residents of Haggerston with equal religious intensity'. I was persuaded by this notion, that figures encountered on streets, benches, canal paths, could be part of a submerged tradition, sanctified eccentricity; the crafting of lives into brilliantly coloured icons, *actual* icons, a focus for devotion, not the abasement of the term as applied to vanity-architecture stumps that have been around for five minutes, or any valiant British athlete who staggers on to the Olympic podium, to weep as required through the national anthem.

'Miracles enacted in a recognisable East End environment,' says the Gentle Author. Margaret Rope's windows recover the scatter of London saints, names we barely notice on local landmarks. She transports their legendary deeds into the preoccupied streets of Hackney, Shoreditch and Whitechapel. St Leonard of Noblac was the patron saint of prisoners, especially chained prisoners held in severe duress in pits or lightless dungeons. In later life he retreated to the forest as a hermit, where some of those freed by his miraculous intervention sought out his den, to hang their manacles and chains on the sheltering branches. Noblac, trading on its association with Leonard, became a halt in the pilgrimage route to Santiago de Compostela.

It is said that there are 177 churches dedicated to the saint, but George Dance's hypodermic spire at Shoreditch got the right man for its dedicatee: a parish of career criminals, hustlers, weekend ravers and paid-up professionals of violence. Out of the devastation of the V2 rockets, the City bomb sites, the tenements of Hoxton, poured the ghosted biographies of sharply-suited Cockney villains: petty pilfering from ruined homes and factories, scrap metal in prams, old man on the run from the military police, deserted mum with heart of gold; could-have-been-a-contender boxing, protection rackets in the dance halls and markets, playing crazy (and meaning it) to avoid National Service, glasshouse to madhouse; gangland affiliations (and treacheries) among warring brothers, fitted up by Old Bill, the Scrubs, Parkhurst, and a comfortable afterlife smoothing over tall tales for bent coppers and gullible media groupies. Among many others, in the shadow of St Leonard's spire, the Frankish saint lent his name to Leonard John 'Lenny' McLean of Hoxton: on-the-cobbles bruiser, doorman enforcer, author, television presenter, small businessman and blacksuit pallbearer at celebrity funerals in Bethnal Green. 'The hardest man in Britain.'

In Margaret Rope's saturated window, St Leonard strikes off the shackles of a bearded vagrant penitent. A red Number 6 double-decker bus pushes north. The spire of Shoreditch Church penetrates a heavenly chamber in which one of the parishioners is taking communion. It's like that epiphany David Jones remembered in the First War, the furtive vision of a Catholic priest giving the sacrament by candlelight in a barn. In Rope's Shoreditch window, the ritual is a glimpse of a glimpse from a secret chamber. Her emblematic figures chime with the crusading knights and threatened Pre-Raphaelite maidens Jones drew for illustrated magazines during his period of war service.

When the Thatcherite realities of the 1980s began to bite, that frontal assault on untidy parts of London weakened by adherence to discredited myths of community, St Augustine's church in Hackney Road was decommissioned. And Margaret Rope's coloured windows were removed, replaced by plain glass.

The Gentle Author visited St Saviour's Priory where the walking nuns found sanctuary for two of the banished saints, Paul and Margaret. 'Both glowed with rich colour,' the blogger reported. Paul's transformative vision, the whiteout of epileptic seizure, happens beneath the dome of his name church, Christopher Wren's cathedral on the summit of Ludgate Hill. St Margaret delivers a model of the red-brick priory into the hands of John Mason Neale, the priest who founded the order in 1855. The sisters arrived in Spitalfields from Sussex in 1866 to help with the nursing of victims of the cholera epidemic.

The six 'missing' windows, not required in the new Hackney, found sanctuary in Munster Square, in the crypt of a large church with six active communicants. Searching them out, yet another unplanned London detour, was the price I paid for brooding on a journey inspired by the seated man of Haggerston Park. I was inflicting my dubious projections on his traumatised and unreadable psychopathology.

I had expected to strike south from the wisteria-bedizened bridge of the Haggerston boat to the river, but that is not what happened. That is not where the benched Buddha wanted me to go. Or where, for the sake of the story, this book, I wanted him to want me to go. He was thawing slowly, wrenched from the ice floes, packed in skins, feeding on his own fat, origin obliterated, floor puddled around him. But his hoarded indifference, his self-sufficient torment, pushed me into an act of reckless literalism: to locate the stain of the window in his stalled consciousness.

After following the Regent's Canal to the Islington tunnel, down a twitchy rule of coffee outlets, blocks of balconied flats, warehouse conversions, mosquito swarms of pinging cyclists, I loped downhill towards King's Cross and the diesel-reef of Euston Road mainline stations.

Munster Square, never previously visited, had lost its identity papers. It was trapped, without status, in Sickertian gloom, between railway tracks, Regent's Park and the parallel rat-runs of Albany Street and Hampstead Road.

Slogging past the stations, buffeted by mad heads-down soliloquists, bruised by invalid carriages, blocked by strings of unlicensed children and dogs, family units confused in tourist hell, deafened by sirens and the yelp and fret of cyclists hammering on white vans or sharing obscenities with U-turning cabbies, I was convinced that the city had reached the limits of human tolerance. We were supposed to be choking on fumes, but the cocktail of familiar pollution fed my frenzy: the cheapest high in town.

Now the interior spaces, the anonymous hotel rooms of back-street Euston were much closer to the paralysing melancholy of Sebald, with his maps and timetables, than the brown studies of Walter Sickert – who exposed sagging flesh behind heavy curtains, cratered goosefeather mattresses, dead-cigar Sunday afternoon ennui after laboured coitus in rented railside properties, and the unlanced boil of the shrouded sun dying in dirty windows. 'I think how little we can hold in mind,' Sebald said, when he found himself, yet again, frozen at a still point among the seething mob on the platform. 'How everything is constantly lapsing into oblivion with every ex-tinguished life, how the world is, as it were, draining itself, in that the history of countless places and objects which themselves have no power of memory is never heard, never described or passed on.'

Even if, as Sebald has it, the covert ways between Munster Square and Euston Station were lanced of meaning, the fading flares of ex-tinguished lives gave a lift to my steps. There is a moment, when you least expect it, when some dim tributary, the equivalent of a lost London river, snags your frustration and carries you forward. There was a magnetic pull now between station and park, those grand white properties enhanced by the fiction of Elizabeth Bowen and the sullen green carpets and sticky doorways illuminated by broken-bottled flashbacks of John Healy's *The Grass Arena*. Vagrants sprawled in purgatorial exhaustion in tolerated hollows between station and traffic. Hotels of passage, with suspiciously pastoral names, throbbed with sullen and illicit conjunctions. Smokers cupped their cigarettes and waited for death on the pavement. Charities and clinics rubbed along with uninviting cafés. Glass walls reared above the action in a Vorticist geometry of disputed dominance. This was not a suburb or a ghetto. It was a nowhere soon to be asked to explain itself, before being swallowed in the next overbudget utopia, authenticated by a major artwork.

Unimproved by planners, Munster Square hung on in furtive ob-scurity, giving shelter, I hoped, to the stained-glass windows from St

Augustine's captured church. My barely formulated ambition was to reunite the windows with the dream of Haggerston. To walk through the stillness of the man on the bench, to ventriloquise his silence. So that, in one flash of surgical intervention, jigsaw fragments of colour would invade the grey fog of catatonic slumber. And, in exchange, something of his integrity, his absorption in the stew of place, would carry to the Munster Square crypt.

The church is locked. Of course it is. That silence has to be protected. The chill. The damp. The guttered candles. St Mary Magdalene. The Magdalene from the red-brick wall of the Haggerston Priory. The Magdalene of railway hotels. But the gate is open and the steps down to the crypt are not barred. There is nobody at the desk, nobody at the tea bar.

'Three and one, thirty-one. Four and nine, forty-nine. Three and six, thirty-six.'

A voice from another room.

'Two and eight, twenty-eight.'

Are they stocktaking? An inventory of chairs? Are they numbering asylum seekers for transit? The crypt is dedicated to the Third Age Project. For once, I've come to the right place. A man pads out from the office. He pours tea into mugs that have been lined up along the bar. He knows when to add milk and a generous dole of sugar. Biscuits are counted on to the plate. They have a nice range of leaflets, if your Third Age eyes can bring the print into focus. Old people, inconvenient survivors, are kept below the pavement, under the church. Numbers. Statistics.

'One and seven, seventeen.'

Zumba Gold exercise for those 50+. It starts early, the Third Age. Third Age Cinema presents: *Suffragette.* 'Carey Mulligan is simply astonishing, ditto Helena Bonham Carter. Meryl Streep has a very small cameo role. It is inconceivable to this reviewer that women had to endure such hardships to obtain the right to vote.' Tactful screening time for those who don't venture outside after twilight, 2–4pm. '£1.00 entrance includes refreshments.'

Older Men's Health. Free 6 week summer course. 'If you complete the course you will get goods to the value of £5.' Bullet points include: 'The importance of exercise as you get older. Know your prostate. What are the top 5 causes of early deaths? Foods to avoid if you're over 65.'

'Biscuit? We can manage one spare.'

I am, it appears, one of the regular pilgrims who find their way to the crypt to inspect these problematic stained-glass windows. There are as many as two a year, always with notebooks and that air of being quietly gobsmacked. The Margaret Rope windows are exhibited like paintings, not set into the wall. It required some subtlety, the man behind the tea bar told me, to explain to his Third Age members, few of whom were Christian, many of whom abhorred religious iconography, that these things should be considered as paintings hung in a gallery, bright and uplifting decorations. Depictions of London, like postcards: red buses, lads playing cricket, St Paul's cathedral. Basically all the things you might now fall under suspicion for photographing.

The bingo session, an ecumenical diversion for multicultural pensioners and prostate-checkers, decanted a shuffle of gamers, in a diminuendo of managed excitement, from an inner chamber. Winners had to be persuaded, prodded forward, to collect their glittering prizes: an Airwick air freshener and an outdated Cadbury's bar.

Before the thirsty crowd rushed the cooling mugs of tea and hoovered the plate of biscuits, the genial custodian, perhaps trying to draw me into his flock, outlined something of the history of St Mary Magdalene's church. There had been two churches in the neighbourhood of Munster Square; pitched battles, fist-fights among the pews. This was formerly a red light district, the church was built where a thriving brothel once stood. Such was the pernicious microclimate of the railway: prostitutes coming down from Birmingham. Irish girls fallen on hard times, fond of a drink. A clergyman with a private income established the foundation. The crypt with its Third Age congregation, all races, all creeds, was the last remnant of the founding vision.

Margaret Rope's stained-glass windows, present but rarely inspected, were stored in a site that was still a going concern. Valued relics drawing the occasional aesthete or local history buff across town.

The glassed saints and the buildings with which they were once associated are representatives of another era. Margaret Edith Aldrich Rope, it is said, liked to tease ribbons of text through the leaded panels. Sometimes she hid a tortoise in the undergrowth, her symbol. She was known as 'Tor' to distinguish her from the other Margaret, her cousin: Margaret Agnes 'Marga' Rope, who was also a glass designer. Both women trained at The Glass House in Fulham. Neither married. Both were established Anglicans who converted to Catholicism. Marga, a dynamic cigar-chomping biker, became a Carmelite nun in 1928.

Six saints. Six windows that are no longer windows. An enamelled graphic novel of East London particulars moved to another place, taken underground: as into a catacomb. In loving memory of something valuable, lost or suspended.

Leonard. Augustine. Anne. George. Joseph. Michael. An improving Victorian adventure story with one female. What larks! What good works we brought to the disadvantaged. We put cricket bats into the sticky fingers of the unwashed. There is a very English blend of fantasy about these eye-level windows. Chaucer's pilgrims handpainted on the rim of a commemorative plate. *Our Island Story*. We are used to looking up, cricking our necks to catch a pale winter sun flooding colour down the cool stone length of the nave.

The Rope windows are coded or layered with numbers, symbols and fragments of text. Margaret's vision of St Leonard's at Shoreditch has the spire growing like a horn from the curve of the saint's shoulder. In 1933, when the design was completed, the Number 6 bus started at Aldwych, travelled north up Shoreditch High Street to Hackney Road, and on, by way of Mare Street and Morning Lane, to Hackney Wick. After 1992, the route was altered, like a tribute to L-F Céline's transgressive *London Bridge*, to ply between Waterloo and Willesden. Much of the madness of Céline's London novel happens on the bus, tracking shots of carnivalesque mayhem and riot. A scene into which Rope has inserted her athlete saint, ready to snap chains with his powerful hands.

PRAY FOR THE SOUL OF FREDERICK HENRY SNOW...
FOR SEVENTY YEARS CHORISTER, SERVER, SACRISTAN
AT ST BARTHOLOMEW'S & ST AUGUSTINE'S.

Spectres of Haggerston etched in stained glass. The Boston Street church becomes a glass factory. The landlord of The Suffolk Arms, according to the Post Office Directory for 1848, was Andrew Motion. By 1938, on the cusp of war, it was a certain Gulliver.

A man marooned on a bench on the island of the park, where HMS *Haggerston* rises from the waves in the wake of the whistling V2 rocket. Now sheep graze on the former Boston Street. The church is an extension of the pub. The figures in the coloured window are all white. The pattern of the leading contains a hidden alphabet. A Gothic script. An illuminated manuscript from which cryogenically frozen human figures begin to stir and shiver.

When the Gentle Author came here, he reported that St George looked 'like a young athlete straight out of the Repton Boxing Club'. What Ronnie Kray would call 'a prospect'. There is a homoerotic nullity about the male saints, their features as smooth as marzipan. These are women as denatured men, if only men were nobler (and stupider) than they are. Or women playing men for the enticement of other women. Fluid gender identities make Rope's muscular Christians into alien visitors to a fabled East London that no longer exists.

I remember walking the morning circuit of Haggerston Park with my wife, with Anna, who sometimes chose to accompany me. We had been listening for cockcrow from the City Farm and wondering how the animals would be affected by the endless building work from the conversion, floor on floor, of the Children's Hospital. We noticed how this dreadnaught development by Mettle & Poise flattered the marine pretensions of the park by not only having the displacement of a cruise liner parked in Palermo, but in its promotional copywriting. 'Shared Owner*ship*.' '*Launching* Autumn 2016.' They even had the bottle to call the vessel: THE GARRETT. No more 'loft-living', no more poverty chic and trust-fund bohemia. The walls are hung with gigantic photographs of a future arcadia.

But check the small print: 'Computer-generated image of the aerial view of Mettle & Poise is indicative and subject to change.'

The shaded Samuel Palmer tunnel known as 'The Woodland Walk' led to a secluded bench where a group of rough-sleepers, Eastern Europeans, were sharing a bottle of raw spirits. I passed first, with a non-committal wave. Anna, who was wearing a blue cap, zipped jacket, jeans, was given a much warmer welcome. One of the men held out the bottle and waved her over. And then, shaking his head, clearing blurred vision, a muttered word or two. Repeated in English. 'It's a woman! A *woman!*'

Some of Rope's panels, crusaders with red crosses on white shields, could serve as UKIP banners. St George in 1933: PRAY FOR ENGLAND. I WILL DELIVER THEE THROUGH THE POWER OF JESUS CHRIST. There never was a greener England, a luxuriant turf island detached from an unseen and unrequired Europe. The crucifix of the naked Christ is driven into the ground somewhere very close to Glastonbury.

At Quidenham in Norfolk, after she converted to Catholicism, Margaret Rope was invited by the Bishop of Northampton to go on a pilgrimage to Lourdes. In 1978 she left Putney for the last time and returned to the family farm in Suffolk. She died in March 1988, her short-term memory obliterated, after a long period in which the past grew brighter as the present faded, a condition loosely characterised as Alzheimer's Disease.

There is a photograph of Rope, in smock or all-encompassing habit, hair short as a boy, perched on a set of high steps, attending to one of the stained-glass windows with a measuring rod. She makes us feel that she could step through the barrier and take the place reserved for her in the composition. Like the man on the bench in Haggerston Park, she would become a blind watcher on the far side, a still point among the floating debris of the city.

BY WEIGHT OF WATER

'You find things by the wayside.'
WG Sebald

Are the coots, patrolling this stretch of the canal, now suffering from smokers' cough? Suffering from London? Small lungs choked with duckweed, beaks knotted with slime? Among the vaulting echoes of the railway bridge, a barking sound, a dry tubercular retching. Like a horse being slowly strangled, its chain caught around its neck, as it tries to mount the ramp to the towpath, after stumbling into the water. It takes a moment or two, halting on my morning walk in a place where it's much safer to keep moving, where wild-eyed cyclists stamp the pedals in furious entitlement, to identify the source of the horror. A small dog, a terrier, is swimming in tighter and tighter circles, clean sweeps of the radiant green surface, coughing for dear life. Coughing like the interior of a nineteenth-century Spitalfields tenement. Coughing, going under, head jerking up, coughing again. While the owner, I now see, waits with his back against the sticky wall, brushing a leather coat, assessing possible spray-can transfers, swaying a little, reaching down for a bottle.

Every time the animal makes it to the edge, gets its frantically scrabbling paws on the bank, the man nudges it back into the water. Not violently, no kick to the head. A playful prod of the toe. It's just a game. And then it starts again. The awful sound challenging witnesses who make no move to intervene. This, I recognise, is a *feuilleton* – as Sebald calls it – to transcribe for future use. A snapshot of Hackney.

Public officials, invisible until they swoop, are not so fastidious. One of the human markers I catalogued, alongside the Buddha on the bench in Haggerston Park, was a rough sleeper in a black bag (the kind in which a body might be removed from a crime scene), on a muddy shelf disputed by a pair of swans, and sometimes rats, along from the Empress Coaches garage, under Mare Street railway bridge. Every morning through that winter, in rain and snow, I passed him; encouraged in my own pedestrian rituals by this person's ability to remain just where he was, breathing softly, unnoticed, unmolested and late-rising.

I worried when a hut was constructed from driftwood and plastic sheets hooked from the canal. When the solitary guerrilla, who melted seamlessly into the canal's rubbish trail, spindrift among Red Bull cans and burger caskets, hooded and hidden, found some company. The shelf became a camp. A mess of supermarket trolleys, oilcan stoves, improvised kennels, rubber carpets. The other men went off about their business, but the solitary original stayed in his bag well into the morning. His unseeing neighbours, yards away, under another arch, were laying out cafetières and croissants for their round-table breakfasts. It was not to be tolerated. Footage of the Calais holding camp made regular appearances on television. This was Hackney. This was the future, the resurrected canal system. This was the film set.

On the morning of 14th April 2016, they came: at cockcrow. Mob-handed, and by the book, insultingly polite, the bailiffs surrounded his nest before the sleeper had time to take in what was happening. HOME OFFICE IMMIGRATION ENFORCEMENT. But it wasn't immigration they were enforcing, quite the reverse. Black vans parked where TV catering trucks were usually to be found, outside that dowager among ruins beside the Empress Coaches garage; a barrel-chested building regularly in employment as shorthand for blight in neo-noir dramas, and as familiar to viewers as the flaking pink house in Princelet Street, Spitalfields, from Dickens and Ripper heritage pieces.

There were six officers in black uniforms. Most of them on phones, walking up and down, with their backs to the humans whose particulars they were checking. Three of the sleepers stayed on their mattresses. Notices had been posted, earlier that week, along this stretch of the canal, inviting ratepayers and concerned citizens to report rough-sleepers. By the afternoon of that same day, the unapproved immigrants were gone. The rubbish was untouched. The hut unbroken. From the dank shelf the sorry troop would be taken into a purgatory of suspended identity, endless paperwork, postponed hearings. They would be held pending further investigation. Sometimes for months, years, decades. Insulted with tokens to spend at an approved store. Forbidden public transport. Removed from sight.

On the following morning, the pioneer bivouacer was back, alone. Dug in among wreckage. But it didn't hold. The balance of the world was disturbed. He was landfill. The magic was cancelled. He disappeared.

That was not quite the end of it. With London it never is. Detouring to pick up an oversize package – *Atlas of Improbable Places* by Travis Elborough and Alan Horsfield – from the sorting office in Emma Street, I found the pavement blocked by a nose-to-tail rank of coaches. Touring models with coffee-coloured paint jobs and *Empress of London* heraldry. The oily puddle of the garage beside the canal was, I presumed, in occupation by a TV crew.

And so it proved. The displaced squatters and the campers from the shelf under the bridge were reduced to leaving painted messages, sentences with missing letters, on the walls of Corbridge Crescent: *raying you won't be beaten up sleeping rough. ife without hope.* It was not easy to tell, in an era of digital cannibalism, if the messages were an authentic *cri de coeur*, spraycan interventions, or set-dressing for a film. *ife without hope.*

A genuine communication, handwritten, was attached to the broken fence alongside the mooring once favoured by the more anarchic and off-grid narrowboats. CREW LUNCH. Film not nautical. This water was no longer water, big-foot coots hopped from bank to bank. The duckweed baize was a glitter of meshed emeralds. A parked camera crane, *Nifty HR12*, waited its moment. The expelled were not quite ready for their terminal close-ups.

What might, a mile or two down the A13, near the smoking landfill dune at Rainham, have been an exotic junk-ghetto of unwanted containers, was a hip retail park, a post-industrial stack set beside the decommissioned gasholder. The investment presented itself as a city of the future: CONTAINERVILLE. Shared space had already been allocated: POP UP PROJECTS, RECORD-PLAY/PHONEFILE/FINDTUNES, LONDON CRAFTED BEER FESTIVAL LIMITED, WOOZLE RESEARCH, MAX BETS, CURRENCY CLOUD, DIGITAL MUMS STUDIO.

From the curve of the wall under the bridge, I had a privileged view of the squatted shelf. *The sleeper was back.* I watched him, fully clothed, trainers ready for rapid departure, tossing and turning on his mattress. He was shielded from the sight of potential informers on the towpath by a strategically positioned slab of plywood.

On the north side of the canal, in alignment with the Corbridge Crescent rough-sleepers, buddleia bushes alongside the bus garage on Sheep Lane offered useful cover. There was also a stinking porch, yards deep in encrustations of pigeon crap. An optimistic junk dealer had two liberated street signs on offer, symbolic markers for the last London: WARDOUR STREET W1, SPITALFIELDS E1. Like trophies rescued from the rubble of the Blitz. Areas devasted by intrusive Crossrail burrowing.

Ah! Reach for that notebook. Freshly sprayed this morning: ANGELS GATHER HERE. Woodsmoke from tin chimneys. Yawning cats. The settlement of the moment isn't brownfield, but the emerging water village. Double- and treble-banked streets of narrowboat dwellers grasping, before the rest of us, that the defining process of the times is migration. Occupation is anarchy. Property is debt. Why not play at riparian bohemianism for a season, while staying as close as you can to the artisan bakeries of Broadway Market. Before moving on, moving out. Accepting in a spirit of enquiry your banishment to Ponders End and beyond.

Used-book barges. Fancy cake-makers. Menders and bodgers and tarot readers. And collectors of empty bottles. The world is turning fast: new-build canalside towers are purchased by Chinese investors while nice middle-income English couples become boat people in a parody of crowded, deck-to-deck Asian harbours and rivers. A new white stencil among the wall-tats on the towpath: SHOREDITCH IS THE REVENGE OF FU MANCHU.

A box of roughly chopped logs, of the kind I last saw stacked in the porch of a farm cottage in the Neath Valley, to see a poet through the winter, is now vividly present and resinous on the roof of a Hackney narrowboat. Tomatoes in growbags. Beans without blackfly. Gardens in wooden trays. And portholes repaired after intruders. And burnt out shells. And *For Sale* notices – without the intervention of estate agents. The canal is about a barter economy.

When they paint JE SUIS CHARLIE on the railway bridge, in the immediate aftermath of the Paris massacre, it becomes as much a post-historic exhibit in the catalogue of London signage as one of the faded Victorian trade signs on some warehouse in Shoreditch or Stoke Newington – or the serial announcements of the innocence of armed robber George Davis, bang-to-rights guilty but fitted up on that particular occasion. George will be remembered as an East End territorial tag when otherwise dead and forgotten.

I abandoned myself to the excited dialogues of joggers and cyclists from Europe, and all the other places too: London was an integrated acoustic landscape in which every culture was free to ignore every manifestation of difference. We keep to our pods, slipstreaming in parallel lines that never touch. The English language is such a rarity that I took to transcribing odd morsels thrown out by phone addicts, robotic transients who used their smart electronic devices as mechanisms for homing in on a target. A drone in the hand is better than two under orders from George Bush.

Information junkies were walking faster, heads down, from flats and boats, from ramps and roads, zeroing on the digitally illiterate, making them swerve and cringe.

'So, essentially, I forgot to take the keys back?'

'So ideally that works for you basically? The 22nd of September? Three days or four days is just fine with me.'

'So the problem is I don't know any proper men. All I know is women.'

'So it might be an idea if you speak to the concierge.'

'So take them. I've got a fridge full of fruit.'

'So he's a chocolate maker, that's very exciting.'

'So dancing with a dog… yeah, honestly, a *dog*.'

'So he said I should get Botox.'

'So I'm applying for a US teaching visa. And I'm also applying for German, just in case.'

'So they're raised in incubators all over the country. But once they mate, they mate for life. Boris is behind all that.'

'People are so hungry, they're *starving*. So it's like sex on your wedding night.'

'So I rang Stacey to say, "What's the air temperature in Melbourne?" Very important.'

'I'm allergic to honey, so I can't eat cornflakes. So do you know Will Smith?'

'Uber to Shoreditch House costs about eight quid.'

There were complicated reasons why I wobbled across the rim of the Cat and Mutton lock gate, before peering down into the sludge, a shifting slop of blue cans and rancid polystyrene cartons. It was the afternoon of the day after the towpath was sealed with blue and white ribbon in yet another malign fiesta. To be guarded by serious, broad-bottomed policewomen in yellow tabards, with comical bowler hats perched on stiff hair: like a *Clockwork Orange* hen party. More officers, males in padded vests, overendowed with torches, phones and weaponry, requiring a waddle rather than a walk, propped themselves against the open door of a black van to blow froth from jumbo beakers of takeaway coffee and to fang at Broadway Market doughnuts. Sugar moustaches and polished hardnut heads.

I thought of Wyndham Lewis and his unfashionable purgatorial trilogy, *The Human Age*. From 1928, when the project began, Lewis laboured to construct the geometrical fortifications for a Magnetic City that could be read, at a stretch, as a prescient blueprint for

Stratford's Olympicopolis (the ugliest word in the language).

'Across the river looms the City of Heaven.' After blasting and bombardiering in the First War, Lewis recognised canals as formidable barriers for pilgrims seeking access to Paradise. In London, man-made waterways evolved into their own suburbs, ribbons of speculative development. 'The Waterman was now only a shadow,' Lewis wrote. 'He had passed through a veil of transparent steel… The blank-gated prodigious city was isolated by its riverine moat.'

A sinister lump floated in the Broadway Market basin. There was a bellying green tent around an object not yet detached from the slime. Impossible to tell if this was how the perpetrator of the crime had left the headless torso, or if the authorities, sirening loudly to the scene, lights flashing, had chosen to mask the horror from public view, while they waited for the arrival of the forensic team. Shit happens. They witness it. And file the appropriate forms. Before tipping off one of Rupert Murdoch's jackals – for a suitable bung. Wetting the beak, as the Sicilians have it.

A pair of mallards stalked a solitary swan. The police presence imported a frisson of traditional excitement to Victorian cobbles over which the rudely expelled cyclists now bumped. News crews arrived later that day, when they discovered the identity of the floater, the butchered woman: Gemma McCluskie. In the first years of the new millennium, McCluskie played the part of Kerry Skinner in 'more than thirty' episodes of the *EastEnders* soap opera. A local woman, living close to Columbia Market, she found herself taking up a position on sets derived from actual Hackney buildings and quiet residential squares.

The last known photograph of McCluskie has her in bright yellow, arm raised in the camera-clutching mime, like a swan's neck, while she records the opening ceremony for the £650-million upgrade of the Royal London Hospital in Whitechapel. Gemma was a woman of modest stature, an inch short of five foot, according to postmortem statistics. In agency snaps, with her long dark hair and holiday-tanned skin, the actress has a challenged Native American aspect.

You might question, finding McCluskie's head circled, what this event was all about. Others in that close-packed hospital crowd have their arms held high in a shared digital salute. We cannot identify the object or the person who excites their attention. You have to wonder why the photographer is making a record of the attendees, the charity mob. But the white aureole around McCluskie's head is a halo of bad news not a beatification.

A new morning with the taste of Hackney in the mouth: sticky lime secretions, musk of mature fox faeces, curtain-filtered bacon sizzle. I was striking south towards Haggerston Park when my sleepwalker's reflex route was interrupted by a previously uncollected figure. On the shaded side of the road, I caught the pungent drift of this man's ripeness, the London miles he had walked, early or overnight, as he headed north on a raised pavement polished by the rising sun. Here, if I was feeling romantic, was a prophecy of my alternative future. The harder path not yet taken. Twilight days of tramping in search of mislaid selves, stories uncompleted, forgotten friends.

The man sported a red wool cap. There was a nautical tilt to his stance, as if he had been discharged, cast off by HMS *Haggerston Park* for the crime of premature motion. The park gates were not yet unlocked and the Vegetative Buddha had not taken his place on the bench. There was, if I insisted on it, a significant connection between the two men: the one who was frozen to his place like an ice-rimed ghost from Shackleton's open boat, and the other, the mutineer or ancient mariner, roaming the city in quest of an audience.

I saw this new lurching pedestrian, advancing at pace, as my own photographic negative. Where I was bleached in sand-coloured shirt and lightweight trousers, he favoured a many-layered, all-weather outfit. He was insulated in a black coat cinched with a brown leather belt. Beneath the ankle-length garment, inherited not scavenged, and carried off with effortless ritz, was a layer of dirty leather with a monkish hood. The man's feet were sockless but shod in very experienced trainers. He tweezered an unlit cigarette in his outstretched right hand like a pedagogue's chalk stub, ready to scatter the blackberry drift of reluctant Academy pupils, kids busy with their electronic devices slouching straight into the traffic. In the belief that these gizmos conferred a magical immunity from damage, a personal force field that flowed out ahead of them. Like that immortality, all too often withdrawn, of being young and foolish.

The new walker on this patch had my attention. There was a lineage I was too quick to project on him: by way of Thomas De Quincey, Henry Mayhew, Charles Dickens and Jack London. Outsiders shuffling from generation to generation as provocations for the tapeworm of interlinked London narratives. 'Life rewritten by life,' as B. Catling has it in *The Erstwhile*. Reluctant tellers of tales to blue uniforms in green rooms. False witnesses. My fetish was to believe that these men and women, randomly encountered, belonged to an older order of the city. They were not citizens of Olympicopolis. The vagrant walkers were disenfranchised and proud of it. Olympicopolis, on the banks of the River Lea, was defined as a space where no ghosts could settle.

The episode becomes another discontinued detective story. I stalk him. Where will he go? Can he sustain this pace? He seems to be heading for a silent-comedy collision with every lamppost, but swerves away at the last moment. A religious dancer gone in the knees, he crosses Queensbridge Road, unmolested by traffic. I am outside the gated Adelaide Quay flats, watching a range of international Londoners emerge and plug themselves in, before heading off towards the City. *Listen for the clang of the gates.*

I am still hoping for the tranquillity of the park, when I decide that I have to turn back, to catch this man's slipstream. He might be one of the *Lamed-Vav Tzadikim*, the thirty-six righteous ones of mystical Judaism. Here presented in its gentile and bastardised form. The thirty-six are unknown to each other, hidden within the city, unknown even to themselves. They serve a higher purpose. If one of them goes missing, falls away or is struck down, the world ends. Sodom is destroyed when a quorum cannot be found. They are *Nistarim*, the concealed ones. Their identities must never be made public. By the Gematria of the numerical value of their given names, our ignorance is kept in balance.

Now the walled garden of Haggerston Park, and my contemplation of the man on the bench, made numbers dance. Six exiled stained-glass window, six lost saints: 6 x 6 = 36. Will London be spared for their sake? 'Death waves from the other side of the abyss,' cautioned Sebald.

At the bus shelter on Pownall Road, school-kids ignore the vagrant's advance. He walks straight through them like a sneeze of dust. Without warning, he veers away to the right, towards the door of a flat that seems to have been left open. It is done so abruptly that I almost miss his disappearance.

He goes inside, emerging in seconds clutching a sheaf of white papers. Evidence to be destroyed? Opportunist theft? Necessary documentation left behind in his own property? A life to be reclaimed. He feints towards Queensbridge Road, whirls around, and back once more into the unprotected flat. Looking through the open door, after he has stormed off for the second time, I register a hallway heaped with chairs, black bags, rolled mattresses. Eviction?

I have passed this way many times over the years, taking in the memorial to the murdered policeman, Laurence Brown, who was patrolling outside Orwell Court when an unemployed 20-year-old, Mark Gaynor, pulled out a shotgun and discharged it into his chest. Recent renovations and the rebranding of the Regent's Canal as a tributary of Olympicopolis have not obliterated aboriginal Hackney attitudes to rubbish. When you squeeze through one of the access tunnels from Pownall Road, you cannot miss the messengers of entropy: collapsed garden fences, wild nature asserting its unyielding authority.

The tall man in the belted black coat, with the swagger of Shakespeare's lowlife Pistol, rolled south. He was a beam of wild light radiating from the eye of the man on the bench. A long-strider, sticking to his preordained course (as I had on my expedition to Munster Square), he came abreast of the convent of St Saviour's Priory. One of a pair of synchronised young Chinese women made a grotesque pinched face and held her nose. None of the other digital walkers – calling mum, dragging the office with them, arguing with lovers – paid him any attention. They belonged in a different universe, a different species: the fixed and the provisional.

And again, like Pistol in the stews of Eastcheap, our discharged seafarer had his crew about him: attendant waifs and strays he chose to ignore. They were waiting beyond Sainsbury's Local on Hackney Road, acting very much like the cheery gang of pensioners who gather on the pavement in Broadway Market, an hour before the post office opens.

Established cash-machine squatters were hoping for a dole. There was a blind man with a blinder dog. A combat casualty in an electrified chariot draped with battle flags. A red-haired woman splayed on the pavement, skirts spread to catch any windfall from the ATM hutch.

The man from Pownall Road hit the cashpoint like a favourite bar. He rammed his card down its throat and had the notes tucked in his coat pocket, and away, before any of the crew could lift a tin cup. I had stopped for a moment to read a new inscription on the wall. When I turned round, he was gone. I sidestepped the immobile security guard and checked the aisles of the shop. My man wasn't there. He was not to be found among the vegetables, frozen dinners or shelves of booze. Walking faster now, I investigated the neighbouring streets and shady *cul de sacs*. He had vanished into the contaminated air. I entered his details in my notebook and plodded back up Queensbridge Road to resume the suspended constitutional by taking the ramp to the canal. A commissioned artwork in the form of a rusted docker's hook had been adapted as a shelf for cans, cartons and silver wraps. The peloton swept past in a yowl of ironised insults and snarling put-downs.

Within a week, like a recurring dream, the man in the black coat was back, and our paths crossed once more in exactly the same place. He was on the west side of Queensbridge Road, heading north, while I was at the gates of Adelaide Quay, making for the park. I had paused to witness an incident at the traffic lights (a hole manufactured by Volker

Highways, who are never out of employment from Hackney Council).

Two showroom cars stopped, bumper to bumper, within the thickness of a coat of paint, electric windows right down and stomping headache sounds blasting out. They were putting on a performance. Two smart young Asian guys wrestling, mock-slapping, swearing – before smearing their motors in shaving cream and cartons of fastfood. Windscreens completely snowed. Yellow curry accidents on passenger seats, on the new leather. Mess swept into the road as the lights change and they bomb away, horns blaring like the Thames on New Year's Eve, neck and neck, zero to sixty in seconds, towards Hackney Road.

The man in the coat ignored the episode, to come over at his favoured place, the blind spot at the crown of the humpback bridge. It was just as before: the sudden lurch down to the flats, the open door. The rapid retreat. The march to the cashpoint. The vanishing. Gone again. For good.

On the fence beside the canal, at the bottom of the Queensbridge Road ramp, was a new notice: CAUTION DIVERS. Police frogmen this morning have the melancholy duty of searching the heavy water, among submerged bicycles, traffic cones and shopping trolleys, for missing limbs, for the head of Gemma McCluskie. We are a quarter of a mile from where the torso was found floating. Have McCluskie's mortal segments migrated through the Cat and Mutton lock, then west towards Islington? Is it a feasible hypothesis that the killer managed to travel the busy towpath dispersing the evidence of his slaughter without being challenged?

Wreaths, flowers, furry bears and cards appear, overnight, woven into the fence above the lock basin where the torso was discovered. Yellows and purples. Flaming reds and pinks. Carnations, tulips, lilies. In funnels of cellophane and twists of stiff green paper. A silver star, helium inflated and tethered by a string, distorts the scene, the solemn faces of those who have come to pay their respects. With plenty of practice, we have learnt how to make a ritual of grief, even for those we have never met and know little about.

Council workers tidy away all traces of the spontaneous floral requiem. They dispose of the upper-case tributes, the letters on yellow and pink paper from friends and colleagues. And those awkwardly intimate communications from total strangers who feel the need to resurrect the identity of a deleted fictional character. Tabloid headlines strain to convert a brutal domestic drama, from the Pelter Street flat Gemma shared with her brother, into a national tragedy worthy of the hysterical conventions of television soap opera.

Pressure to blackbag all traces of the crime, a heady drench of morbid perfume, is made critical by the positioning, at just this moment, of a docking station of blue bicycles: the latest extension of a hire scheme allowing clients, for a modest charge, to pedal around inner London advertising Barclays Bank. The clunky bikes are sponsored by a financial institution, but the Mayor of London, Boris Johnson, soaks up the credit. And 'Boris bikes' must not be associated, in any way, with towpath horrors. At this stage in his vertiginous rise and rise, the old Etonian charmer is never photographed out of the saddle.

Staring down into the trapped water of the lock basin, I noticed the pages of an open book. There was a book barge, a narrowboat crammed with paperbacks, moored on the far side of the bridge. A quick search, passing through here on a dull afternoon, secured one item: *Land Under England* by Joseph O'Neill. Gollancz, 1935. A dust-wrappered first edition with bright black boards. 'He has elevated the thriller into literature,' says the Irish poet Æ (George Russell) in his foreword. 'The story that I have to tell is a strange one – so strange indeed that many people may not believe it.'

But this drowned volume, its sheets detached, drifting in loose arrangements of threes and fours, is not a Gollancz novel. The text, when I studied my photographs with a magnifying glass, was German. WG Sebald's *Austerlitz*? Sebald wrote in German and was then translated into English. The submerged text comes in solid blocks, soft focus under the smoky surface of the canal. I compared this page number, 162, with my English version. 'All interlocking like the labyrinthine vaults I saw in the dusty grey light, and which seemed to go on for ever.'

The place where the two rubber-clad policemen were diving was a bridge with history. It was where all the old Hackney villains staggered to dispose of knives and guns. Tony Lambrianou, the Kray foot-soldier, chauffeur to the carpet-wrapped body of Jack the Hat, lived in the flats on the far side of Queensbridge Road. When we stood on this spot in 1992, Tony was proud of his legacy, waxing sentimental about the canal where he dumped the keys from the two-tone Ford Cortina he had used to carry Jack through the Blackwall Tunnel.

'Yes,' he said. 'The weapons went into the water here, after the murder of Jack McVitie… When they sent the diver down to search the canal, he found two pieces they thought *resembled* a gun and a knife. It was never proved. It's like an armoury down there, in the mud, goes back generations… There have been allegations of other things happening around here, not down to us, going back to Victorian times. It's got a great history, Hackney, when you come to think about it. If you ever dredged this stretch, you'd be surprised what you'd find. It's part of the mystery of it all. It's part of your tradition if you live on the canal.'

A few days later, a leg was found. It was identified as belonging with the recovered torso. McCluskie's brother, Tony, was formally charged with the murder on Monday, 12th March, 2012.

And now I understood the concept behind the docker's hook art-work. The curved arm was pointing to the spot in the water where Tony Lambrianou dropped the knife that killed Jack the Hat.

Starting with the man on the bench, wondering how he got there, how he survived, my simple-minded curiosity had led me once again into a detective story that was all beginnings, arbitrary photographs shuffled across my father's desk, unsatisfactory stalkings through the parks and alleys of East London. I was reminded of Walter Benjamin's vision of the 'angel of history'. Jean-Luc Godard spoke about this in a 1978 interview. 'His eyes are staring, his mouth open, his wings are spread… His face is turned towards the past. Where we perceive a chain of events, he sees one single catastrophe which keeps piling wreckage upon wreckage and hurls it in front of his feet.' Godard's cinematic angel is charged with waking the dead, bearing witness before the storm carries us forward into an unknowable future. 'This storm is what we call progress.'

For no good reason I thought of my angel as a woman. And I asso-ciated her with the winged warriors on a plinth opposite the Royal London Hospital in Whitechapel. Here, I suppose, was another link to Gemma McCluskie.

In the state that manifests itself when projects are launched, and when they dictate their terms by way of coincidences and excited discoveries, unexpected phone calls, emails from strangers, I found it difficult to sleep. The streets had become a displacement dream. A not unpleasant fugue of liminal insomnia allowed me to know the night, to step outside among the dramas of foxes and cats. An engagement with these false glints of a new day could be glossed as preparation for the nocturnal walks I planned, when I would be doing without sleep for many hours, in order to achieve a dissociation of sensibility through which the hallucination of London would reveal the secret of mysteries worried at for fifty years.

Pelter Street, rechristened in 1905 in honour of a sixteenth-cen-tury landowner, was formerly known as Willow Walk. It is still a lane impregnated with memories, bucolic aspirations, running in a

curve from Ravenscroft Street to Columbia Road. The flats with
their balconies of fresh laundry and flowers have a pleasing Dutch
or German sense of community. Nicely preserved stone setts are
contemporaneous with sections alongside the Regent's Canal that
have not yet been improved by bitumen.

When I lost my man in the black coat at the Sainsbury's Local
cashpoint, I carried on south, struggling to form some impression
of the property where Gemma McCluskie had been murdered by
her junkie brother after a domestic disagreement. Studying the in-
voluted pattern of the shadow-bathed setts on Pelter Street made me
appreciate how the old equation of light and stone, leaf and masonry,
was a more reliable register of London's changes than the histories of
people and events that passed in the blink of an eye.

The signs were ominous: invocations of 'dragon' and 'river' spirits. I
photographed collages and stencils in which skulls and voodoo devils
were dominant. IS THIS LIGHT FAULTY? Pelter Street had been
infected by pressure on the optic nerves, a queasy electric pulsing in advance of a fit. On a 'Customs Declaration/*Déclaration en Douane*' pasted
to the wall, a totemic black head had been painted with horseshoe lips
and huge white eyes. A mask. A head on a stick. Another skull wore a
full Sioux headdress from Little Big Horn and was winged with fire.

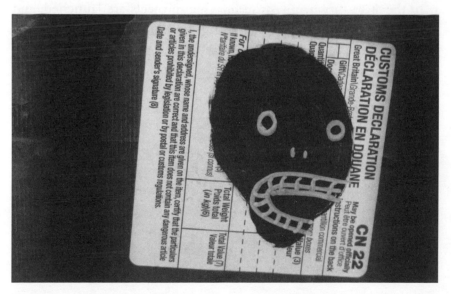

Only when we walk with no agenda does the past return. A police van was shadowing me as I tried to record my impressions. They were, as ever, photographing the photographer. Or so I thought. In reality, in the drowsy suspension of a warm afternoon, they were killing time between busts, hiding in the shade. If I had a phone with me now I could call my son in Brighton to ask him about his first mainstream directorial job in television, in at the deep end with multi-camera pressures and the volcanic egos of *EastEnders*. Had William known McCluskie out there in the cod-Hackney theme park at Borehamwood? With Barbara Windsor and the rest of the Stamford Hill gang.

Where Pelter Street emerges into Columbia Road, the Columbia Market Nursery School survives. That's where my older daughter went. Anna remembers pushing the pram through Shipton Street and swerving to avoid a bloody missile, when a first-floor window opened and a woman flung out a dead rat. On several occasions, they carried on to Brick Lane to meet me coming home from my stint in the ullage cellar of Truman's brewery. The nursery hung on, where Columbia Market, the fantastic mall-palace designed by Henry Darbishire for the charitable banking heiress, Angela Burdett-Coutts, in the late nineteenth century, failed and was erased from the landscape. The deserving poor were not impressed by a monster market with a proscriptive housing element; ill-fitting doors and no glass in the cloister windows, in order to keep the atmosphere bracing. Markets in Bethnal Green and Whitechapel favoured unpoliced street stalls, a weekend clearing house for stolen goods and illicitly imported animals. The gateposts and railings of Columbia Market now enclose the nursery school.

After remaining submerged, out of sight and mind during the cold rains of the Royal Jubilee, and the delirium of the 2012 Olympic regeneration of the Lower Lea Valley, the missing head of Gemma McCluskie broke surface in the Regent's Canal, close to the lock basin where her torso had been pulled ashore. Six months in Hackney water before rising through the duckweed carpet. Like an unsightly bump in the ironed surface of a snooker table.

A television crew set up lights and a crane on the far side of the canal for another episode of London *noir*. As witnesses, memory thieves, we are all implicated in the formulaic iteration of a limited stock of dark motifs. My younger daughter, Maddie, worked as a script editor with the original *Luther* writer, Neil Cross. He surprised us both by revealing that, as a student in Brighton, he'd been inspired by my novel *White Chappell, Scarlet Tracings*. And that one of the episodes in the second series was 'meant to be a bit of a homage'. Which the director never 'got'. But it was disconcerting to think, even as a Xerox of a Xerox, that those scarlet tracings laid down so many years ago were now surfacing in the scenes I watched, with scepticism and a reflex shrug, on my morning walks.

The scenic gasholder would soon be decommissioned to make room for a riverside container stack. The narrowboat dweller with a pirate flag, a man who uncovered stories of radioactive contamination around the Olympic Stadium, told me that he had been fitted up and was facing trial for the crime of protesting an illegal incursion on centuries-old Lammas land, one of the last of the unenclosed Lea Valley spaces. This, he said, was standard practice, a tactic for muzzling voices of opposition at a sensitive time. When the games were safely over and the cheers had faded, his case would be allowed to slide.

McCluskie's return to newsprint, that tight smile, that dark hair, haunted my attempt to write my way towards a London different – in ways I couldn't yet define – from anything that had come before. There were plenty of violent deaths in the record, but none, in the thrust of the regeneration moment, so much like found footage from a deleted file. The unmanned cameras that monitor our lives were beginning to make their own reality programmes.

As the trial of McCluskie's crazed brother moved to its inevitable conclusion, news channels ran surveillance footage in its raw form. The tragedy began with a phone row over an issue of personal hygiene, the state of the flat they shared in Pelter Street, taps left running. The sort of hopelessly loud, one-sided rants we hear all the time, on buses, outside betting shops, on park benches.

Deed done when it was done, and the awful consequences coming slowly into focus, the progress of the bloody-handed butcher is
tracked through a tissue of stitched together, low-resolution CCTV
images from the local cab firm. Soap opera to freak show: a précis of
cultural shifts in terrestrial broadcasting. The heavy, dripping bag is
swung into the opened boot, when Tony McCluskie summons the
nearest firm, for a short ride to the canal. He must have repeated the
excursion several times. He will serve, the judge says, at least twenty
years in prison.

Shortly before Boris Johnson stepped down to lend his well-
rehearsed charisma to the Brexit campaign, a story by Adam Lusher
was flagged up in the new tabloid version of *The Independent*. BORIS
PLANS TO PAVE UK CANALS FOR BIKE PATHS. A shameless
lift from a *Hackney Gazette* scare story had come to pass. There was
a headshot of Mr Johnson, glossed as 'a keen cyclist', in a helmet
spattered in Oyster branding. And it did look as if he'd managed
to ram his golden mop into a giant mollusc. The story was hung
on the inevitability of the Mayor's ascent to Cameron's throne. As
prime minister, Boris would tarmac a Euro-severed England, land
and water, in a network of true-blue bike tracks.

> Building the multimillion-pound 'great British cycle super-
> highway' would involve filling in all 2,000 miles of Britain's
> canal network… One branch would link with 'Boris Island', a
> new airport in the Thames estuary. He plans to open the net-
> work jointly with Sir Bradley Wiggins in a ceremony involving
> 'semi-naked women' playing beach volleyball in the middle of
> the old Grand Union Canal, glistening like wet otters.

The piece attracted little attention when it appeared on April 1st,
2016. But like all the best jokes, it was close to reality. In the post-truth
era of Johnson and Donald Trump and Nigel Farage, asserting and
denying with the flick of a thumb, the wilder the statement the more
effective its carry. Olympicopolis happened. And it will happen again.

AFTER SEBALD

'Popinga was still walking. This had become half his life, wandering
through the streets, across the light cast by shop windows, mingling with
the crowd.'
Georges Simenon

Elbows spread wide, hooked to the rail at the edge of things. This
view. Breath held. As motionless and drained of animal warmth as
the man on the bench in Haggerston Park. And thinking about the
DVD of the film I have dropped off in Shoreditch, on my way down
here, the study of a catatonic patient released from hospital and escaping, who knows where, for a lost week never to be documented,
before he surfaces again. *Escaping from the questions, the voices.*

They want him to watch two men, actors, having sex on a bed.
They shine intrusive lights in his face. He was dressed by his brother
in clothes that did not belong to him. A soiled grey raincoat. Speech
was far away. But they spoke *at* him: relations, psychiatrists, social
workers and camera crew

Far enough out and there is nothing left to be said. Listen to
the fear. They are looking at you. They are reading your lips. You
repeat their questions with sufficient delicacy to spare them shame.
Midnight. A railway station. A bus station. Stations of the cross. Listen
to the beat of a telltale heart. Listen to London light remembering
the ocean.

Look down into the nave of the great railway cathedral from a
high walkway punctuated by sealed doors, fantastic war memori-
als and tin receptacles for pre-trash newspapers, bins waiting to be
emptied. Take care to avoid the bronzed Kindertransport models,

dwarfish aliens with empty suitcases. Sentiment betrays memory. Contemplate the scuttling dance of inky figures on a ballroom floor: the retail concourse of Liverpool Street Station.

How do they avoid collisions? Heads down, eyes in their hands. Every one of them pokes and prods, making it seem that the devices are malfunctioning. They do not trust what they are seeing. Mass addiction. They barge across one another. Always late, they panic along predestined diagonals towards numbered platforms. They never appreciate in their neurotic haste that they are a lowly manifestation of the human soup, something akin to the viral democracy of the public swimming pool painted by Leon Kossoff.

The master artist of this neighbourhood – Arnold Circus, Spitalfields – Kossoff was shipped out in wartime, evacuated with other pupils from Hackney Downs School, sent into Norfolk. He never forgot the scene from the train window: sheds, canals, allotments, gasholders. An elasticated landscape witnessed in transit, he knew better than most, is never the same as walked ground.

Coming down stairs that move for you, move as you stand still, and avoiding clipboard missionaries, beggars, dispensers of promotional leaflets, you are in it, part of the soup. I walked straight over to Platform 12, where the Norwich train was about to depart: with the notion of identifying a WG Sebald *type*, a literary phantom freed from the labyrinth of text. Scurrying businessmen. White raincoat women with lidded beakers. Two Chinese postgraduates, with cameras and laptops, in excited conversation. Not an authentic rucksack in sight. Not a grey moustache.

I was early at Platform 8, where Stephen had suggested we meet. The held train was advertised as EMPTY TO DEPOT. PLEASE DO NOT BOARD. The station, considerably revamped and draped with screens of advertisements and rolling news, still accommodates that solemn forest of branching cast-iron columns with palmate capitals. The nave is endstopped by high walls of religiose (but non-denominational) windows, through which shafts of city light are projected, bouncing from the panels of new towers, to illuminate saints and sinners alike. Liverpool Street references an era of tropical hothouses, refuges for drippingly fecund vegetation. Trees that might flower, magnificently and defiantly, once in a hundred years.

I worked in the old carbon-coated station, at night, from a hut where seasonal postmen rested, read their tired science-fiction paperbacks, and kept warm between sessions loading and unloading mailbags, to be shuttled to other metropolitan termini in a period of parcel bombs, utility strikes and blackout conditions that invoked the remote heroism of the 1939–1945 war. My recollections of that smoky, male-fetid bothy, where wool-capped figures in fingerless gloves scooped cold baked beans from the tin, are patchy. And probably based on the prison-camp escape films I saw as a schoolboy. *The Colditz Story. The Wooden Horse.* One student mistook me for a face in an obscure vinyl band, and took my absolute denial as a wink, to put off the uninitiated, those who didn't trawl through the long night in a cannabis fug. 'OK, *right*, man.' His unshakable conviction made me doubt my own biography. Could it be true?

I used the downtime to patrol empty platforms, mesh-protected caves and cobwebby offices. Sebald's description in *Austerlitz*, his 2001 novel, of the abandoned Ladies' Waiting Room, may have been embroidered but it caught the atmosphere of the pre-development Liverpool Street with preternatural accuracy: a Bluebeard's castle of locked doors, ramps without function, cancelled corridors; spaces in which the lost souls of the city took up residence on hard benches. Drinkers trembled and lifted damp collars against the hour when the first bar would open. A television actor from *Last of the Summer Wine*, a man specialising in stuttering incapacity, wandered in, alone, after midnight, to rest with an attaché case for a pillow, until the morning commuters allowed him to vanish, once again, into the faceless crowd.

When I could, if there was a predicted interval of a couple of hours between trains, I cycled home through clammy streets to Hackney, where my chill return to the marital bed, fully clothed, was not especially welcome. It might trigger a disturbance for a pair of lightly sleeping infants. And another challenge as I tried to close the door.

In those days it was necessary to keep three jobs in play: private gardening around Finchley and Golders Green, a bookstall at Camden Passage in Islington, and nights on the station. A casual lodger in our house, a young woman from a family of established Marxists, asked me to drive her, with numerous bags and cases, to the station, where she intended to take a train for Harwich, and on, without much in the way of tickets or papers, to Moscow. She dressed for travel in a fur hat and a balding fur coat, worn over a thin nightdress and a pair of black rubber boots. The van of state-employed watchers, parked across the road from our house, at a period when there were few privately owned vehicles in the area, broke away as we reached Shoreditch and the silver dragons with red eyes who mark the boundary with the City of London. When the telephone crackled, we assumed that it was tapped, but it was still possible to walk in and out of the station without appearing on a dozen monitor screens. Surveillance was *personal*. Watcher and watched formed a bond. To be one of the observed, or to claim it, offered a certain status.

As the crowd thinned, after 9.30am, Stephen Watts appeared from the direction of Bishopsgate. I didn't spot him on the moving stairs, even though I was staring, expectantly, in that direction. He manifested, quite suddenly, very much in the manner I encountered him over the years as we wandered Whitechapel and the riverside reaches on our quite separate projects. If I were talking to a German or Dutch documentarist, say, in Fieldgate Street, close to Tower House (the 'Monster Doss House' from Jack London's *People of the Abyss*), Stephen would be attending, keeping his distance, paused in his own trajectory – just close enough, with a friendly but undeceived smile, to make me acknowledge the crude theatricality of the pitch I was offering. You can be in a place and of a place, Stephen implied, and you can even visit, for a day at a time like Professor Sebald, but you cannot asset-strip locality. It is permitted, as Max often did, to smooth over facts, change names. But you must not insult your readers or exploit the integrity of a sacred terrain. White Chapel: exile. Enclosed burial grounds with their bridled ghosts.

There is nothing of the appearance of the philosopher Wittgenstein, as we know it from photographs, in Stephen. That challenging impersonality of gaze is not to be found in the owlish stance the poet adopts, as he rocks, in measured and arduously constructed conversation, in the midst of the traffic, side-swiped by stampeding city workers. Was this another of Sebald's fictive smokescreens? He casts his *Austerlitz* station-haunting character as an eidolon of Stephen Watts, but dresses him with another mask. 'I had been thinking at some length about his personal similarity to Ludwig Wittgenstein, and the horror-stricken expressions on both their faces. I believe it was mainly the rucksack.' And then, helpfully, Sebald provides a snapshot portrait of that same rucksack, 'bought for ten shillings from Swedish stock in an army surplus store in the Charing Cross Road'.

It is a rucksack of character; canvas, womb-shaped, and glamorised with an assortment of straps and buckles, book-bulging from a naked hook. The photographic capture, cropped tight, takes on the romance of Vincent Van Gogh's flapping hobnailed boots. Here, among the lines of Sebald's generously spaced text, is a poignant insert, a signifier. The author's own rucksack, we assume, retrieved from European trains and platforms, from his tramp out of Norwich to the house of Michael Hamburger. Did Max carry home a cache of the poet's windfall apples? Drowsy country wasps burrowed into an intoxicating interior. The sepia mulch of alcohol and printed paper. The stalking cameras of Tacita Dean.

The Charing Cross Road shop was right, Stephen said, but the price was wrong. More like a fiver. It was *his* rucksack. Sebald rang, late in the day, the finished typescript of *Austerlitz* on the point of being shipped to the printer. He would come to London, meet Stephen, as usual, at Liverpool Street, walk through to the library cave among the studios of Toynbee Hall, and take a portrait of the rucksack. It had precisely the character Sebald required. I had never noticed this bag on Stephen's shoulder, as he made his compulsive drifts down favoured alleys, through the courtyards of flats, to the Thames and across the river, by foot tunnel, to Greenwich. Doubtless it accompanied him on reading tours and holidays among the villages of his forefathers in the Swiss Alps on the Italian border.

He arrived in Whitechapel from the island of North Uist in the Outer Hebrides, emerging from the underground into a shock of dusty sunlight in 1974. He was overwhelmed, at once, by a sense of molecular recognition that never faded and which now conferred on him the impression of a man a beat removed from mundane reality. Clocks, iPhones, driving licences, credit cards: they were no part of his discourse. When you needed him, he was there. Most often at poetry readings and unheralded presentations; his own and those of others he chose to support.

'I walk along the pavements carrying with me words / spoken by tired schizophrenic old men,' he wrote in the title poem of his book *Ancient Sunlight*. 'I walk the streets of Whitechapel with the blue bag / of language slung across my breast.'

Stephen struck north out of the station, through the agitated pavements of Bishopsgate. Free of his rucksack, prophetic hair swirling, he explained how Sebald, perhaps with a sense of mischief, or because such details are of no account, wrote of advancing on the river by way of Shoreditch: the wrong direction entirely. 'I can never be sure,' Stephen said, 'if Max is quoting me or if I am quoting him, some remark from one of the books.' Sebald came to Spitalfields for the first time to visit a female colleague from the University of East Anglia who lived in Princelet Street. Max was always scribbling in his notebook, Stephen said. He wrote poetry, steadily, with no particular fuss, from the Sixties. And he published, as we all did, in small magazines.

We decided to head east, in the muffled footsteps of the numerous expeditions on which Stephen had led the professor – or allowed himself to be gently prodded by one of Sebald's critical but unexplained quests. Our pace picked up. Recent developments, abrupt road closures and suspended permissions, had Stephen struggling for breath. The new city tasted of iron: bitter shavings left at the bottom of a dirty cup. Without obvious enthusiasm – and Sebald was a person in whom rising levels of enthusiasm were well concealed — the *Austerlitz* author would trawl through shoeboxes of postcards in plastic envelopes offered for sale in Spitalfields Market. Stephen, fresh from his North Uist hut, brought a scavenging instinct to London. He swooped on broken packing cases, chairs without legs. There were richer pickings, Sebald hinted, in Norwich junkshops and the somnolent villages of Norfolk. 'Woodsmoke in the city,' Stephen said, 'there is nothing like it.'

The poet reckoned that he made contact with Max Sebald around 1990 or '91. He was contemplating a dictionary of European poets in translation. The professor was sympathetic. There were meetings, grants for research, invitations to conferences. Stephen was charmed by a story Max told: how, maybe ten years earlier, driving back from the university to his house in a village five miles to the south of Norwich, Sebald had caught, with shocked appreciation, a prize-winning poem the Whitechapel wanderer was reading aloud on Radio 3. Reception was uncertain. The Norfolk air was busy with white noise from US bunkers and masts, hissing interference from listening stations among coastal dunes and gravel spits, acoustic debris from the beginning of time. This poem, beautifully voiced, soared above the chaos. It was Stephen's seizure by place, his original Spitalfields epiphany. He floated above the gravity of the houses. A sensation, impossible to repeat or recover, stayed with him. And with Professor Sebald too. As they arranged to meet on the station platform and to set off in search of Jewish burial grounds and galvanising postcards.

'We never drank in the Great Eastern hotel, as they do in *Austerlitz*,' Stephen said. The hotel was one of my own places and much as Sebald describes it: involuntary stasis, submersion in a tank of furniture rescued from the *Titanic*. A museum of loneliness, as the film-essayist Chris Petit saw it, between flights to Berlin. There would be twilight conversations, when a poet and sculptor of my acquaintance, recently removed to Oxford, returned to the memory grounds of our earlier adventures and poverty, to sip whisky, and watch the stiff-shirted City Boys and Bishopsgate detectives shuffling through to their secure Freemasons' temple. Sebald invents a

Portuguese business manager to give him the architectural tour. 'A vaulted ceiling with a single golden star at the centre emitting its rays into the dark clouds all around it.' I tried, after three or four doubles, to tempt the Oxford poet towards prose. He was a natural storyteller and he had fed on London's museums since childhood, the further out the better. What I was groping towards was the conviction that different writers, laying down different maps of the same place, enlarge the potentialties of the city. Geography shifts. Individuals dissolve. Place is burnished and confirmed.

At the back of the former brewery, a Bangladeshi man in a white shirt with flapping cuffs engaged Stephen in polite chat. Old acquaint-ances. We were in that half-hidden corridor, moving in parallel to busy traffic ditches and approved highways; we channelled tenter grounds, rough meadows seen from commuter trains, where shaggy ponies cropped alongside scrapmetal caves and arches of unwanted furniture. The achieved balance between private islands of public housing, closed in against the outside world, and small parks shaded by peeling plane trees, proved how one version of the city sustained its ancient self-belief.

'Stencl sat on that bench for hours. He liked to talk to vagrants, street people.'

Stephen was conjuring up the Yiddish poet, Avram Nachum Stencl. Stencl, according to rumour, was one of the good things to come out of the Olympics of 1936. Born into an ultra-orthodox Hasidic community in Poland, he migrated to Berlin, where his work was praised by Thomas Mann, and where he formed an at-tachment to Dora Diamant, mistress of Kafka. Lovely stuff for East London heritage buffs to savour, such tales enriched our threatened turf. Rachel Lichtenstein, whose grandparents had welcomed Stencl to their house in Westcliff-on-Sea, wrote about how the poet had been smuggled out of Germany in a coffin, with the help of an athlete returning from the Berlin Olympic Games.

Now on our Sebald walk, Stephen employed the name of Stencl as a quotation of legitimacy, a way of conferring virtue on the ground, of confirming that our blindfolded drift was a proper passage through Whitechapel. The flat where Stencl lived and died, in Greatorex House, was pointed out. But the slender alley, carrying pilgrims through the tenement complex without recourse to public highways, was gated and padlocked. Stephen flinched, turned up his collar against the cold, and seemed, when we stopped to talk, to be massaging his heart in an attempt to fire the vanishing daemon of place.

'There was a problem with his health.'

He meant Max. I said that my sense of the Sebaldian voyage was of a man who is not quite well, walking through a landscape of coincidences and elective affinities in search of a sepia photograph of a discontinued self. Trembling slightly, Stephen thought I was commenting on his own reaction, the physical difficulties, the struggle for breath provoked by a confrontation with overwhelming blocks of reflective glass, security-controlled parking spaces under supermarkets, gaudy Ideas Stores in place of serious book-lined libraries.

'There *was* a sort of breakdown, as in *Austerlitz*, perhaps brought on by overwork, the usual conflict between the demands of an academic job, which he took very seriously, and his compulsion to write. I don't know.'

This breakdown, in whatever form it manifested itself, struck me as significant, a state of consciousness uncannily connected to the area through which we were walking.

'And I also believe,' Stephen said, 'there is that old familiar writer thing, money. Even when Max's books were selling well, he had his family and a big house to keep up, the rectory at Upgate in a funny village called Poringland.'

Arriving at the high wall of the Jewish burial ground in Brady Street, I realised that the site I pictured as crucial to the close-woven topography of Sebald's Whitechapel was not here, but further to the east, off Alderney Road. Another hidden Jewish cemetery and one that Stephen said Sebald would have seen when his train from Norwich ground to a halt, as it inevitably would, on its approach to Liverpool

Street. Brady Street was my own itch: the fact that I'd never, in more than thirty years of beating its bounds, succeeded in gaining access, gave it a special potency. The cemetery, bolstering the long-demolished Peabody Buildings with the open-air chapel, and close to the vanished Roebuck pub on the corner of Durward Street, was a cherished riddle in the eccentric mythology that informed all my negotiations with Stephen's beloved territory.

Once again, he stood confused. 'It's so hard to remember where I walked with Sebald and where I'm recalling accounts of fictions deriving from our conversations. I used to go through Shadwell to Limehouse and over to Greenwich all the time – but did I ever do that with Max?'

Being with Stephen, such a youthful veteran, an articulate ghost among ghosts, opened the wall. Builders were taking down the lodge, the cemetery guardian's house, and we were free, for the first time in years, to stroll into the screened enclosure.

'When we were together,' Stephen said, 'one walker always absorbed the other. Walkers became the walk, the place. But Max also ventured on his own. He talks about stepping out, as darkness falls, and wandering for hours, as far as Chigwell and Romford, Hampstead Heath and Richmond Park.'

Inside the Brady Street burial ground, we moved apart. I was trespassing on a carpet of dry brown leaves, nettle beds, star-blue anchusa among the overwhelming green, but Stephen, following the line of an erased path, was at home. He didn't need to speak or to make reference to any of the fortuitously revealed details. He stood, fluffing his feathers: as poet, priest of place, shoulders sloped like folded wings; magenta scarf, scarlet lining to anorak, black-rimmed spectacles and aureole of wizardly white hair. I photographed decorations on sepulchres; a grey cinema of arms reaching out of clouds, chipped angels balancing the scales of judgement.

When we reached the far corner, where the bright yellow tubes of some new development opportunity rose above the old walls, Stephen recalled one particular walk with Sebald. They came to Wilton's Music Hall, near Wellclose Square, to witness Fiona Shaw ripping into Eliot's *The Waste Land*; blarneying the voices, perched on the high stage before an immense plaster backdrop, a slab of masonry that caught the shadowy outline of the performer and threw it back, in my conceit, towards Ratcliffe Highway, Wapping and the Thames. I had been in that audience too, without noticing this pair, who had broken away from an unresolved expedition, to make the double hit of Eliot and the recently opened music hall (former bar and brothel).

I returned, with Stephen, years later, when we met on that same stage, to give readings in honour of Sebald, and to launch a number of commemorative volumes. Chairs were arranged in a semi-circle as for a séance, while witness after witness stepped forward, making their sober testaments and hoping to invoke the shade of the absent author. 'One Well-Known, Yet Unknown': as it says above a waterless drinking fountain on Whitechapel Road.

AS Byatt, I remember, was suffering from a heavy cold. As if being there, in the cabin of that cold room above the theatre, was a required territorial penance. When the disciples and posthumous publishers droned on with their heartfelt tributes to a loss we all felt, a line from Brian Catling came into my head: 'Safe but elsewhere'.

After Brady Street, it felt like a few minutes' stroll down Mile End Road before we reached Alderney Road, which had never been anything to me but a Sebald divination, a chapter on which I was not permitted to trespass. Stephen struggled, visibly, with split vision, past and present; buildings he didn't recognise, buildings that had disappeared or migrated to places they were never supposed to be. Wrong city, wrong country. Wrong author.

The *Austerlitz* burial ground was secure, and not to be accessed, not today. YOU MAY BE REQUIRED TO WAIT WHILE WE CONFIRM YOUR IDENTITY. YOU MAY BE REQUIRED TO RETURN. Too many intrusive readers. Too many photographs. Respectful groups of folk as old as we were played with notebooks in the deep pockets of their sensible rainwear, as they tried to identify the house in which Austerlitz suffered his fugue and knew the clamp of death on the heart: the terrible recognition of the fact of having 'never really been alive'. One of the stillbirths of literature.

And then the convalescence, which is Sebald's way of writing about St Clement's Hospital, a bleak institution overlooking another East London wildwood, the tangled nature reserve of Tower Hamlets Cemetery. And here Sebald's album does overlap with my own. I spent many lunchbreaks, in my period as a Limehouse gardener, carrying my sandwiches to this park; listening to the trains, contemplating the prison block of the hospital-asylum. Pale lights in barred windows. No visible human traffic. Tall chimneys and an Italianate clock tower. Suffering is not contained, it burrows. It contaminates. We carry it away.

BRITISH STREET, it says on the road between hospital and cemetery. Like the title of a state-of-the-nation film by Lindsay Anderson: *Britannia Hospital.* British Street leading to Hamlets Way. Glades. Dells. Groves. Meadows. Sanctuaries. A cemetery plan like a jigsaw map of Texas.

Slow down. Lose yourself among walks laid out with sufficient complexity to confuse the dead. To keep them to allocated spaces. To the chipped ballast of memorial slabs holding them in the ground. It is the dry whisper the trees make, the worrying at a catchment of leaves. And there is *another* sound beneath and beyond all that. Trains in the trees. Tangled poplar and horse chestnut, linden and ash, as a buffer against the agitation of Mile End Road, the sullen mass of the hospital.

Stone ships tossed on the pubic curl of waves. Severed hands, in oval dishes, pointing at the earth in Masonic allegiance. Autointerners. Premature hibernators. Ironworkers, medical men, widows without number. Tribes of children, new arrivals borrowing the identity of the latest loss. Babes who stayed here just long enough to register names they would never occupy. And the keeper of the Dog Inn at Upton: *Her short sweet life was as the dream of an angel.* I plant myself on a green metal bench dedicated to the memory of Bob Shorter, in the shade of Lime Tree Walk. It is a good place, but I am too restless to stay there, dawn to dusk, learning to let go. Rooting and rootless.

I wondered if Sebald ever wrote about driving. The published books deliver a man most comfortable with a repertoire of waiting: station hotels, Swiss lakes, views of snowcapped mountains, flights into northern cities, hikes through salt marshes on sandy paths. And always in expectation of that single justifying encounter: the trapdoor of flashback, the skewed quotation. The misremembered echo of a translated text. The page floating beneath the surface of an urban canal.

The Sebald story, the one he would never be able to reconstruct, ends in a car. It was a heart attack, Stephen thought, on the road between the university and the Poringland Rectory that demanded so much care and financial support. His daughter Anna was with him, a swerve into the path of an oncoming lorry. In the only photograph I have seen of the celebrated walker's house, two large cars are parked on the flooded gravel drive.

Elegies to Sebald, especially *The Rings of Saturn*, became a cultural industry, stalking footprints that were never there, unpicking the play of meticulously crafted fictions, making them ordinary. And bringing the faithful, in the spirit of pilgrimage, to venues like Snape Maltings, for readings, recitals, concerts and confessions. A cult of managed English melancholy and weekend breaks in moody winter resorts.

At one of these sombre gatherings, yet another Sebald *Festschrift*, Rachel Lichtenstein was shown a photograph of the author standing outside a hotel, a bunch of books under his arm. She wrote to me in a rush of excitement.

> *Stephen Watts came for the weekend, wonderful to spend time with the legendary poet and with Robert Macfarlane…*
> *During the evening I was approached by an academic from UEA who worked with Sebald for many years and who has spent the last few years compiling a 600 page volume of essays and newly translated works by and about him. She told me, for the front cover, they are using a photograph of Max, standing outside a hotel in*

Aldeburgh, holding, amongst other things, a copy of Rodinsky's
Whitechapel. *You can imagine how thrilled I was.*

I asked Stephen if he had presented Sebald with Rachel's book,
her illustrated tour through the labyrinth of family history, an out-
reach of the Princelet Street recluse's room. He thought not, but he
couldn't be sure.

The interrogation of the photograph of this man, under what I
look to be the overhanging thatch of a tree, outside a seaside hotel,
a bundle of books clutched against his heart, became as momen-
tous for Rachel as her first encounter with David Rodinsky's garret.
Sebald's brow is deeply gouged in ripples of concern. One eye is shut
against the sun, the other wary. I looked again: no tree, but a hanging
basket with geraniums and daisies.

Lichtenstein, in *Estuary*, her 2016 publication, said that Sebald was
'the person whose writing had had a deeper impact on me than
any other artist'. She felt that, in discovering her Whitechapel book
clasped by this man, she had been given 'a blessing from beyond the
grave'. So she decided to abandon previous plans and to strike off
into Essex for her account of the Thames Estuary. Her impulse was
a standard literary conceit: in stepping away from what we think we
know, we magnify our debt to the ground we leave behind, mother
of stories.

Poring over the Aldeburgh photograph with my magnifying glass,
I identified a scrap of paper on which Sebald might have been making notes for his Snape Maltings lecture. You can pick out the name
Joseph Cornell. Discussing the way Max seeded his texts with images,
and the status of those images as 'found' and manipulated, it became
an accepted critical reflex to make the comparison with the New
York artist/collector. Jim Schley, reviewing *After Nature* and *On the
Natural History of Destruction*, wrote: 'Photos are used in most of his
books, not as illustrations but rather as visual detritus, ciphers or
enigmatic flotsam, as in the sculptural collages of Joseph Cornell.'

And just as the snapshot of Sebald with his copy of Rodinsky's
Whitechapel haunted Rachel, so a minor discovery of my own, when

I went searching for background information on the enigmatic German author, and pondered his choice of the commuter village of Poringland for his years of employment at UEA, struck home. Poringland is known, if at all, as the inspiration for John Crome's painting *The Poringland Oak* (1818–20); a work which is now to be found in the Tate Britain collection. Crome is frequently credited as the founder of the Norwich School, a group of nineteenth-century artists notable for the elevation of landscape painting as a serious concern: the primary subject of the craftsman's attention, rather than a strategic backdrop against which to show off clothes, property, possessions, children, dogs and wives.

I was interested in the ambiguity of that name, Poringland, as it hovered undecided between humours, wet and dry: *pouring land*. A clothed boy looking at a naked child who is reaching for his naked mother: Crome's figures are an extension of terrain. Sexuality is distributed through the soft thrust of an ancestral oak and the play of diaphanous clouds. Local historians say that the tower on the horizon 'could easily be All Saints Church'. The sky will darken, the bathers disappear. Sebald is buried at St Andrew's in Framingham Earl, a short walk from the Rectory.

Returned to Liverpool Street station, after parting from Stephen Watts, I took my notes to a Caffè Nero on London Wall and wrote them up while I waited for the photographs to be processed at Snappy Snaps on Bishopsgate. A blue plaque on the north side of the road recorded the site of the second Bethlehem Hospital, the Bedlam of infamous legend.

Wallet of photographs safely tucked away, I thought I was done, but that was not the end, it never is. Now the Jewish burial ground in Alderney Road, and the fading red notice – BEWARE GUARD DOGS – on the high wall, was established as a meeting point with Stephen, leading us, after necessary diversions, to a particular grave in Tower Hamlets Cemetery. An amputee angel on a tilting plinth. A remnant from a city of the dead, as Sebald has it, after an earthquake. *Until the day break, and the shadows flee away.*

'A terrible weariness overcame me at the idea that I had never really been alive, or was only now being born, almost on the eve of my death,' Sebald wrote. The author's private face, in snatched photographs, like the capture outside the hotel in Aldeburgh, seems to pass through the alchemy of copying and recopying, layer after layer, until it fades from reach. 'At some point in the past,' Sebald said, 'I must have made a mistake, and now I am living the wrong life.'

We return to Alderney Road with the ambition of identifying the house in which Jacques Austerlitz lived. The notion is absurd, house and man exist only in the context of the novel. Standing on the pavement outside Carlyle Mews, an address you can locate, listening to the voices of children in the little park across the road, we persuade ourselves that the atmosphere is right; decades of grime on dull yellow bricks, darkly indented windows, the mews passage.

On the buttress of the crumbling whitewashed wall of the burial ground, I registered – but only when I had the photograph in my hand – black marks hinting at a full-face portrait. The holes for the eyes, nose, mouth are too accurately placed to be the result of natural decay and damage. I felt uncomfortable, towards the end of Grant Gee's film, *Patience (After Sebald)*, when smoke in a hedge is frozen, like a miraculous revelation, as a profile of the author; a premonition of his road accident and death. But here I was, in Alderney Road, behaving in the same way, and treating a very ordinary wall as a death mask. If I had stumbled on anything, it was a nice example of Sebald's humour.

From Alderney Road, travelling along less familiar ways, through railway tributaries and tranquil squares, we felt as if we were stepping on the faces of the dead, a causeway of unreachable histories. The burial ground with its section reserved for the post-1657 planting of Sephardic Jews from Portugal and Spain, returned to England by Cromwell, flowed into a second cemetery, now open to outsiders, set among the building site that is Queen Mary College. Dark envelopes dressed with a super-abundance of Spanish bluebells.

On Bancroft Road, with direct access to the university denied while mechanical diggers chewed up the ground, we confronted episodes from our different pasts. I regretted the 'temporary closure' of the Tower Hamlets Local History Library and Archives Reading Room where I had been given the freedom to rummage through file-boxes of pamphlets and cuttings, when I was a gardener looking for information on Hawksmoor's churches. The memory of that dusty chamber with its insulation of mysterious volumes summoned the photograph Sebald inserts in *Austerlitz* to suggest the 'crowded study' where his character works, 'not far from the British Museum'. This airless box is 'like a stockroom of books and papers' with hardly any space left for its occupant. Here, surely, was the studio Stephen had occupied for many years beside Toynbee Hall in Spitalfields.

Stephen, who was vague about certain sections of our walk, showed no hesitation among the bifurcating paths of the overgrown reservation of Tower Hamlets Cemetery; one of those places where I invariably succeed in losing myself. We were soon standing beside the plinth referenced by Sebald, his armless angel.

In a haunted voice, slow and steady, Stephen intoned the passage about 'statues of angels, many of them wingless or otherwise mutilated, turned to stone… at the very moment when they were about to take flight from the earth'. I could believe, quite easily, that Stephen, like the traumatised Jacques Austerlitz, 'had learnt by heart the names and dates of birth and death of those buried here'.

A few weeks later, courtesy of a radio programme on Sebald's heritage, and after brief visits to Manchester and Norwich, we found ourselves inside the Alderney Road burial ground. Max had reached the point where he confessed that black and white photographs were 'all that was left' of the life of Austerlitz. The fictional character rings the bell, beside the locked door in the wall, and is admitted to the resting place of the Ashkenazi community, the lime trees and lilacs.

As with so many private London gardens, complacent behind a screen of houses, strategic plantings, time slows its momentum, and visitors reach for the right place in which to sit or stand in silence. The young radio producer, with her typed list of questions, to feed cues into an approved script, employed Stephen as the spirit of place – with the unspoken requirement to channel Austerlitz. A predatory ghost who had already occupied his studio and stolen his rucksack.

'What rough circle in our language / has brought us back to here?' Those are Stephen's words in his memorial tribute, 'For My Friend, Max Sebald'. The Spitalfields poet paces the cell of his studio 'mewling' a name – and summoning another room in Norwich. A room 'full of photographs', in which his friend, the beloved academic, keeps his 'realm looked after by trees'.

We were accompanied that afternoon by another London poet, and by a young and engaged rabbi. The Talmudic scholar provided the history lesson, dates and details. He confirmed the integrity of this hidden garden. And the Mile End community it once served. The spectre of development, as ever, was hovering. But the rabbi explained that the earth in which a Jew is interred belongs to that man and to his family forever. Until the trump of judgement.

If any material object sits comfortably in Velho, Old Cemetery, it is Stephen's rucksack. Retrieved from *Austerlitz,* it was returned, this afternoon, to the road. The poet's trailing lavender scarf is precisely the colour of the flowers dividing the grey slabs of the burial ground at Queen Mary College. A crown of silver hair is wool to his neck. The vein at the right temple pulses like a worm of the Thames.

'These last weeks I have been writing you postcards in my head.' The canvas womb of the rucksack has weathered another walk. Its neck is tied with twine, hooped around a padded leather collar like something on a mountain mule.

'Max, I am listening,' Stephen says, letting ellipses play out... Implying continuity, the distance still to be travelled.

FINDING

DIGGING FOR VICTORY

'Es WAR ERDE IN IHNEN, und / sie gruben,' wrote Paul Celan in *Die Niemandsrose* (1963). 'THERE WAS EARTH INSIDE THEM, and / they dug.' And with those words I felt the scratch of curved claws against the distended drum of the belly. Earth calls to earth. But the earth I pictured, when I employed that disquieting quotation in a book of poems published in 1973, was ballast in the intestines of a deranged European archaeologist, sunstruck in the desert, uncovering a Sumerian ziggurat, deciphering cuneiform tablets. Or that earth was hardbaked and red in Yucatán, with the giant poet Charles Olson, sweating and striding, fingering Mayan shards, to provoke a spark of inspiration to carry him forward. The earth was inside them, certainly, *but it was not here*. It was never London. We had allotments beside railways and canals, poisoned land in recovery. Modest gardens waiting on the next grand project: oblivion. 'They tear up the earth,' I said, 'searching for their fathers.'

And again they dig and the earth is sweet. The Hackney Hole is eight square metres, straight down, through the tidy lawn of a former rectory, close to the heart of the village settlement on the banks of the buried Hackney Brook. This private garden is separated from St Augustine's Tower by a wall of weathered brick. The periscope thrust of the square tower is all that remains of the borough's oldest ecclesiastical building, a sixteenth-century revision of the thirteenth-century church founded by the Knights of St John.

The Hole is a statement and it is properly capitalised. The labourers, a self-confessed art collective, work the Hole by hand, with pick and shovel, turn and turn about. It takes them four days to complete the shaft. And this is achieved without any of the tortured grinding and screeching, the gouging that attends uncivil engineering projects that carve so recklessly through tarmac and concrete, the heavy clay of this loudly regenerated fiefdom. And down, down again, through the pipes and wires of utility companies who treat their cone-protected pits as art installations organised to impede traffic, to block junctions and towpaths for confidently announced, but frequently revised, allocations for months or years. As a many-tongued militia in yellow tabards retreat to their all-day breakfasts and tabloid-insulated Portakabins. Easy to believe that Mare Street and Morning Lane have been rebranded as VolkerHighways (Considerate Constructors).

The noise! The din those improvers make. The decibels of patronising signs. The notices that appear in advance of demolition. The defining political requirement of our era is the art of getting your apology in first. And often. Letting the world know that you are sorry about being sorry. Wet-eyed, stiff-lipped on the cusp of another upwardly-mobile resignation. There is not a plugged Victorian sewage pipe without a headline boast. Not a dustcart without a grandiose statement of intent. Utilities are billboards. The propaganda of signage is funded by ratepayers like all those 'free' newspapers clogging our letterboxes. Ecology of excess. Slow death of meaningful language. Lies like lies.

TRANSFORMING WASTE
INVESTING TO IMPROVE OUR STREETS
BUILT TO OUTPERFORM
WORKING FOR A BETTER TOMORROW
INVESTING IN THE WALKING ENVIRONMENT
PUTTING PEOPLE FIRST
CREATING SPACE TO INSPIRE
JUST ENOUGH IS MORE
OUR PROPERTY KNOWLEDGE GIVES YOU POWER
TURNING IDEAS INTO BUSINESS
TRANSFORMING AND RESTORING LIVES
A HOME FOR EVERYONE
WORLD LEADER IN PAINTBALL
THIEVES BEWARE:

WORKING IN PARTNERSHIP WITH HACKNEY
COUNCIL
OWN A PIECE OF EAST LONDON HERITAGE
CCTV CAMERAS INSTALLED FOR THE PURPOSE
OF CRIME
DELIVERING GOOD DECISIONS
INVESTING IN COMPETITIVENESS
IMPOSSIBILITY IS NOTHING
HACKNEY IS MORE INTERESTING THAN
HISTORY

Ears plugged, gaze averted, the rectory lawn-despoilers launch their modest project at the summer solstice; before returning every single grain of soil, with willing volunteers, in October. This Hole is an *action*, not a budgetary solicitation. Not a plea for sponsorship. It's not for charity.

A filmmaker who went down into the pit spoke of being condemned to fall asleep every night to the clatter of helicopters 'circling the milky sky of Hackney'. She relished, by contrast, the silence of the burrow, and the 'damp, perfumed scent' of living earth. Here was an embrace that baffled all the sirens, the screams and shattered glass, keeping her safe. 'I felt cradled by this bare soil,' Chiara Ambrosio told me. 'Contained and absorbed by a place of origin and convergence.'

When the skin of the world is so overdrawn with competing narratives, shrill boasts hung from every blue fence, plastered over buses and police cars, there is an understandable impulse to go underground. Oligarchs and over-compensated money-market raiders, Premier League footballers and their agents, have burrowed under Chelsea and Kensington for generations, commissioning *Dr No* swimming pools, cinemas, and state of the art gymnasia. These windowless sets, finessed by fashionable architects, are as remote from the experience of ordinary consumers as the CGI facilities promised for the Queen Elizabeth Olympic Park in Stratford. What could be more empowering than to contemplate an immaculate rectangle of water, a 3-D David Hockney ripple never to be violated by a thrash of ticket-purchasing recreationalists? Neighbours, lacking this obscene quantum of liquidity, might well bleat about the noise, dust and damage to their foundations: it doesn't signify. Trump off, peasants. Money means power. *Bad*. Very bad.

Without fanfare, and with no shame, the domestic mining fetish arrived in Hackney. I visited Wilberforce Road, an avenue running south from Finsbury Park. This is a transitional zone of large mid-Victorian properties rationalised into flats. I noticed a Methodist church with a wood-faced turret. And a choice of uninviting hostels for backpacking passerines. But despite such awkward neighbours, and a degree of spillage from Finsbury Park kerb-crawlers, preying on the bruised desperation of addict-prostitutes, Wilberforce Road throbbed with the thump of earth-shuddering excavations.

Here is a rising street with estate agents boosting achieved selling prices and stimulating the neurotic impulse to treat a home as a vulnerable asset. The canny speculator must be alert for the optimum moment to cash in the chips. In late 2014, three-bed flats are on offer at £750,000. The average rent in the street is calculated at £1,666 per month.

Inspired by a febrile vision of progress, householders dig like moles. There are seven basement excavations in progress. Wilberforce Road is unlisted and schemes for enlarging properties are waved through in the mistaken belief that more housing units are being created. Specialist earth-removers mask their activities behind grey plywood shields. Which prove to be the ideal surface for yelps of protest: NO EXCAVATION! TEN MORE YEARS. NO MORE EXCAVATING IN WILBERFORCE. It is claimed by protesters that mining operations can last for anything between two and eight years. Giant compressors thunder. Security guards – bored, edgy, poorly rewarded and waiting for that tap on the shoulder from immigration enforcers – lurk in the shadows, warning off snooping photographers. Rear elevations have been torn from properties and cavernous pits revealed. Disturbed rats are moving out. Plagues of mice take up new quarters in the flats of the unambitious. The fashion for digging moves across the borough with viral enthusiasm.

More holes, more dust, more grey security sheds. After the first deep-trenching, they all go down.

This compulsion to dive beneath the skirts of river terrace deposits, Hackney gravel, shale and mudstone, down through old workings, the slag and clinker of doomed estates and lost theatres, is soon demonstrated by every stratum of society, from City Hall and the major developers, the off-shore speculators hidden behind front companies and proxies, to art collectives and 'place-hacking' crews posing for hi-res selfies in Secret State bunkers, sewage outfalls and ghost stations filled with forgotten archives. Subterranea, an uncolonised country of childhood imaginings, is the coming battleground. The epidermis of the city is so heavily policed now, so fretted with electronic babble, so corrupted by a strategic assault on locality, that civilians unable or unwilling to engage in a war they can't win respond by exploring forbidden depths. A Wellsian subtopia without maps or frontiers.

The burrowing reflex has a long history in London, as in other cities – Rome, Paris, the Warsaw of Andrzej Wajda's *Kanal*, the Vienna of Carol Reed's *The Third Man* – dominated by rituals and regulations. When the first Thatcherite towers sprang up in Docklands, and forgotten reaches on the Isle of Dogs agreed to behave as if the fictions of JG Ballard were planning documents, the painter Gavin Jones, working alone, excavated a wartime bunker hidden beneath a mound in a block of council flats in Bow. He disguised the entrance with an upturned boat, ran out electricity cables, and made himself a set of dank studios. He offered one of the four chambers of this Pharaonic tomb to an eccentric urban wanderer – who brought back museum-quality plunder to be fitted into a space that very soon became a single compacted block; a primitive curation in the spirit of Joseph Beuys.

The taller they stretch vanity towers, the silos of target architecture, the more those condemned to live in the shadows dig and scrape. Underworld is the condition of being resolutely off-grid. It registers as a free state, a pirate liberty, in the way that party-loving hipsters followed cells of the French Resistance into a labyrinth of quarries and catacombs beneath Paris. This is, as idiot interviewees are always mumbling on morning radio, 'Surreal. Completely surreal.' Meaning: unusual, but unspectacularly. A surprise.

An urban dowser called Alan Hayday, retired from the assembly line of the Ford Motor Company in Dagenham, contacted me to pass on his research into a tunnel he claimed to have discovered running from Sutton House, a Tudor mansion on the ridge above the vanished Hackney Brook, to a church on the other side of the River Lea. There was evidence, Hayday suggested, of mineral exploitation, speculative mining. He had tapped walls with dowsing rods made from strips of metal recovered from the factory floor.

Just as estate agents treat the warehouse communalists of Hackney Wick as pilot fish for virgin territory to exploit, so the bureaucrats of progress engineer regime change for land beneath London. The fences around swaggering construction projects in Shoreditch and London Bridge – THE GREATEST LIVING SPACE IN HISTORY, SYNCHRONISING THE WORLD OF COMMERCE, LEVEL 32 SKY LOUNGE & TERRACE – are now aped by grey sheds knocked up to hide the scooping out of bigger and better basements.

How far down can you go without planning permission? Nobody seems to know. Crossrail's heavy plant is so expensive, and so comprehensively promoted in approved documentaries, that it can't be retired to some transport museum in East Acton. Invasive boring is fated to become a permanent feature of London life. The Crossrail blitzkrieg, west to east, tracked by property speculators, boxes the compass. Tunnelling monsters summon up the prehistoric Megalosaurus referenced by Charles Dickens at the dawn of the first railway age for the opening of *Bleak House*: an 'elephantine lizard' waddling up Holborn Hill to die. The beasts are insatiable. They are hungry for the earth inside them. The earth in which they will soon be lost.

Fracking is the latest invasive wheeze, a US import. Ground war on the home front. When I visited the poet Gary Snyder in Kitkitdizze, his retreat in the Sierra Nevada foothills, he alerted me to the hunger of the frackers. 'A lot of public land,' he said, 'has to be converted, in the most organised fashion, into hundreds and thousands of gas wells. It's like the original oil era. They've tricked a lot of public land by offering inducements that haven't been followed up on.'

Our local frackers have their piggy eyes on the Weald Basin, from Kent to Dorset, and after that they're ready to take on London. Anything that can be talked up as ecologically sound, any quick-fix solution to the energy crisis, is going to receive immediate support from celebrity politicians who will always put green bridges and cable-car rides before the impossible business of troubled hospitals, failing schools and a shortfall in public housing.

A consortium trading as London Local Energy has applied for permission to bore into the crust, to pump water, chemicals and sand into shale rocks, and to release the gas. 'We want to light a fire under the debate and we want to make money as well,' said frackist pundit Nick Grealy.

The fracturing will start at Harrow and follow a track across town, in the footsteps of Tory grandees such as Winston Churchill, all the way to Downing Street. The gimmick is that urban fracking will be a *horizontal* manoeuvre, missionary position. Like sliding poker chips across green baize. A blind grope rather than a full-frontal assault. And as for that NIMBY whine about insults to the geophysical mantle, Mr Grealy pointed out that hydraulic fracturing (and the protest shrieks of tree huggers) would present no problem in London suburbs where neighbourly conversation is already drowned by incoming aircraft and the soothing hum of orbital motorways. We can take our chances with contaminated groundwater and a bracing snort of greenhouse gases. Chemical roulette offers a Darwinian edge to life in the metropolis: survive and thrive.

'We should leave no stone unturned,' Boris Johnson said, 'in the cause of keeping the lights on in London.'

This mania for boreholes, at whatever cost, reminded me of a cautionary tale by Arthur Conan Doyle, 'When the World Screamed'. Doyle's crazed *Übermensch* scientist, Professor Challenger, who would now be seen as a BBC4 natural, Patrick Moore channelled by Brian Blessed, sinks a shaft in Sussex, going deeper than anyone has ever done before, to prove that 'the world upon which we live is itself a living organism, endowed... with a circulation, a respiration, and a nervous system of its own'.

Challenger's project begins with a politic falsehood: he says that he is out to prove that there is petroleum under England. Perhaps the frackers have just such a post-truth agenda. Perhaps they believe that entropy can be reversed by a course of acupuncture for sedimentary rocks.

The professor uses an inherited fortune to construct a model village, after the fashion of Poundbury, the Dorchester Legoland sponsored by the Prince of Wales, as a smokescreen for his penetration of the earth's core. And it should be noted that the Duchy of Cornwall has already registered mineral rights for all the land under their control, including Poundbury.

When Challenger's miners break through the crust and pass the coal measures, an 'iron dart' is fired into 'the nerve ganglion of Old Mother Earth'. With the resulting howl of 'a thousand sirens in one... echoing along the whole South Coast'. A savage rent letting out, in one terrifying instant, future blitzkriegs, the chattering skulls of medieval ossuaries, terrorist bomb outrages and the uncapped shame of the refugee camp across the water.

'No sound in history,' the narrator tells us, 'has ever equalled the cry of the injured Earth.' Spectators are drenched in a foul and reeking substance. Volcanoes erupt in Iceland and Sicily. Mexico and Central America suffer the consequences of 'intense Plutonic indignation'. 'When the World Screamed' was published in 1929, the year of the Wall Street Crash.

Noises off also inform the launch of the Hole project in the rectory garden. Petrol bombs, breaking glass, stones hurled at cars: the riots of 2011 travelled from Clarence Road, at the northern end of Narrow Way (Mare Street), to the nexus of commercial enterprises, the betting shops that used to be banks around Hackney Central station. Funds provided by central government for regeneration were siphoned into an upmarket shopping hub; factory outlets for Burberry, Aquascutum and Pringle of Scotland, in neighbouring Chatham Place.

In some unintended way, the Hole became a focus for resistance without slogans. The Church Commissioners, landlords of the property alongside St Augustine's Tower, took the decision to sell house and garden as a development package, more flats. Windfall revenue would help to fund a community centre for St John's church. Meanwhile, the existing community living in the Old Rectory would be scattered, house and garden obliterated. Up to the moment of threatened disappearance, few Hackney citizens knew that this bucolic retreat existed.

On a wet November night in 2014, a month or so after the Hole had been filled in, and before the commune dispersed, I visited the house by invitation of William Bock, who acted as spokesperson for the collective. As might be expected, Will looked pale and convalescent. He hugged himself under a poncho of blankets, drawing up his legs on the sofa, before he launched into his story. The atmosphere of the room, the soft candlelight, the fire, the heavy curtains absorbing and containing outside sound, was familiar, but I hadn't experienced it in three decades or more. Will had taken the metaphor of the Hole, the maimed biosphere, into his body. He spent the weeks immediately following the conclusion of the archaeological event shuttling backwards and forwards to Homerton Hospital. A stomach abscess and a leaking wound.

'His spirits are higher now,' his collaborator Alberto Duman told me, 'or is it the drugs that are fed to him?'

A public ward at the Homerton was another kind of community altogether, less sheltered, more disparate in background and affiliation. Clients were united in pain, in the grudge of dormitory imprisonment and diminished motion. They drifted into reverie or chemically induced suspension of reality. 'Hasidic Jews, mad old Cockneys,' Will reported with relish. 'A clinically obese man, a monstrous giant of flab, being spoonfed by his mother.'

One by one, the other members of the collective straggled in, shaking wet coats, warming their hands around mugs of tea. Will, with his green beanie pulled right down, his hipster beard, explained that his partner Andrew was the official guardian of the building. Bock had lived here for a year and eight months. He was interested in photography and performance – and, in the wake of recent excavations, local history. The four-day removal of Hackney earth led the collective towards research into the place where, by some trick of fate, they found themselves.

Alberto Duman, the most politically engaged, had the notion that if a significant 'discovery' was made during the dig – a Templar relic, a sword or grail cup – then the demolition process might be halted. He recollected prankster actions in territory beyond the former watercress beds now overlaid with a 24-hour Tesco Superstore.

When council officials ushered representatives of the Manhattan Loft Corporation around the development site, just one day before a planning application for the conversion of Chatham Place went through, Alberto and a summoned flash mob began to sweep the area with brooms. They surrounded the old industrial warehouse, the monolith with a Burberry outlet on the ground floor. They climbed on lampposts, scrubbing and polishing with fanatical zeal. Security couldn't arrest them for civic altruism. The corporate suits stood bemused, staring at their phones and tablets, wondering what dark stain had to be scoured away. What crimes were being erased to make way for the coming era of retail adventurism?

Further research by Duman tracked Hackney Brook across Mare Street, where a railway bridge carrying London Overground to the malls of Stratford had replaced the footbridge seen in period engravings. And on, under Morning Lane, towards the River Lea. Alberto was amused to note that the constructors of the Holiday Inn, shoehorned alongside Hackney Central (amid rumours of a bigger station for the coming Crossrail 2), had been less assiduous in their searches. The foundations of the new building, on the rainy night when we met for the first time, were a black lake. An unplanned basement swimming pool filled with sump oil.

Exploiting the practical skills of Sophie Mason, a garden artist, and the person who recognised that they would need a bucket and rope to remove the soil, Duman and the other diggers laid out tables of archaeological finds: broken clay pipes, bits of bone, unidentified shards of pottery, junked forks and spoons. There was no requirement, as there had been with the pre-Olympic remediation of the Lower Lea Valley, to produce an exhibition of their spoils. The Hole dictated its own terms. Earth is not sieved. They penetrate a crust of grey conglomerate, older houses, older pubs and cinemas, shops reduced to crumbs that resist the pick. Working together provokes intimacy. The artists are excited by how they hear themselves telling each other stories; how they rhapsodise and forge a fellowship of resistance. This, I remember, is a commonplace of any labouring job for wages. It is the best of it. It is what we choose to carry away.

William Bock made the Hole into a camera obscura with lid and lens. The collective painted the walls of the pit white with gesso and gum. Those who came down the ladder into the earth cell, after their eyes adjusted to the absence of light, found the experience captivating. The world above appeared in phantom form, inverted; a ribbon of articulate shadows, trees like underwater clouds, the ivy-covered rectory building, and people leaning in over the grave. A primitive projection of cave drawings spilling out from their heads. *They were remembering as much as experiencing.*

By now, each member of the collective was reading from a different script. Will privileged the performance aspect, a provocation for rituals. And for the manufacture of images, including a carpet-sized print made on the floor of the pit, when the excavated space became a pinhole camera. Sophie Mason treated the garden as a world unto itself. Alberto Duman, with sceptical eye, and knowledge of événements in other cities, listened and plotted; he took the diary of the Hole as a future manifesto. Mark Morgan, an excavation theorist, biding his time at the edge of the gathering in the candlelit room, revealed that he had made a calculation. According to values per square metre of towers going up in Hackney, basements being hacked out, every pint of earth salvaged from the rectory lawn was worth £2.50.

They climbed down the ladder, all the strands of local activism; poets, musicians, oral historians, solicitors who spent years battling over doomed music halls and Georgian terraces trashed in arson attacks. They read their texts with their voices barely reaching the surface. Performers twisted and turned, trying to find their special spot, before they dared to look up at the trees and the stars.

Jess Chandler, publisher and curator, said that being in the Hole made her feel *completely* alone. She voiced poems by dead makers, spirits of place: Derek Jarman and Steve Moore. In this 'grave-like setting,' as she described it, Jess felt 'as though the audience could choose to bury you at any moment.' She wanted fire and honey to ooze from cracks in the earth, but the ground was arid and unforgiving.

Chiara Ambrosio used her descent as an invitation to balance temporary inhumation with the silence of the soul. The sudden chill entering the bones was a defence against a manifest of what had been left behind on the surface. 'As the pavements are lifted from the ground, I can see the soil beneath it glinting like moist flesh.'

Bill Parry-Davies, taking time off from a court battle with Hackney Council over the treatment by the developers Murphy of the last rind of Dalston Lane, blew his saxophone from the pit in feisty lament. He had issued his jeremiad before this. 'The conservation plan is to demolish them all. To create a *tabula rasa*. A year zero solution. After demolition the houses will be rebuilt, in heritage likeness, with machined bricks, with machined slates, with machined joinery, as Georgian replicas to create a Georgian theme park.'

Bill's words were swallowed, but the sounds he blew reverberated around the pit. He told me that he experienced his solo penetrating the earth and going out with the spoil and the worms. And it felt good. And it felt right.

Another voluntary prisoner in the white-walled kiln ran into technical difficulties with her presentation. Karen Russo, a young Israeli artist, cultivated a fascination with William Lyttle, the so-called 'Mole Man' of Hackney. Lyttle, talked up by estate agents promoting the auction of the tragic shell of a property wedged like a ghost ship in the pack ice between Mortimer Road and Stamford Road, was puffed as 'a civil engineer'. The engineering project that won him local notoriety involved a labyrinth of tunnels beneath a house from which all other occupants – family, lodgers – had been expelled. Rumour had the abandoned rooms filled with rubble, walls papered with yellowing newsprint. And catacombs, chewed out by the solitary digger, running into cellars, cutting through utility cables, and causing cracks in the road surface into which double-decker buses tipped.

Mr Lyttle's exploits inspired a cult. Young boys swapped Mole Man headlines from the *Hackney Gazette*. They pictured a chainsaw cannibal in moleskin hood netting lost children and populating the underworld, between buried rivers and coming Crossrail tunnels, with monsters, hybrid creatures, gypsum zombies. Russo heard the first furtive whispers of the Mole Man in 2006.

I met her in one of the surviving but revamped pubs in Broadway Market, where she lived in a small flat. She would be leaving soon for Walthamstow, rent hikes made continued Hackney residence impossible. There was a young family to support. She went down into the Hole, so she told me, to give an ethnographic account, supported by photographs of her expeditions with Mr Lyttle into what was left of the tunnels. The Mole Man had been removed by Hackney Council. They plugged his caves with fat concrete boles. The site was hidden behind a corrugated iron fence, but William said that he knew a way in.

The performance in the Hole faltered. Russo's laptop did not respond to premature burial. There were no images and her voice did not carry. She had to adapt, physically, to the absence of light. She was sustained by the singular illumination she found in darkness. She felt like an animal. Her eyes shone as she recalled the initiation of becoming an earth battery with no pictures to project on the walls of the excavated hide that was now her place.

Plunged into an investigation of 'the psychogeography of underground environments in London', Russo determined, whatever the risks, to track down the elusive Mr Lyttle. And to forge a relationship. To make a film.

Our table in the pub was soon spread with books, papers and the flickering laptop. The Mole Man presentation looked like an auction promo in which every pristine CGI interior has rotted into a crime scene photograph. Stone steps went nowhere. Porcelain basins for midgets, Morlocks with warped spines, were set a few inches from the floor. Sofas sagged under the weight of coupled bodies cast in mud. Tunnels were blocked with the Caesarian sections of cars and propped up with salvaged deep-freeze units. Where you might expect a devotional picture on the wall, Lyttle hung a keyboard or a three-bar electric fire.

After the Mole Man vanished from the secure accommodation to which he'd been banished, and official channels claimed to have lost track of the unsanctioned excavator, Russo ran him to ground at Crisis Skylight Café in Commercial Street. William was taking acting classes. It was said that he had a part in a radio play, but nobody knew when, if ever, the broadcast went out. Despite being stitched up, so he claimed, by a television company doing a piece on property makeovers that went wrong, Mr Lyttle was happy to engage, in person, with Karen Russo. He agreed to make recordings and to be filmed on the platforms of Underground stations at Holborn and Aldwych.

When the tapes eventually rolled, the Mole Man opened his throat and spewed out a venomous diatribe of inappropriate sexual dalliance with racist sidebars. Russo, who came to this confrontation by way of Novalis, Hoffman, Hoffmannsthal and German Romanticism, the folk tale of a young miner brought to the surface in a state of perfect preservation, seventy years after the accident that killed him, found her interactions with William Lyttle challenging.

'How come you have a small nose? Jews don't have blue eyes.'

On and on he went, trying to probe her intimate preferences. Russo remembered legends of lovers who descended into the depths to reclaim partners enraptured by the goddess of death. Now she was involved with a dribbling Celtic Minotaur in gabardine whose wife had moved out, disappeared from the story, leaving him to his drills and shovels. Mr Lyttle posed in the rubble, silver hair combed back, in open-necked shirt and a trenchcoat that was literally that, veteran of the trenches.

'Artists don't need to take on a moral tone,' Russo said. 'I kind of like the idea of the artist as devil's advocate.'

Psychotic rants rolled and echoed through tunnels that ran in every direction from the basement of the Mortimer Road house. In the new Hackney, a property of this size, in this location, was worth well over a million pounds. The council were demanding hundreds of thousands from the expelled householder for the damage he had inflicted on his own underworld. Mr Lyttle dropped hints about a fortune buried in one of his caverns, biscuit tins with £50,000 bundled up in greasy rolls of banknotes. The bait kept the remediating crew interested.

Then the crisis came. William Lyttle made a physical assault. He seized Russo's tapes and kept them as bargaining chips. In her original thesis, Russo glossed the Mole Man's rogue archaeology as an outsider version of orthodox art practice: a self-funded parody of the rhetoric of Anselm Kiefer's labyrinth at La Ribaute, the compound near Barjac in Provence. Mortimer Road was La Ribaute without budget or status. Without the support of the art establishment. Or a visitation from John Berger. The psychosis of William Lyttle was naked behind its inadequate security fence. Naked and dancing in a stained republican trenchcoat. The fetid soliloquy accompanying the excavations was obscene. 'Curiosity is my curse,' the Mole Man said. 'If I make a start, I must know where it ends.'

Kiefer's labyrinth was constructed by a crew of trained workmen: as a metaphor. In meticulously calibrated layers of darkness, solemn pilgrims would be reminded of the light. 'Everything that happens in the tunnels is reflected above.' Haphazard towers on a private estate, with entrances to the underworld, are designed to tumble. Their essence is their fallibility. Bulldozers cough and snarl. The artist finesses the alchemy of ruin: a spill of lead here, a scatter of ash there. Film crews arrive to pay their respects.

The monumental German artist, supporting a nation's guilt on his shoulders, boasted to documentary-maker Sophie Fiennes: '116 lorries have already left'. Kiefer oversaw the break up of his Barjac studios and the removal of artworks to hangars in Paris. The new accommodation was convenient. It was 'out by the airport, beside the motorway to Germany'.

William Lyttle's effects, when he absconded from his council-sanctioned room, were seized. The tapes of the interview with Karen Russo were mislaid among books and shoes and shirts. He asked her to pretend to be his lawyer. The deception shouldn't be a problem, he said, after all she was Jewish. If she agreed to fight his case with the officials, he *might* return the impounded material. But it all was too late. When Mr Lyttle presented himself at the housing offices, they told him that his belongings had been destroyed. He died soon afterwards.

When the news broke, two years after the death of the Mole Man, that his house had been bought at auction by a couple of second generation YBA stars from Shoreditch, for north of a million pounds, the triangulation between land value, conceptual interventionism and psychopathic burrowing became critical. David Adjaye, the ubiquitous architect of the moment, was already onboard. Adjaye was responsible for the Idea Store, a glitzy toy box that replaced the old book-burdened Whitechapel Library. Set alongside Sainsbury's car park, this colourful intruder looked like a Rubik's cube made from acrylic perspex. The moving stairs didn't move but there was a nice café with a view over the Jewish burial ground in Brady Street and the improved and extended Royal London Hospital.

Alberto Duman, recalling his action with the broom outside the designer shopping hub in Chatham Place, told me that the Pringle sock shop on the corner, the one flagged up as you step from the Overground at Hackney Central, was soon to be replaced by a David Adjaye tower. The impetus that brought the media-friendly architect responsible for the International Finance Corporation headquarters in Dakar, Senegal, and the modifier of the presidential palace in Libreville, Gabon, to a trashed shell in Hackney, was friendship. He had fond memories of an earlier collaboration with the artists

Tim Noble and Sue Webster. That gig featured a conversion that was also a signature work in which the raven-haired couple could hang out and manufacture their branded products: the Dirty House in Shoreditch.

Redchurch Street, a borderline between the selfie-spattered, tourist-cruised, retro reservation of Brick Lane and the islands of public housing, the small furniture and shoemaking operations of Bethnal Green, was about to detonate. To implode with cool. The area had been cooking quietly for years. Coming artists, taking advantage of opportunities offered by decamped industries, found the space they needed for contemplation and family life. It was a period of inward migration. In harsher times, established and successful immigrants escaped the ghetto by moving to Stoke Newington and the leafier purlieus of Victoria Park. Now, being taken up by Charles Saatchi, White Cube or Nicholas Serota meant a shift in the opposite direction.

'There's real estate and unreal estate,' Don DeLillo said. And the Mole Man's tunnels were as about as unreal as London can manage without actually turning inside out. Sewage trench to trophy installation in one jump.

Tim Noble and Sue Webster mastered the rubbish racket in a more calculated and rewarding fashion. They scavenged, swept up: transforming, by smart curation, the least required into top-ticket essential. They were addicts of entropy. They remodelled junk heaps and projected silhouettes on gallery walls. And these shadows, by some mysterious trick, evolved into self-portraits. It felt as if all the grunge traces of the embattled city were auditioning to become avatars of the twinned artists.

The Dirty House, a former timber factory, was recast by Noble and Webster, with some professional help from Adjaye, as a light-devouring black monolith; a stockade that had been there all along, waiting for its moment. Trading in novelty, the Shoreditch artificers, under the insidious influence of place, engaged with whispers from the past. They liked the idea that their designer bunker had once been a pub called the Blue Anchor.

But then the landscape changed, changed utterly. It was no longer so pleasurable to gaze south from a high window. The Bishopsgate Goods Yard development went ahead. Pop-up shops were stacked like brazen Tilbury containers on a lurid carpet of artificial grass. It was party time for cross-town transients, intersex retail vamps delivered by the Ginger Line. Customised *stuff* was being sucked up with malarial relish. The twittering of cell phones replaced the dawn chorus of sparrows in the London plane trees around Arnold Circus. Artists with property portfolios feared for the exclusivity of their patch.

It's great to be where it's happening, before it actually is. The conversion of a tea warehouse into Shoreditch House members' club, with swimming pool and cacophonous, monkey-house dining, brought numerous satellite galleries in its wake. High-end schmutter pits offered unticketed minimalist stock – two shirts, one cardigan – on naked tables for a business-class customs inspection. Lights were low-slung like a Victorian coffin warehouse: in a film. Bare bricks. Bulbs without shades. Investment coats swaggered from racks in the private changing rooms of performance artists. Males favoured tight trousers with highly polished brown shoes. And sculpted lumber-jack-fundamentalist beards. Young women channelled the fearsome disdain of Bond Street. Happening bars were brothel-scarlet like antechambers of hell. Boutiques were indistinguishable from galleries in the permanently skewed and tilting Redchurch Street opening night. There was a great fondness, now that sweated labour had suffered extraordinary rendition, for the word *artisan*. Cut-price denim from Cheshire Street stalls, by coming indoors, and migrating a hundred yards north, gained £500 on the price tag.

Sue Noble cycled past the Mole Man's Hackney ruin and recognised the possibilities. A new obsession was born. The very clean interior of Adjaye's Dirty House, white as the painted walls of the rectory Hole, was unreadable behind treated glass. Neighbourhood drug casualties and blank-eyed self-medicators, caught in the cracks of an ever-widening social and financial chasm, lurched up against the building like matchstick boats against a thunderous rock. The impenetrable surface, coated with a thick black wash, repelled all contact. Mirrored windows, some of them indented, were a display of negative prints reflecting spray-can panoramas from the opposite side of the street. By the magical repulsion of money, they stayed clear of defacement.

Webster had a vision. The roof of the Mole Man's house had fallen in, bringing down all the floors. She would construct a three-storey home with the infamous basement as a studio. Whatever could be preserved of the tunnels would remain as quotations, gingivitic molars from a spooky London past teased into the bright light of the now.

I waited where I had mooched so many times, at the perimeter of the Mole Man's house. Sue Webster agreed to give me a tour of her property. She arrived on the button: a slim, brisk woman on a slim-wheeled bicycle. She wore her fame lightly with an aura of post-punk, think it/do it realism. We slipped through a magic door and were soon ducking under scaffolding and jumping from ledge to ledge above the pit in which a team of builders laboured, clearing tunnels, securing foundations. A solid slab of concrete had been laid over the water table. William Lyttle couldn't go down any deeper beneath his basement, so he branched off in every direction. He had a relish for *en suite* fittings, toilets hidden in cheese cupboards, rat holes equipped with broken basins and light switches cut in half. He imagined his hidden kingdom as an underground Piranesi prison for lodgers.

The half-completed passages and perpetual burrowing reminded me of the fractal architecture of the Elizabethan palace contrived by Michael Moorcock for his Spenserian 1978 novel, *Gloriana, or The Unfulfill'd Queen*. Moorcock, in his turn, was paying his respects to Mervyn Peake's *Gormenghast*. Being outside the literary mainstream, and seeing the spread of the city as just a single draft for a multitude of parallel universes, stimulated the urge to invent secret spaces behind mirrors, behind walls heavy with velvet drapes and faded portraits. 'There we find corridors within corridors, like conduits in a tunnel, houses within rooms, those rooms within castles, those castles within artificial caverns.' Moorcock knew how to wait for the past to come round again. That smell of sodden wood pulp and dry rot in the latest loft conversion.

I traded information with Webster; we were both collectors of unreliable Mole Man anecdotes. I mentioned Karen Russo's experiences and the sour sexual monologues that bubbled up, incontinently, from mephitic depths. Webster told me that her builders had not unearthed any biscuit tins of banknotes, but they had discovered caches of pornography, specialist magazines featuring very large ladies. Mr Lyttle buried his own fertility figures, tubers encased in white fat, Willendorf Venuses splayed in chemical colour on water-damaged stock, reeking of semen.

I said how I'd heard that the Mole Man had inherited the property from his parents and that he'd lived there with wife and daughter, until they walked away. Then he took in lodgers, but they proved too much of an imposition when he began digging. Webster pointed out the traces still visible, like spectral imprints in the cast of Rachel Whiteread's 1993 '*House*' in Bow, of the tabloid newspapers with which Mr Lyttle improved the walls of tenants who wanted an upgrade to ameliorate the damp.

It was thought that the reluctant landlord had once worked as an electrical engineer. He did all his own wiring and plumbing. The aborted caverns, tunnel entrances with supporting columns, had a fungoid charm Webster associated with Antoni Gaudí and his unfinished *Sagrada Família* in Barcelona.

The Mole Man's great work, like a story by Kafka, could never be finished. But Tim Noble and Sue Webster, as his elective heirs, would honour the heritage. The assault on the subsoil of Mortimer Road was a neurotic scrabble, a butting and gnawing at earth that poulticed the haunted prose of Kafka's 'The Burrow'. 'So I must thread the tormenting complications of this labyrinth physically as well as mentally… and I am both exasperated and touched when, as sometimes happens, I lose myself for a moment in my own maze, and the work of my hands seems to be still doing its best to prove its sufficiency to me, its maker, whose final judgement has long since been passed on it.'

Kafka's mole-creature hears terrible noises. *There are other things in his tunnels.* New occupiers are coming. 'Yet if these creatures are strangers, why is it that I never see any of them? I have already dug a host of trenches, hoping to catch one of them, but I can find not a single one.'

Mr Lyttle's excavations are an MRI scan of paranoia constructed to hold off the predatory owners he senses on the horizon. To hold off rival artists. To hold off the future itself. And the investors who will invest in the residue of his madness. And the writers who will exploit his legend.

Tim Noble joined us, another slim-wheeled bicycle to padlock. His hair, once as inky black as that of his collaborator and former wife (they were married by Tracey Emin on a Thames boat), is now bottle blond like a hitman from a Barry Gifford story. The couple got their start in East London as factory assistants to Gilbert and George in Fournier Street. They laboured on the ground floor, while the celebrity conceptualists took their ease upstairs, reading the *Telegraph*. 'But they were always very prompt in paying their invoices.'

You can see how well it went for Tim and Sue. They are one of those hardworking, faux-slacker, pretend-dangerous couples doing their spiky best to look menacing. They love the fabric of what they have acquired. They admire Mr Lyttle's DIY expertise and the way he made moulded pillars carry a load. The persistent lung-teasing stench of brick dust and albino mushrooms, drains and drowned leather, carries an aphrodisiac hit that takes the artists back to their first date: a visit to the house of Fred West, the Gloucester serial killer. West was another builder and bodger. Tim Noble remembered the way that a side return had been roofed over, using a tree for a supporting column. The house of horror in Cromwell Street was demolished, reduced to dust, made into a landscaped footpath. And now Noble explained how, once the cage of scaffolding had been removed, they wanted to retain the Mole Man's historic façade, so that the house appeared to outsiders as a ruin lost in time, while behind the untouched and peeling sour-cream paint, the sticky-gravy window frames of ugly coal-smoke London, an uncluttered contemporary home would be created. 'I love the way light falls here,' Noble says.

★★★

After we parted, and intoxicated by my tour of the site, the burrows and ledges and lumps that confused all previously established notions of scale, of what constitutes inside and outside, I decided to return home to finish reading the book I'd extracted from the narrowboat moored beside Cat and Mutton bridge, at the end of Broadway Market: Joseph O'Neill's *Land Under England*. The towpath, a fraught negotiation with cyclists, joggers, carts like supermarket trolleys stacked with small children to be delivered to schools and nurseries, had become a dormitory for those who preferred not to join the property ladder.

The morning smell of woodsmoke is enticing. Freelance operations of the kind that once found room in Portobello Road or Camden Passage have transferred to the canal. They sell tea and homemade cakes, knitted hats, haircuts, yoga and Tarot readings. *Word on the Water*, a book-barge based at Paddington Basin, sometimes chugs downstream to Camden Lock and Hackney. The Paddington mooring is threatened by demands for yet another quintessential coffee franchise, in keeping with the speedy buzz of the development. The book business, started by a man who spent twenty years helping to rehabilitate former addicts, and a partner with a shop at Archway, caught the eye of sympathetic journalists by displaying a full complement of shipboard cats and open boxes of Beatrix Potter. The floating *bibliothèque* drifted for a time, up and down the River Lea, until the bookmen were wearied by threats of fines from the Canal and River Trust. Stewart Lee came aboard to record a message of support. 'This is a land grab,' he said. 'I'm not sure what of: the air between the edge of the boat and the quay?' It is all a question, he concluded, of making a case for eccentrics, of what we decide to value in our culture.

As a former professional in the scavenging trade, a *Merz* collector (school of Kurt Schwitters), I went through the narrowboat stock in about two minutes. Harmless reading fodder in paperback ranks. Glossy art books, slightly weathered. Then there was *Land Under*

England, a first edition from 1935, in pristine yellow Gollancz jacket. The title sat nicely with my current preoccupations.

O'Neill was Permanent Secretary to the Department of Education in the Irish Free State, and an occasional, but always interesting novelist. The cover copy describes *Land Under England* as 'a work of genius'. And goes on to say that 'on the spiritual plane it is a book of the most profound significance for our time'. Æ, the Dublin poet and mystic, glosses the novel as a political satire against totalitarianism and the insidious seductions of dictatorship. 'The highest form satire can take is to assume the apotheosis of the policy satirised and make our shuddering humanity recoil from the spectacle of its own ideals.'

At the period when *Land Under England* was written, the glamour of fascism touched Æ's friend and associate, WB Yeats, who pledged his support for Eoin O'Duffy's militaristic Blueshirts. Francis Stuart, a self-condemned Irish Dostoevsky, who was also published by Gollancz in the 1930s, had a special gift for putting himself on the wrong side of every political argument. He took off for wartime Berlin, where he made broadcasts, and dreamed of heading further east into the firestorm of Russia.

O'Neill's subterranean fantasy absorbs these currents. Finding a copy in contemporary Hackney, smuggled in by water, feels like recovering a message rescued from a bottle washed ashore after almost eighty years, at a period when the entire city, from politicians, corporate entities and property speculators, to psychogeological artists, is digging. Going under. Ripping up the surface. Hacking out pits and shafts in a demented bid to turn the world on its head and to colonise the land under London.

The conceit of O'Neill's novel is that a decayed gentleman with an inherited pile, up north, returns from the First War with nothing left except his high-Tory passion for the classics, for Latin, for the values of the Roman *imperium*. He tramps Hadrian's Wall, poking into every cranny, tapping at stones like Tony Robinson and his hyperventilating TV archaeologists. Until, one day, he succeeds, and vanishes somewhere beneath the ground. His son, in a lather of Oedipal conflicts, follows him down.

The technical aspect of the descent is overwhelmed by the Miltonic conviction of O'Neill's eschatology, a terrifying slither across dust and pumice to a dead inland sea. Descendents of the Roman legions, minds sucked to an affectless conformity, work at their tasks, controlled by Masters of Knowledge. They are like so many shared-desk digital zombies, all individuality leeched into some flickering universal screen in a Shoreditch container.

'I saw that I was the only human being left in that world outside that machine,' O'Neill wrote. 'Under that dome, which was the land of England, I must make a stand for humanity.'

The insanity of attempting to impose a limited version of history, an apology for conquerors and occupiers, while burning the brains of token resisters, incubates the threat of future war. 'The danger would be greater because nobody could suspect that, under the green earth of England, an outcast offspring of its own people… was gathering itself for a spring into the upper world again, under the urge of a madman who combined the evil of the light and the darkness.'

I came home to find a piece of paper on my doormat.

> *Dear Sir/Madam. You are receiving this letter because your property or business is located within 200 metres of land that may be needed in the future to build the proposed Crossrail 2 underground rail line.*

We lived, so it appeared, in 'an area of surface interest'. If the shadow of the Crossrail pit queered any potential property sale, we were free to make a claim for 'statutory blight'. I thought of the actual blight of the enclosure of Finsbury Circus, an oasis among the towers of the City, sacrificed to the impossible ideal of smoother, faster transit for workers at the financial hub.

We had come full circle. Forty-five years ago, we moved into a terraced Victorian house with outside lavatory and tin bath, under threat of demolition, when the towers of the Holly Street estate marched south. The previous owners were emigrating to the liberties of forest-fringe Essex. The terrace survived and became, in the course of time, part of a conservation area.

Given the struggles of present day artists, inspired to dig holes in rectory lawns, or to excavate wartime bunkers, we were fortunate. London moves on. It always does. But this time it felt different. That invisible cockpit of pollution, rising from the loop of the M25, the orbital motorway, had closed against the rest of England. London was now an island, open for business only if your business is business.

Coming off the canal, up the ramp to Queensbridge Road, I was barged aside by a man on the run, ranting into the air, balancing his phone out in front of him like a very small tray of slippery cock-tail sausages. 'I bought 2,000 bottles of poppers, thinking the price would be *incredible* when they were made illegal. I speculated. I took a legitimate punt. Post-Brexit I am always angry.'

OVERGROUND SOUNDSCRAPE

While an unreported war raged in tunnels under the parks, the lost market gardens and brick kilns of Haggerston, an approved future was made visible in the form of the London Overground railway, an elevated circuit familiarly known as 'The Ginger Line'. You could see it and hear it (and smell the burnt air too), if you lived within the right set of real-estate contours. Much of the time – weekends excepted, sections closed for perpetual Crossrail improvements – the Overground worked. And worked well. It linked Haggerston with Denmark Hill, Willesden Junction with Canonbury: a single self-sufficient railway doughnut rising above the status of less fortunate neighbours. Think of the Overground as one of London's transmuted Olympic rings.

I spent months walking the loop, watching the transformation of spaces under the tracks, oily caves metastasised into coffee outlets and exercise boutiques. The high fences around development sites, brilliant with predictions, told me just how many minutes it would cost to arrive at a more desirable place, a better class of station.

The sound of the railway was a lingering sigh, shivering the bike-rack balconies of new-build flats. A gentle, life-affirming zephyr summoned those agitated walkers, who are always late, app-informed that the only train (for the next three minutes) is about to depart for Highbury & Islington.

Certain specialised beggars, inflictors of unsolicited magazines and peel-off chemical sachets, staked out the fringes. Mounds of free newspapers, with bulging property supplements, were distributed at key stations: Whitechapel, Shoreditch, Dalston Junction, Hackney Central. Haggerston qualified for the morning *Metro*, but not for the *London Evening Standard*. Paper handlers, sidesmen for some discontinued parish church, lurked at the station entrance passing out folded newspapers like prayer books. Always with a smile, a courteous nod of acknowledgment for regular parishioners.

A fit young black man, like a personal trainer from the gym in the railway arch on Stean Street, squatted into his dominant position on the pavement right outside Haggerston station. There was no way around him.

SPARECHANGEFORFOODPLEASE.

SPARECHANGEFORFOODPLEASE.

SPARECHANGEFORFOODPLEASE.

No variation in pitch or emphasis. SPARECHANGEFOR-FOODPLEASE. More of a mantra than a practical demand. SPARECHANGEFORFOODPLEASE.

Later in the morning, there is a transitional phase when this man shares the pavement with a barista coffee cart offering rush hits before a run at the barriers and the stairs. Then he's gone. But his chant stays in my head, accompanied by weary sighs from Overground trains, hitting the brakes before climax, before peaking again at Hoxton.

SPARECHANGEFORFOODPLEASE.

Follow the railway, follow the beggars. Under the bridge, emerging from Shoreditch station, there are substantial holdings of pavement polishers, flattened cardboard mattresses. Rough-sleepers endure the din of street musicians and crews of spray-can professionals. And the crusty droppings of pigeons dodging their spikes.

There are not many beggars working the trains. One Dubliner tried her luck. A small woman in ripped tartan trousers. 'I don't want to impose now. Can anyone help with a few pennies?' Women respond more generously than men wedded to their screens. But they are relieved to see her move on. 'I don't want to impose…'

London voices. They are talking to their hands. Between Haggerston and Shoreditch, it's money: owed, withheld, promised or stolen. It's property, viewings to be arranged. It's rehearsals, recces and shoots. It's meetings in bars. Between Dalston Junction and Highbury, it's domestic. Grandmothers and minders checking in. Outings to the Olympic Park. Until all the fragments we are forced to share become a single acoustic block. A soundtrack to the view from the window nobody has time or inclination to experience. I'm looking out and listening hard. Certain phrases are imprinted over the Snake Park, the canal, the Geffrye Museum. 'A weird *crow*, man.' 'Speaking from Tokyo, Major Johnson.' Small dramas of strangers in transit who allow me to share an unearned and undesired intimacy. 'As soon as he walked out of the door, I called the Fraud Squad.'

I'M SO HAPPY I'M NOT DOING THE 'SPECIALS' ANYMORE. LOOK AT THEM AND THERE'S NOTHING THERE, MUM. COMING INTO CANONBURY STATION, A BIT LATE. COULD YOU GET ME A LAGER? I TRUST JACKIE'S JUDGEMENT. SO – MY NAME'S SAPPHIRE? PUT YOUR MONEY AWAY. SO IT GOT TO THE POINT WHERE WE WERE GETTING ON EACH OTHER'S NERVES. WE HAVE SOME SPACE FOR A LITTLE WHILE. YOU KNOW CHARLES DICKENS? HE WAS A MAN IN THE VICTORIAN PERIOD. I TRUST JACKIE'S JUDGEMENT. I'M GOING TO HAVE A BIT OF A WARM UP, 'COS I HAVEN'T STRUCK A BALL IN WEEKS. WE HAD A GOOD DAY IN THE OLYMPIC SWIMMING POOL. *LEARNING ENGAGEMENT* – WHERE WAS IT? EALING BROADWAY? PUT YOUR MONEY AWAY. THE TURKISH CREW IN HACKNEY. OH YEAH, THE GUY WHO DOES THE BOILER CHECKS IN BRAINTREE. DO I DETECT AN IRISH ACCENT? SO – MY NAME IS SAPPHIRE? IT'S FUNNY. IN SECONDARY SCHOOL, I WAS ONE OF FOUR CHARLOTTES. THEY GET FIRST CLASS ON ALL FLIGHTS. YOU RUNNING WITH MUSIC OR WITHOUT? THANK YOU FOR YOUR EFFORTS, AS EVER. YOUR CONTRIBUTIONS ARE REALLY APPRECIATED. PUT YOUR MONEY AWAY. WE WANT AS MANY YOUNG WOMEN AND FLOWERS AS POSSIBLE. IT'S SHACKLEWELL LANE. SOMEONE OR *SOMETHING* IS IN THE HOUSE. YOU SAYING YOU MUM CRAZY, YOU SISTER CRAZY, THEY ALL CRAZY? I'M GOING TO PICK UP A FRIDGE

NOW FOR A TENNER, INNIT. NO MONEY CAN BE PAID IN BEFORE SEPTEMBER. I GIVE YOU MY CARD. I *HAVE* MONEY TUCKED AWAY. NO NO. I'M WAITING TO PAY. SAY AGAIN. DO I DETECT AN IRISH ACCENT? SHE NEEDS A RE-START, I THINK. IS MYRICK STILL IN THE OFFICE? HIS PHONE WAS OFF. WHAT APPROACH DO YOU HAVE? DON'T CALL ME *EVER* AGAIN. I'M JUST GOING TO PICK UP A FRIDGE NOW FOR A TENNER, INNIT. PUT YOUR MONEY AWAY. DON'T CALL ME *EVER* AGAIN. WE WANT AS MANY YOUNG WOMEN AND FLOWERS AS POSSIBLE.

PIGEON FISHING

'Unexplained, but not suspicious.'
Police report on the death of George Michael

I took up my position and allowed slowly thawing stones to become my throne, while I waited. And waited. I'm not sure what I thought was coming or how long it would take to arrive. The Bethnal Green church portico, with its view across snarling lines of traffic held at the lights of a busy junction, absorbed my token resistance. The virgin morning air was ripe with the poisons on which we feed. It was a good day to go fishing for pigeons.

The Vegetative Buddha of Haggerston Park had taught me the value of staying still, rooting like a shrub. London needed its specialised witnesses, disaffiliated monks trained in silence. Involuntary momentum has to be bled out of the human machine, along with ambition. That hunger for stories and patterns. Church-sitters are on the far side of this thing: trauma. The worst has already happened. Now they are all waiting. And watching over nodal points. Halfway to becoming statues. Halfway to vanishing into the stone. As unloved as the great tribe of feral pigeons, those shit-machine rats in avian drag. Warm bodies like oil-lamps, vulnerable necks. Pecking mobs force-fed on crusts.

I tried to read the fossil evidence left by former squatters, human and animal, at the church of St John. And I thought, as so often before, about the poet John Clare, rambling into town, during the slow years of his graveyard existence in Northampton General Lunatic Asylum. How he identified his shamanic spot on the porch of All Saints' Church; tucked away in an alcove, hat at his feet, staring down

Gold Street, snatching awkwardly at phrases that would no longer knit. A recorded presence at the civic centre of the market town. A premature heritage piece established by a drawing in which he seems to levitate, hands on thighs, bareheaded in a spill of bounced light.

Across Cambridge Heath Road, Daniel Mendoza, the bareknuckle Jewish pugilist and author of a classic book on the noble art, had his house on Paradise Row. His mythic blindness, as I stare across the diesel fug, shifts into a softer, pearlier glow than anything electricity can provide. His blue plaque becomes a medal of honour, not a satellite dish.

At another window, left open against a hot night, above the Salmon and Ball public house, you are never free, once you have seen it, of Jock McFadyen's painting from 1994. Jock has zeroed in, with the telephoto lens of a tabloid snoop, on a meaty Francis Bacon geezer doing a bit of business on the blower; an instrument which, gripped in that gnarled fist, becomes its rhyming-slang self, a bone.

Another figure, a concussive negative in a white beard, loiters in the outer darkness of the upstairs room, under a bare bulb. More bulbs, coloured, constellate a flickering sign: MINI CABS. This is a termite operation working the gap between boozer and elevated railway. Under a lovely brain-damaged sky at the end of a long day's drinking. A golden dazzle of meteor showers before we retch into the gutter.

McFadyen, at this era, was the paparazzo of blight. He covered the waterfront and much beside, populating his turf with muscular, hoop-legged tarts, drawn from his own mirror image in a leather skirt. Tongue-sharing bombsite lovers chew and tug like James Ensor's *Skeletons Fighting over a Pickled Herring*. Ill-matched creatures, beaten by fate, dry hump in condemned doorways, watched by one-eyed dogs. The hobbled horses of Travellers crop the central reservations of arterial roads.

As the dawn of the new millennium approached, humans disappeared from Jock's Underground stations, his canal paths and steaming landfill dunes alongside the A13. Place required no auditors. The painter had learnt how to balance repulsion and reality. Even in his colonisation of the upstairs window at the Salmon and Ball, Jock noticed – and we have to notice it too – a gargoyle mask with rubbery features set in a niche among the bricks. This grotesque spirit of place rhymes with the face of the lurker in the room behind the cab despatcher. And it floats across the traffic to the church porch where I am sitting, victim to the unedited spill of memory and anticipation, the imagery that drowns us when we are not allowed to walk, make notes or move.

An instinct for upturns in the markets for property and painting kept Jock in play: trading one against the other. When he lifted his camera, I never knew if he was contemplating the acquisition of a chapel or providing the raw material for some huge canvas for the museum trade, the latest warehouse conversion. Our paths sometimes intersected in the afternoon, when Jock was running his dozy, studio-sharing greyhound alongside his bicycle, and I was plodding off, eyes on the ground, in the general direction of the Lea Valley. To be sure it was still there.

I was conscious, while I waited for my man, the pigeon fisher, of Jock's house, on the far side of the Museum of Childhood park. The Scottish realist painter, as he described himself, had been in the news. Driven to the edge of madness by the perpetual drone of idling engines, with attendant pollution, from police cars parked on the kerb outside his door, keeping all systems ticking over to support their computers before the next siren chase, Jock stormed out to hammer on metal and rant with enough fervour to get himself arrested and locked up for six hours. As he intended. And into the headlines.

Today the 63-year-old said he was at his wit's end. Sometimes there are as many as four police vehicles left unattended with their engines running for periods of an hour and a half, throughout the day, so in effect there is always a police vehicle belting out diesel fumes 24/7 unnecessarily. Mr McFadyen yesterday received an apology from his local station for being handcuffed and fingerprinted but police cars on his road are still left running unattended.

Jock was back in the news. Estate agents were invited to take the tour, with Idris Elba as a neighbour, property prices were rising fast. A bit of drama is an aphrodisiac.

But we had been partners in modest subversion long before this; embarking an inflatable kayak, borrowed from the photographer Stephen Gill, for slow raids around the back rivers of the Olympic site. Chains had not yet been set across points of access. It was an Amazonian pilotage, picking our way through curtains of creepers, witnessing the blue flash of a kingfisher, saluting work gangs brought in to bury unsightly pylons.

Jock came away with a substantial topographic record, manipulated on his own terms, in order to hold in permanent suspension the after-image of doomed industries and dispersed communal enterprises. The paintings played alongside Gill's Lea Valley elegy, the photographs he curated as *Archaeology in Reverse*. Yellow lines left by surveyors as outlines for coming media centres, blue fences in progress. All the rituals enacted up to the moment when the temple of the Olympic Stadium began to rise from the ground.

Stephen, who kept a studio overlooking the railway in Bethnal Green, soon learned what those wide horizons had to teach him: when to move out. And how to haunt the places that haunted him. In his books there is always a cumulative momentum. He is a transient in a place that has lodged in his heart, knowing that, all too soon, he will have to give it up. His Hackney reportage is like a letter to a friend, filled with unexpected detail. Nothing has to be explained, but this is what he saw *today*. Out-takes can be safely laid aside, catalogued and left for the next adventure in refracted autobiography.

I was happy to wait on the church porch in Bethnal Green. Perhaps this would be the end of the story. I might have made the successful transition from walker to watcher. Staying where I was, I could trawl back through the mind-movies of my encounters with Stephen Gill. The pleasure I took from the independent books he produced, the unexpected angles of approach he brought to his engagement with Hackney, the marshes and the Lea Valley.

Our expeditions usually begin at first light. This time, Stephen explained, we would be better to hold off until the worst of the rush hour had burnt itself out. I waited, admiring a procession of those bright red obstacles known as buses. In my unopened notebook I had transcriptions of mad monologues from rear seats on the upper deck. The mobile phone gabble that was so distinct from the money chatter and party gossip of the Overground. The new demographic of hipster Hackney spurned the viral crush of buses, preferring to cycle or take the Ginger Line. Buses were heavy with coughing out-patients, illegals of every stripe, nightworkers, mothers battering for space with double-buggies, old folk hanging on anything they can reach like bats. The words, in English, broken or deranged, were about sleights, insults, withheld benefits. There was also a powerful strain of the occult, the casting of spells, encounters with local demons. Talk had its fists up, ready for the next challenge from snoops and inspectors.

'Gotta ask for a refund for the toilet, man.'

'I feel worse than yesterday. I actually left work already. My piss smells like barley wine.'

'Get the boys down, sort that out? Got it, man! Take photographs before and after we go in. Right!'

'You want *money*? I give you money. Nobody wants money anymore.'

'He stitched me up and called to tell me the bad news. You're a horrible man, you are.'

'She's gutted. And Terry's gutted. That's what they're like down there, innit Mum? That's what Lennie was saying. I feel bad not talking to him. But for why? I dunno. He's got that over me as well. All the same, innit? They hang round with each other. They started cracking up in the office. I didn't grin, Mum. I'm really upset with her.'

'What you in *bed* for, man? It's half-past-one. *What*? No, I won't deal with that shit. That's really clever when you've got a child. Stupid cow, stupid cow! You should have a job, have prospects, know what I mean? Drift then, drift into sleep. Well, I'm *sorry*. Back in the forest then. Set fucking fire to it. Don't be a pansy. Do you want to speak to Little Man?'

'How's it hanging? I'm waiting for a yes or no. See if I can move into this place. Detox. Have you heard from Yankee? Last time I saw him was at Cousin Tim. Mo? Oh yeah. Ha ha! Moaning Mo! Alright. All good now. I was drunk, innit? Slipped. That's how good it was. Happy New Year.'

'Can you see a camera? How many bodies in the car, man? You fucking wanker. I'm sorry about this. OK then. Just let me know. Cheers. Goodbye.'

'I find that so much of my energy is directed to someone else's life. It's not a question of love. It's a question of putting myself first. It's not a problem, but it *is* a problem. *What am I doing?* I can say it to you – as a telephone call. But actually implementing that call after I've met with Alex… OK, sweetheart. Goodbye goodbye.'

'If you don't send your kids to school, the policemen come and take them away.'

'They put him in a cell, know what I mean?'

'Where are you? Where you be? Still in hospital, mum? Mum mum, *mum*?'

'This is a new cheese, my brother. Know what I'm saying? And it's fluffy as wool.'

'She was an absolute fucking alcoholic drug addict waster. They trapped her into disclosing it. I was like, shit. It wasn't up to me. So fucking terrible. So there.'

'I don't give a shit, man. I don't give a fucking shit, man. That's all shit. I don't give a shit. I don't give a fucking shit. That's shit, man. I don't give a shit.'

The new Stagecoach buses parade in packs, showing off their NOT IN SERVICE destination windows. They stall, eager for shade, under the railway bridge, shuddering slightly like overbred racehorses.

'I love the blue of Bethnal Green bridges, the way it's disappearing.' Stephen Gill.

Gill's art – and I regarded him as a major resource, a master of territory – is about a state of mesmerised attention so concentrated that it has to be called love. Love as righteous anger. Love as *notice*, alert to flaws, follies, bureaucratic impositions. He catalogues the proudly mundane: junked betting slips, cans of energy drinks and albums of wedding photographs. Hackney couples, in a scavenged set of prints that he acquired, are taking their first married kiss. Domesticated vampires rigid in stiff clothes, more suitable to a funeral, airfixed hair, are swooning to bite, submit, endorse. A heartbreakingly poignant portfolio of engagement in pinched times. *Hackney Kiss*, Gill called the book. It was published by the Archive for Modern Conflict. 9,000 negatives purchased, blind, on eBay.

'All the images were made by one person,' Gill said. 'But since the negatives passed from hand to hand, no one is sure who the photographer is.'

Brave Hackney citizens are marrying and remarrying in the grey years after the Second World War. Cakes like maquettes for icing-sugar tower blocks. Like models of Nicholas Hawksmoor's Christ Church, the front elevation in Spitalfields; disparate architectural blocks flirting with collapse. Crittall windows. Tired lace curtains. Jewish pennants. Fringed shades on standing lamps. That tragic cigarette in the bride-groom's trailing hand. Boot-polish hair. The clock at five-past-three on the sideboard, next to the bottle of port. Fancy mirrors. Exotic wallpaper. The porthole of a squat Coronation TV set looking like a primitive microwave. On the wall, earlier couples are frozen into their frames. There are more dead floral tributes on long tables than on the coffin lid of a Kray funeral in Chingford Mount.

But Stephen is always positive. Take away his camera and he'll draw on his eyeballs with a felt-tip pen.

'Years of sunlight went into making that texture of ironwork,' he said, looking across the road. 'The blue has faded so beautifully.'

Stephen is one of the few people to appreciate old railway bridges as *bridges*. Portals to the next zone of London. He needs to let the first frenzy of traffic play out, because he'll be standing right in the middle of the road poking a long pole into crannies under a succession of railway bridges. And there are many bridges, many feathers, many fallen nests along our tarmac riverbank.

We walk west.

My guide is dressed as an urban fisherman: soft blue hat with no flies in the band, blue jacket, loose trousers, heavy boots. He is carrying a bulging bag and a silver pole. He calls a halt where Collingwood Street emerges from Three Colts Lane.

'Look at *that*,' Stephen said.

The arched roof of the road tunnel under the railway is scored with claw marks, yellow-orange striations revealing the original glow of the bricks beneath generations of thick grey sludge-varnish.

'Overloaded vans heading south to the scrapyards.'

White goods heaped on numerous Transits have gouged at the curve of the low ceiling. The lane going north is untouched. Stephen is a connoisseur of pigeon habitats, but this bridge doesn't answer. It is not a promising spot to begin our fishing. The photographer knows all the secrets of the silver stream of the railway. A hunter-gatherer of images.

On our walk from Cambridge Heath Road, Gill pointed out the warehouse where he had kept a studio for many years; the grotto from which he launched his dawn raids on disputed landscapes. The former inhabitants had been priced out, then expelled: radical printers, painters, performance artists and invisibles. Even the junkies shooting up in the metal box of the lift had left for Hastings.

'I could watch the trains from my window. I could cycle up the Lea Valley. I could work all night in the darkroom. Then make a coffee. Go for a wash to York Hall.'

The silver fishing pole is extended. Stephen is satisfied with this new pitch, the pool of light under the second bridge.

'Listen,' he says. 'Can you feel it?'

The ripple and shudder of the Stansted Express. Planks tremble. Girders sigh. Now the fishing pole looks like the prosthetic arm of some manic soundman trying to trap the yawn of expanding metal joists. Gill purchased it, so he told me, in a hardware shop on Hackney Road. The telescopic pole is intended for use by window-cleaners. Stephen has adapted it for his camera.

People don't like pigeons, Will Self said, because we never see the young, the cute ones on *Countryfile* calendars. 'No fluffy little pigeon chicks or hatchlings to arouse our sentimental feelings.' But we don't need to see the prey on this fishing trip, we can smell their dens from the other side of the road: burnt marzipan in diesel soup. Marsh gas trapped in the bones of a plague pit. Stephen has the clothes, the camera and the whippy rod. But he's forgotten his surgical facemask. The reluctant subjects of his ethnographic survey into sexual habits are the feral pigeons who have infested these arches since the coming of the railways. They have seen the days of trading in exotic animals, imported lion cubs, parrots, monkeys, come and go.

The enchantment of the area derives from the Victorian invasion by canals and railways: secret caves among the brick arches for dealers, hucksters, illegitimates. Stephen is honouring the private life of the much-maligned, shit-endorsed pigeon colonies; spectral coops within the ironwork of railway bridges. Birds are London's dead souls nesting on stalagmites, on conical mounds of their own droppings. Aeons of acid waste eating into metal. We have never observed these creatures in such enclosed settings: so defenceless, taken by stealth. They are ruffled, agitated by the shock of the harsh white flash. The avian portraits, over which Stephen has limited control, are pure revelation. They chart previously unrecorded Bethnal Green life, one of those tiny pockets of origin left outside the intrusion of surveillance systems.

Breeding pens, high above the cars, stash fresh eggs among spikes laid out to frustrate potential landing strips. Prison eugenics in a rusting iron vault. Pigeons are a swaggering underclass hopping around on diseased feet and too few legs. They operate best as a mob, holding off bother-boy corvines who try to muscle in on the confetti trails of stale white bread lobbed out by mad old women, emerging from insecure flats, and pretending that the crumbs are nothing to do with them. A leak of body waste it would be unmannerly to mention.

Pedestrians, mostly Asian, heading through the tunnel, notice the image-fisher, but elect to leave him alone, without comment. The long pole wavers. Stephen stands among the cars, he raids. Traffic swerves. He counts aloud, his camera is primed: 'One. Two. Three…'

After twelve seconds, the flash detonates. Stephen is shooting blind. He won't know what he's got until he makes the print. The birds explode in an aggrieved fury of wings. They circle, swoop, settle on the roof of new flats erected where the Kray family home used to stand in Vallance Road. Such souls as managed to transmigrate from these original terraces, interior lives as tribal as the birds, have been reborn into a secondary existence in pigeon purgatory.

A fledgling, fallen from the nest, pink of belly, thrashes on a ledge, unable to take flight; but unwilling to fall to the ground. The demented creature is trapped in Sisyphean torment. Nothing to be done. Down on the pavement or pulped under the tyres of a white van.

In soft focus, the birds cohabit with their own dead in a space that is both larder and crèche. A ledge on which thick nests of twigs are frosted in white droppings. This is a final colony from which the tenants have not yet been unhoused by power hoses. A use has been found, at last, for Boris Johnson's expensively acquired water canons.

But the strangest aspect of Stephen's pigeon séance is that nobody challenges us: two men poking a long silver rod under a railway bridge. A rod with a camera attachment. And a brutal flash (the kind that conspiracy theorists claim blinded Princess Di's driver in the underpass). In our surveillance city, where image-making is always suspect, if not criminal – 'Don't you know there's a war on?' – fishing for pigeon portraits passes without comment. Until a local matron, dog on a string, approaches. 'You're doing it all wrong, gentlemen. You'll never get rid of the bastards that way. I've lived here thirty years and I've tried everything. They still crap on my head every time I set foot on the street. Those pigeons, they think they fucking own the place.'

When we'd finished our day's fishing, Stephen carried his pouch back to the studio. In the dark room he would discover what he had caught with his camera on the end of a rod. Rivets like steel eggs. Nests like crowns of thorn for a heretic messiah. Subtle blues and greys of metal and feather. The domestic life of birds in crannies under railways.

Walking home to Hackney from Stephen's own nest and private place, with all those processed layers of light, the rescued objects and boxed archives, still playing in the sump of my crocodile brain, I washed up against a well-intentioned obstacle that I recognised as a public artwork. The level of collaboration between promoter and commissioned artisan achieved an over-loud political correctness that cancelled itself out; waiting for the years of neglect to break it down to a condition where it was worth a second glance. Even a photograph of record.

In Weavers Field, as so often with these interventions, local school kids have been brought in on the act. They have been invited to invent upbeat slogans, which will then be baked into interlocking bricks. A chorus of voices around a spindly sculptural dance symbolising everything implied in the park's title. I transcribed some of the messages immortalised on the rosy bricks.

GIVE US MORE TO LIVE FOR THAN WAR. PEACE. ART. NEVER DOUBT THAT A SMALL GROUP OF THOUGHTFUL COMMITTED CITIZENS CAN CHANGE THE WORLD INDEED IT'S THE ONLY THING THAT EVER DOES.

We had been talking about bricks. The relationship with baked clay and text goes back so far: to Mesopotamia, to shards lovingly preserved and displayed in the great museums. Stephen is a committed scavenger. And what he finds and uses, carries home from his expeditions, is neatly boxed and labelled as future evidence. I think his practice is exemplary, the way he strives to allow place an equal share in every photographic project he undertakes.

Before I left the studio, he showed me a box filled with pieces of brick, conglomerates, rocks with chipped edges. We'll return to that story. Everything in the new CGI London, in Olympicopolis, denies stone, mistreats wood, spurns the sloppy mud and dribble of poisoned creeks. It is time, no doubt, for a period of pyscho*geology*, navigating by glacial erratics dropped behind municipal flats, the hunks of Cornish granite exposed in parks made from demolished terraces. The stones are beginning to sing. Thick lips of kerbs exert a powerful magnetism, twisting the blade of the compass, like that moment in *Moby-Dick* when lightning strikes and the ship sails *against* the advice of its fallible instruments. We are coming back, so misdirected by electronic gizmos and information overloads, to the stone core within ourselves; ice memories, diamonds in the blood.

Stephen spoke of bricks made from the residue of the Beckton Sewage Works; human waste being used, as in the first settlements on Thames marshland, to pad the walls that contain us. *First London*: silt, straw, smoke, shit.

I remembered my own fetish for picking out tide-smoothed pieces of brick on the foreshore, in Wapping or East Tilbury, London bricks with lettering, broken alphabets. And, like a kneeling child again, trying to make sentences from the traces of vanished buildings.

All of which is a long way around to arrive in the streets of Hackney at the time of the riots in August 2011. Stephen Gill is so deeply embedded in mapping and recording that he felt obliged, as a moral duty, to document the event in some way. But he struggled to avoid a reflex response. You could identify in news reports such a relish for apocalypse. An ecstatic acknowledgement that the fires and trashed cars and supermarket sweeps were the perfect pre-Olympic trailer. Those confused souls, TV journalists, parachuted into Tottenham war zones to provide reportage, stood stiffly at their posts, while all around them danced the children of the estates, tweeting and twittering and teasing the action on. Flames seemed to run by some malicious instinct right down the fuse of the Overground Line, from Dalston Junction to a veteran furniture store in Croydon. End of the line.

A harvest of stones was gathered by pram and bicycle. Stephen toured the aftermath of the riot zone, in Clarence Road and Narrow Way, and by broader sweeps through the territory, like an urban archaeologist evaluating axe heads and grapeshot, picking up chunks of rock that had bounced off police cars and fondling them for bruises. Tenderly, he transported the relics to his studio, where they could be afforded the dignity of forensic examination. He logged each exhibit with a microscopic high-definition lens. At which point the bricks and chunks of projectile were revealed as lunar landscapes; surfaces seething with lichen clusters, plasma stains and violent fissures.

The history of small wars – and these riots, overheated by new technologies, were a minor manifestation of regular seasonal friction – is told through a photographic interrogation of spent bullets and shells recovered from the battlefield. Every one of these bricks has a narrative. Some of them were recovered by Gill, after he had noted, from his laptop screen, the trajectory of flight picked up in a news report. Sections of garden wall and pressure-cracked flagstones were pressed into service at a moment of social upheaval. Gill's prints restore gravitas. They are a truer portrait of the crowd atomised into individual units for judgement and retribution than that ugly parade of smudged surveillance mugshots in the tabloids.

Cities can be mapped by missing cobblestones: Paris in '68, London at the burning of Newgate Prison, Budapest, Belfast, Prague. Streets are dug up in displays of reverse archaeology. The stones redistribute themselves, flying through the air like Magritte's loaves, towards the wall of Plexiglas shields and visored helmets. If you can't trust those mobile-phone snatches of women leaping from flaming buildings or street actors brandishing their swag, the bricks in a box are naked evidence. We can be grateful to Stephen Gill for finding a way to animate the riots so modestly, without prurience or the politician's boast that he alone has the solution. No recipes on his desk, only rocks.

John Minton's 1951 cover drawing for Roland Camberton's Hackney novel, *Rain on the Pavements*, takes the same view of Mare Street offered by eye-in-the-sky helicopter coverage of the riots. But there is one striking difference. Minton's aggrieved marchers, holding up political placards, are heading for the right place to lodge their protest: the old Town Hall. The 2011 consumerist communards converge on JD Sports, on betting shops and windows featuring widescreen televisions and designer handbags. Camberton's ambition, like that of Stephen Gill, was to know every stick and stone of the borough. The contemporary flash mob, like those grand-project promoters and offshore property collectors, want to tear the borough down, to remake the world as a future ruin, a *tabula rasa* undisturbed by previous history. Gill's portraits of stones, grey and self-contained, are a telling record of this episode.

In Weavers Fields I sat on a bench, facing south, my back set to the noise of the riots. I tried to think about nothing. To empty it all out. But the irritation was still there. The voices of unsponsored oral historians offering chapters of their fragmenting lives as they race through the park, almost colliding with other ranters, jabbering into the cold air.

'I turn out my pockets. If I find a monkey, I'm going straight to Heathrow and buying two tickets to Bolivia. And a fucking big camera.'

'Reluctantly, we're going to have to say "no" to that. You'd better stick it out, John. It's going to take proper money. I want to see *landscape* on my desk. There are huge numbers of jobs available in London. The company will change a lot over the next year. You can't master the same costume when you're in a different culture.'

'I got a job today, mum, property development.'

FREE BREAKFAST FOR BIKES

'Free breakfast for cyclists! Free breakfast for cyclists!'

The jived-up T-shirt gang at the stall, hopping from foot to foot like incontinent missionaries, waving plastic water bottles and making threats with bowls of green apples, have been accredited to offer the bounty of the earth to the indifferent swarm of cyclists on the blacktop perimeter of what used to be London Fields. This is a council initiative. There is a well-staffed office dedicated to cycle politics, to getting the world to mount and ride. They want to convert the lumpen masses of Hackney – and the impulse is messianic – to a velodrome of committed athletes streaming to their Pilates classes and shared desks through an obstacle course of branded recycling bins and flagstone revisions by Volker Highways (Considerate Constructors).

'Free breakfast for cyclists!'

The Mayor of London is in complete agreement. Cycling is Zen. Cycling is holy. Cycling is the answer to everything. To this end, Will Norman, coincidentally a global partnership director at Nike, has been appointed cycling commissioner. He will work with Transport for London (Every Journey Matters) to invest £770 million on new cycling infrastructure. Mr Norman said: 'Cycling can play a transformational role in improving our health and happiness, and building better communities for everyone.'

'Free breakfast for cyclists!'

And, by implication: nothing for the rest of you. Not a crust for pedestrians, elderly ramblers without affiliation, sniffers of the chemically boosted and sadly mortal strip of wildflower meadow.

'Free breakfast for cyclists!'

Free breakfast: if you agree to sign on, become a positive statistic.

And, by the way, while you are at it, there are other forms – no matter if you are just passing through, dowsing an app trail – to confirm your approval of proposed road schemes, green-route cycle paths barring other forms of traffic, throwing more work to favoured contractors: Volker Highways (Considerate Constructors).

When they are not hawking fruit like Mexicans working a road-block, the dedicated friends of the bicycle are covering the Broadway Market exit of London Fields, harvesting signatures from the slowing peloton. 'Does it matter that we live in Kentish Town or Archway?' Not one jot. Have an apple, a free pen. Anyone in possession of a legitimate bicycle belongs to Hackney.

'Free breakfast for cyclists! Free breakfast for cyclists!'

A 70-year-old black man, tapping along on a silver-topped cane, arrives at the dedicated cycle highway from the direction of Helmsley Place. He pauses, listening out for the rubberised swish of the un-broken morning stream. The Darwinianism of wired pedal pushers with their gaze firmly fixed on a distant horizon. It's fortunate that he doesn't qualify for the free breakfast, because he's never going to make it across the road. Those apples from the sponsored Garden of Eden are out of reach.

In my early Hackney years, London Fields was a destination for communal football. It is now a zone of transience and approved health routines. It is *en route*. Or a party rug for weekend balloon sniffers who are not aesthetically affronted by the terrible purple skirts hung from dignified London Plane trees to tell revellers how to conduct a barbecue. Like neck tattoos on a dowager.

Recreation has been corralled into small neat packages: wire fence, single basketball hoop. For the squeak of rubber on rubber, circle and shoot. Table-tennis slabs providing a tap-tap-tap soundtrack in windblown precincts. The rough sleepers and morning drinkers who used to perch on benches to congratulate each other on making it through another long night have been expelled to the coast.

London Fields is open on all sides. It has been promoted into a traffic island sandwiched between two active cycle highways; the official one that hurtles past the children's play park and day nursery, and the leafy aisle of the central avenue for those who want a gentler approach to Broadway Market, dodging and weaving among a drift of joggers wired to bleeping devices like so many near misses from an emergency roadkill unit. Exercise covens of already-fit young women are put through their paces by personal trainers, while red-eyed men embellished with knapsacks of child accessories negotiate a passage through dog accompanists making a brave show of waving their poop trowels and colostomy bags. And all of this motion, this life-affirming routine *business*, is ignored by the gaunt casualties of former times parked on their benches with yesterday's free newspapers, their scavenged roll-ups and a bit of a book. The odour exchange, skunk, sustainably perfumed sweat, artisan coffee in take-away beakers, is democratic.

PEDESTRIAN PRIORITY. CONSIDERATE CYCLISTS WEL-COMED. Strategic post-truth signage greets newcomers to Victoria Park. Where there is still space for old-time benchwarmers, conversational joggers (all languages), and dog people composting open spaces. Even the right kind of walker. Figures are established here for a time, or tolerated as they pass through, nodding at strangers, rollerblading, trancing and exercising. Or being harnessed to drag huge rubber tyres in preparation for Polar porterage: if that is your thing, seeing East London's silver tarmac as an ice shelf.

I was heading for the canal when I saw disaster unwrap itself in slow motion. Two young mothers, propped on their bikes, texting and nattering, shushing babes in wicker baskets, did not police the satellite child on two wheels as she circled, wobbled, avoided a jumping dog – 'he won't hurt you, babe, he's only playing' – to take off, picking up speed, down the gentle ramp. And to splash, in the gap between two parked narrowboats, with barely a ruffle of the surface, into the dark and lifeless water. Where a disembarking cyclist dropped his machine, to grab her by the hair, almost as soon as she slid under the surface. All was well. Nobody screamed.

The park is a site of elective infantilism: mature adults on psychedelic skateboards bopping to earworm infills, wearing football shorts and romper suits and scooting along with ponytails swishing. One intrepid voyager in a tight black leotard is propelling a paddleboard down the centre of the canal, at something around the pace of a brisk walk: a busy money-market recreationalist looking like a tribesman from the upper reaches of the Amazon. He draws a straight line through the pondweed duvet. It is four years now since I saw an eel, and longer since the last pike loafed under the railway bridge, snacking on small fry and dumped pets.

'Any issues on your side coming in?'

A couple, in matching designer camouflage, side by side, impervious to the etiquette of towpath survival, rattle towards shared desks in the canalside Portakabin colony, supporting between them a bag stuffed with slim laptops: ROYAL BOTANIC GARDENS KEW. Within seconds they are forcibly separated by the first surge of the peloton. The man fumes and trembles on the edge of water. The woman, clinging to the Kew bag, scrapes under overhanging blackberry bushes, pierced by savage thorns.

'So: that nice Chris was there, yeah? Angus gets, like, a grand. My job... A 19-year-old... She said could she come up to lunch? So there was, like, *no* lunch? I said, "Can you give me a lift to the tube?" He's *such* a bad driver. She sat there eating, like... a sandwich? So, it's me, isn't it? She will *not*...'

'My wife was a *senior* manager.'

'She's *forty-seven*. Has she thought about the future?'

The wolves of the peloton express, in a blur of territorial imperatives, from the dark bore of the bridge, sharp elbows poking for position on the constricted run to Victoria Park. You can hear snorts of entitlement as the pumping thighs of Canary Wharf mercenaries are frustrated, for as much as six seconds, by a floaty Bloomsbury woman on a rattletrap. As a walker, you don't see the whispering assassins until they are past you. A sudden cut of air. A bell that doesn't ting. The goggled scorn of dismissal for anachronistic life forms.

Motorised traffic on adjoining streets, already slower than the saintly cyclists, is being regulated to 20mph. Which gives more time for texting and checking messages. 20mph on the towpath is *launch* momentum as gladiators, hepped to the gills by Tour de France footage and the triumphs of pollen-suffering Olympians with Therapeutic Use Exemptions, weave and accelerate. Those sneaky foreigners are swapping bags of piss before testing. Our boys, it is now alleged, take the same shots. But they have genuine hay fever allergies and Belgian doctors' certificates. And unexplained Jiffy bags with innocent medication.

The skinny wheels of a man caught in the middle of the pack slide in a groove left by recent improvements to the towpath. He plunges, at pace, straight into the canal. The peloton race on. Survival of the fittest. There is no fraternal support for the second leg of this unofficial Iron Man triathlon. You're not supposed to swim while you are still on your bike. The man sinks in the saddle.

It takes me a few minutes, dodging through the next wave bombing from the tunnel to reach him. The cyclist hauls himself out and lies gasping and shivering on the edge, fanned by the backdraft of the swish of wheels. The bike weighs nothing and I pull it out. It must feel like riding on an idea, a line drawing. He seems like a decent chap, in shock to be grounded. He shakes his head to get the water out. The bike is undamaged. The man is most concerned about his phone. He pats lycra padding with multiple pockets to find where it is lodged. The glinting wafer didn't appreciate the sudden baptism but it still works.

That morning, up to the moment of drama, was a quiet one: sixty-six cyclists used the towpath on my ten-minute stroll between Victoria Park and the Cat and Mutton Lock. Along with an almost equal number of joggers. At weekends, there would be more joggers, fewer bicycles. On this day, myself included, I counted four walkers. Two of them, South Korean martial arts practitioners, had a heated discussion before moving into the next phase of their discipline. I recognised a regular, a woman wedded to the towpath. Despite everything, she bustled along for years, staring ahead in paralysed disbelief. Now she held an open newspaper in front of her like a Plexiglass shield. Two of the sixty-six cyclists, both women in hats, approaching the railway bridge, sounded their bells.

★★★

How did it begin, the cycling initiative? The grand thesis, paid for in lives, that getting London mounted on two wheels would solve our problems; not only transport chaos, but quality of life. We would be better people in a healthier city. We would be almost Dutch or German or Scandinavian, while negotiating killer junctions, lethal bridges, alongside fleets of authentically European lorries heaving material to the new Lea Valley frontier, the building sites of the City. No aspiring politician could be caught at the garden gate without bicycle or helmet. Boris Johnson's machine was surgically implanted. Jeremy Corbyn, the people's tribune, was obliged to confirm his integrity by being grumpy with TV crews, before shoving off, helmet secured, towards the day's grave business. No more motorbike and sidecar tours of East Germany. The modern leader is an urban centaur.

Hard to picture Margaret Thatcher embedded in any vehicle other than a Crusader tank or a spanking new British motor. Ethical cycling was a New Labour initiative. In his retirement from the front line, the grand *consigliere* of the movement, Lord Mandelson of Foy, single shareholder in the late-lamented Millennium Dome on Bugsby's Marshes, talked confidentially to an unseen interrogator for a televisual portrait by Hannah Rothschild. How privileged we were, within the kabuki stylisation of eyebrow ballet, the heart-rending sighs over the shortcomings of colleagues, to be granted a glimpse of the child behind the man; young Peter's induction into political life. Picture this: the juvenile New Labour dignitary on a Hovis bicycle! Lord Mandelson cut a smile. And rested his head on leathered support as the camera-car cruised him through London, the city he had done so much to revive.

Triggered by an archive clip of his maternal grandfather Herbert Morrison, another ennobled socialist cabinet minister, Mandelson launched into a cherished memory of cycling around Hendon, committee room to polling station, bearing leaflets, carrying messages as proudly as the freshly baked loaves in Ridley Scott's celebrated commercial, shot in 1973, on the picturesque slopes of Shaftesbury. Carl Barlow, the youth who featured in the advertisement, underscored by the slow movement of Dvořák's Symphony No. 9, arranged for brass, went on to become a fireman in East Ham. And to find himself caught up in the aggravations of the Thatcher period: belt-tightening, union-bashing, the cracking of rebellious coal miners' heads. Lord Tebbit's helpful remarks, delivered to a sea of nodding grey, at Blackpool in 1981, in the aftermath of the Handsworth and Brixton riots, will have carried a special charge for Barlow. 'On yer bike!'

Hovis, thanks to Ridley Scott, preceded New Labour and Boris Johnson as sponsors of the cult of cycling. (Scott was a cycle obsessive. His first short film, made in 1965, in his student days at the Royal College of Art, featured his younger brother Tony schlepping around Hartlepool, and was called *Boy and Bicycle*.) Every inch pedalled is a gesture towards saving the planet. YouTube is blistered with propaganda for cycle schemes funded by the generosity of corporate bankers. And cyberspace has been wormed by guerrilla footage of the real Boris Johnson chuntering on his mobile phone as he labours towards City Hall – as well as faked sequences of a clone with a flop of golden hair stunting on underpasses and concrete ramps. Cycling was invented for the internet, the pirate phone-snatch at twilight, and the GoPro helmet.

The Tebbit sound-bark – *On yer bike!* – has returned, to remind us how neatly cycle rhetoric rhymes with agitation in the streets and the slashing of social services. Thatcher's Employment Secretary, a former BOAC pilot, not yet parachuted into the House of Lords, recalled the defining moment of his childhood – and, as with Peter Mandelson, it involved a bicycle. 'I grew up in the Thirties with an unemployed father,' Tebbit avowed. 'He didn't riot. He got on his bicycle and looked for work.'

Man and machine, molecules shaken by the cobbles, intermingle in a rapturous genetic blind date. Tebbit's paterfamilias, puffing from factory gate to factory gate, becomes a symbol of the decade, half-man and half-bicycle, in the fashion of Flann O'Brien's *The Third Policeman*.

'The gross and net result of it,' O'Brien wrote, 'is that people who spent most of their natural lives riding iron bicycles over the rocky roadsteads of the parish get their personalities mixed up with the personalities of their bicycle as a result of the interchanging of atoms.' When O'Brien's novel *The Dalkey Archive*, in which James Joyce returns to Dublin as a bar curate, was adapted for the stage, they called it *When the Saints Go Cycling In*.

But it wasn't just Tebbit who exploited Ridley Scott's brand of sentimentality to summon an England that never was. John Major, a gap-year prime minister sleepwalking through a job for which he was never intended, offered a reprise of George Orwell's cycling spinster to bring back common decency to an England imagined as a *Midsomer Murders* village green. But neither of these conservative philosophers, Major or Tebbit, appreciated the inflammatory effect that bicycles have on the libido; the erotic impulses unleashed by the potentialities of the open road. That intimate contact with a hard leather saddle. The steady pumping rhythms. The gasping for breath on a steep ascent. The ecstatic, effortless, downhill swoop, hair blowing free: *aaaaaahhhh!*

The pataphysician Alfred Jarry was so excited by the crotch-hugging kit of the years before the First World War that he took to dressing in the uniform of a cycle racer. He caused a scandal by following the poet Mallarmé's funeral cortege on a bicycle. Jarry's text, 'The Passion Considered as an Uphill Bicycle Race', was the acknowledged inspiration for JG Ballard's 'The Assassination of John Fitzgerald Kennedy Considered as a Downhill Motor Race'. The psychosexual derangement of Ballard's *Crash* (1973) would have dissolved into low *Carry On* comedy if the humble Raleigh had replaced the Ford Cortina as the vehicle of choice for navigating the perimeter fence of suburban promiscuity. Jarry, in a vision admired by the surrealists, gazed into the window of a bicycle dealer to discover 'a reproduction of a veritable crown of thorns as an ad for puncture-proof tyres'.

HG Wells, right back at the start of the cycling craze, was quick to recognise the liberating possibilities of this new technology. In *The Wheels of Chance* (1896), a draper's assistant uses his annual holiday to take to the roads of Surrey and Sussex, where he encounters a young lady whose head has been turned by romances featuring New Women in rational costume pedalling towards independence: by way of the coaching inns of Haslemere, Midhurst and Bognor.

Hoopdriver, the Wells excursionist, is encouraged, before he sets off, by advice from a non-cycling co-worker: 'Don't scorch, don't ride on the footpath, keep to your own side of the road.' A reasonable code now being shredded by the urban middle classes as they haul themselves, with the odd tumble, on to a flotilla of Bromptons and Marins. Hoopdriver's informant makes the premature claim that cycling is fashionable: 'Judges and stock-brokers and actresses, and, in fact, all the best people rode.'

In Hackney, by 2010, this century-old prediction was confirmed along canal paths, parks and pavements. Judges and bankers and actors, stand-up comedians, radio producers, script editors, architects, junior doctors, cadet drug dealers, broadsheet journalists, graffiti photographers, libel lawyers and website designers from Old Street: they did their bit to complicate London's traffic chaos, by staying away from stuttering buses, where they would be brought into contact with the sweltering mass of immigrant humanity. The social status of cycling, thanks to propaganda campaigns spearheaded by Bullingdon Club toffs such as Boris Johnson, David Cameron and George Osborne, underwent significant revision.

In the late Sixties and early Seventies, when the path alongside the Regent's Canal was mud, forbidden to pedestrians and cyclists alike, I rode to my gardening job in Limehouse on a wreck bought from Kingsland Waste market for £6. Municipal gardeners and labourers were supposed to get around, tea shack to work site, on bicycles. Some students and food-for-free survivalists also chose two-wheel transport. No self-respecting narrowboat was complete without a bicycle on deck. With the surge of canalside development in the run-up to the 2012 Olympics, I noticed a standard feature of the emerging new-build blocks: the higher the floor, the more bicycles on the balcony. These machines, with their fashionably slim wheels, heralded a new demographic: the liberated short-haul commuter.

The British Waterways authority found it necessary to issue a green pamphlet, in verse, to instruct cyclists in towpath etiquette: 'Two Tings. Ting your bell twice… pass slowly, be nice!' And there followed a long list of rules for the peloton to ignore: rules for bridges, for bends, for wildlife habitats. *Ting ting.* 'Earphones/head-phones should not be worn.' *Ting ting.*

I interviewed Jock McFadyen, an inveterate haunter of the tow-path. 'Every time I hear that ting,' he said, 'I feel like kicking one of the bastards into the canal. Don't ting me! You can't walk. You've got to be constantly standing aside, standing aside. If you hear that ting and you ignore it, then you get called a muppet, a fool. Every trip down the Regent's Canal is an exercise in confrontation.'

By the time, stepping westward towards Islington, you arrive at the courtyard development that has grown out of the former Gainsborough film studios, the convoy of cyclists, fretting and ting-ing, is a permanent sound installation: squeak of brakes, rattle of loose paving slabs. Curses are lobbed at obstacles, including pedestrians.

Behind a ground floor picture window in one of the blocks, resting bikes have been arranged like an indoor docking station, waiting for sponsorship from Barclays or Santander. The deserted gymnasium belongs to that tragic period, maybe five years ago, when cyclists preferred to play safe by avoiding the hazards of the road, and pumping away, to piped music, without going anywhere. Their tranced gaze was fixed on a screen: landscape pornography, satellite sport with irritating stockmarket statistics dripping down the border of the frame. One room in every new development has been set aside to stack bikes.

Security is a major consideration. Bicycles are both the instruments facilitating a local crime wave (ram raids, drug deliveries, phone snatches) and the object of crime. The theft and redistribution of bicycles, rapidly liberated with bolt-cutters, is a substantial element in the black economy. It is rumoured that container loads disap-pear, weekly, in the direction of the Balkans. When a utopian cycle scheme was launched in Cambridge in 1993, all 300 machines were stolen on the first day; broken down for spares or shipped out by free-marketeers quick to spot an opportunity. Halfords attempted a similar programme in London, distributing ten bicycles around the city, in order to publicise the health benefits of cycling: lose weight by seriously emptying your wallet on a replacement upgrade. When the six-week scheme concluded, the bikes would be sent, as a charitable gesture, to Africa. There was a zero return at the end of the experiment.

'Never in my puff did I hear of any man stealing anything but a bicycle when he was in his sane senses,' says the Sergeant in *The Third Policeman* (begun in the 1940s and published in 1967). 'Surely you are not going to tell me at my time of life that the world is changing?'

Urban cycle promotions, as Lord Mandelson would recognise, are about entitlement and ecology. Entitlement to credit by politicians and planners. And the sound ecology of recycling ideas that have bounced around for generations. Kulveer Ranger, dapper transport adviser to Mayor Johnson, swiped his card at a docking station for the benefit of the early evening television news: the first man in London to release a Barclays bike without having to go through the tedious online application process. The card was refused. He moved swiftly to the next slot: no go.

Ranger explained away the glitch as a translation problem between incompatible systems. When he finally got on his bike, for a charity rally across Europe, he ran slap into a pedestrian on an unmarked road in Tbilisi, the Georgian capital. 'He came out of nowhere,' Ranger protested, before his passport was impounded.

Boris Johnson is airfixed to the saddle: fit for purpose, blundering into scrapes with other journalists, unsinkable, in your face, a polar bear on a unicycle. David Cameron pedals too, shadowed by security in the big black car; a bizarre parody of the industrial worker, as represented by Albert Finney in Karel Reisz's film of Alan Sillitoe's *Saturday Night and Sunday Morning*. Back in 1960, the most exciting young actor of his generation jolted across Nottingham cobbles. He was tracked, as Cameron in Notting Hill is now, by an unseen camera truck. The freedom of moving through a city, weaving around crocked pedestrians, doing the banter, in full English weather. Well paid, smart, cocky: up for it. Time to mould wet hair in a dirty mirror. British industry is thriving. Exports are good. Everybody is spending. Onward and upward. It would last forever.

Sleeves rolled over muscled arms, Finney knocks out parts for Raleigh bicycles in the industrial heartlands. End of regimented subservience to unseen bosses. Foremen in dun coveralls. Cigarettes in cupped fists. The bikes streaming from the factory gates are bought at discount, like the cars of workers on the assembly lines at Dagenham and Cowley.

The first episode of the black and white soap opera *Coronation Street*, also screening in 1960, used a bicycle as a symbol of class division. Ken Barlow (William Roache), a live-at-home student, paralysed by infusions of the *Manchester Guardian*, is outraged when his father and brother mend a puncture on the carpet, in front of the living room fire. Cilla Black's recorded memory of watching the launch of *Coronation Street* involved trying to peer at the screen, to witness Barlow's inner-tube wrestle, over the back of her father, who was carrying out the same operation in the parlour at Scotland Road, Liverpool.

The bike, that aspirational prize gifting the migrant poor a better shot at city life, suffers a long period (c.1960–2000) of cultural invisibility, before re-emerging as a transport solution for New Labour. There was something noble, in the years after the Second World War, in Vittorio De Sica's *Bicycle Thieves*. Noble and sentimental. The simple machine, offering employment in a depressed Rome, is solicited like the thighbone of a saint. The narrative pitch is so convincing that it is reprised in 2001 by Wang Xiaoshuai as *Beijing Bicycle*. In pre-Olympic China, possession of a bike guarantees employment as a messenger. The city, not yet in thrall to devastating development between six orbital motorways, is powered by bicycles: factory labourers, schoolchildren, office workers – and street gangs pretending they are riding with Marlon Brando in *The Wild One*.

The cultural historian Patrick Wright, in *Passport to Peking* (2010), quotes the Labour politician Morgan Phillips, who visited China as part of a delegation in 1954. 'As I saw the great mass of cycles on the road I was reminded of a day in Bedford during the last war… The workers were leaving the factory for the lunch hour break. All at once I seemed to be submerged in cycles. Peking is just like that.'

In England, before the great New Labour push, the bicycle belonged to treasured eccentrics: Oxbridge academics, metal-scavengers festooned in electrical cables, youth hostellers with chapped knees and laminated maps. Cycling was an existential Iris Murdoch novel: no padlocks required, no helmets. A becoming flush to the cheeks between afternoon assignations. Murdoch batted around Oxford, head full of Sartre, gown flying. There is a bicycle silhouette by Charles Mozley on the dustjacket of *The Sandcastle* (1957). English schoolmasters, in the woodsmoke twilight, disappointed and damply lustful, trundle over weeded gravel to reach 'the smooth tarmac of the arterial road'.

Wicker basket. Tweed jacket. Corduroy. Camden Town, in Sickertian gloom, to Regent's Park: the national treasure Alan Bennett writing television plays about members of a cycling club soon to be obliterated in the First War. Poets cycling by default (they are lethal in cars). Philip Larkin, the Eeyore of English verse, pushing his hefty machine through a Hull graveyard, white raincoat and bicycle clips, misted spectacles, for a John Betjeman documentary.

The surrealist poet David Gascoyne, after years of silence, came to Cambridge for a poetry festival in 1975. He was knocked down by a cyclist and appeared on stage with his arm in a plaster cast.

The only photograph of the mandarin poet JH Prynne, who operated privately, even hermetically, and as far from Larkin as could be imagined, was made public when a broadsheet responded to large claims from Randall Swingler in *The Last of England* (2004). Prynne, in black jacket, orange tie, had his image stolen as he rode through Cambridge on his bicycle. Soon afterwards he began to make extended visits to China. And it is clear now, reading a transcript of an interview with Jeff Dolven and Joshua Kotin for *The Paris Review* that the poet would have been happier in the old bicycle China of Mao than among the choked avenues of imported cars. 'They've become a capitalist country with reckless commercialism, which has replaced any sort of ideological purpose that gave direction to their social aspirations,' he said.

By 2000, thanks to neo–liberal political initiatives, the marginal status of cycling was revised and upgraded. London was a gridlocked mess with every journey coming to a standstill in contemplation of the horror of the Blackwall Tunnel. White-van traffic seethed and texted. Underground trains panted (when they operated at all) in hot tunnels. Buses lurched in convoys. It was time to take stock of Lord Tebbit's advice and jump on our bikes. After the bombs in July 2005, towpaths alongside the canal became cycle tracks. The overnight shift in the cycling demographic was spectacular. Public transport was left to the disadvantaged: economic migrants and bendy-bus freeloaders. You could categorise the new tribe of urban cyclists as belonging to three dominant classes: pod, posse and peloton.

The peloton stamped, wheel to wheel, without compassion or respect for regulations, between Stoke Newington and Shoreditch, Clerkenwell and Mile End, Docklands and the City. They ventured to Portland Place, White City (before the Westfield supermall), and Goldsmiths College in New Cross. They were waiting to take over London with cycling superhighways.

Coffee outlets, which double as bicycle repair shops, have mushroomed along towpaths and the railway fringes of London Fields to cater to this tendency. At Lock 7, over the bridge from Broadway Market, the hook was: 'Love Cycles, Love Food'. No-nonsense women rip rubber and mend punctures, while clients sip barista coffee at monkish tables. The peloton gathers here to exchange information before heading off down the canal. Their hard–shell helmets are ribbed like condoms. Like exposed, acid-stripped brain stems. GoPro cameras *on*. Red eyes blinking at first light. The peloton is a many-wheeled centipede hogging a path no wider than a single, sleeping nun.

The posse, who bossed it here before the eco-classes took to the saddle, ride the wide pavements of Queensbridge Road and Hackney Road: hooded, no hands, coming out of nowhere. Like the account Thomas Berger gives, in *Little Big Man* (1964), of the Pawnee appearing over a bluff to a westward-rolling wagon train. Our postcode posse, back in pre-Olympic days, favoured thick-wheeled mountain bikes. Right now, the guerrilla raiders of outlying regions operate as irregular BMX units, called together by phone, cruising kebab joints and isolated bus halts.

Zdenek Makar, an office-worker from the Czech Republic, after a precedence dispute in the queue at a Perfect Fried Chicken outlet on East Indian Dock Road, was chased by a gang of youths on mountain bikes. He was felled and beaten with a metal chain. A passing civilian cyclist, who found the victim lying 'in a pool of blood', near All Saints DLR station at Poplar, attempted cardio-pulmonary resuscitation. At 12.20am, paramedics pronounced Mr Makar dead.

In Hackney, scouts patrol their twilight turf, reporting likely prospects on stolen phones. They do not use towpaths or sanctioned cycle tracks. They do not acknowledge the peloton. Or pedestrians. Unless they are carrying interesting packages or chattering, oblivious, on devices that are begging to be recycled.

Warriors cut straight across the busy boulevards. They know all the secret ways through estates. If by some accident they find themselves on a main road, they hold the centre of it, with Samurai swagger, oblivious of frustrated utility vans and honking builders. When the posse meet, they circle and weave in elegant figures, so slowly that it seems impossible for them to stay upright. The essence of their style is never to break sweat, never to acknowledge other road users (except as prey). And never to sound, or even possess, a bell. You don't have to like them, but it's hard not to admire their Apache appropriation of territory. They are seeding an inevitable expulsion, soliciting retribution.

A skunky contrail of indestructible fastfood cartons and crumpled cans of synapse-abusing energy drinks boasts of their passage. The posse are never seen to park or padlock bicycles. Sometimes they double up, as if one of the horses had been shot out from under them by John Wayne or Jimmy Stewart. You see a wobbling pair coming back to the reservation on a stolen Santander steed, a lumpy Boris bike.

Hackney Council funded bus-stop advertisements to warn the unwary: KEEP YOUR PHONE SAFE. BE AWARE OF YOUR SURROUNDINGS. But that is asking the impossible. Cell-phones cancel surroundings in their addiction to a false intimacy; the illusion of travelling inside a shroud of protection while chattering to some unseen other. Until the swooping posse introduce these digital addicts to the reality of the street.

A more recent discrimination is the pod: Cameron's *kinder*, the babes of Boris. They lodge in the new territories – Hoxton, Shoreditch, London Fields – so that they can roll from bed and get to work, in the splash-zone around Silicon Roundabout, Old Street, in five or ten minutes. Barney Rowntree, a radio producer, explained how it goes.

'We live on bikes, all my friends. So we can regulate time. We know exactly how long it takes to move between clubs, pubs, wherever we're going to meet.'

These cycles, for security, are chained together in a nest, a metal pod from which it is impossible to extract a single separate machine. Members use two sets of locks. Kryptonite devices cost from £75 to £100. The individual machines are slender, weighing less than the bondage chains required to protect them. Members of the pod approve of the Boris bike scheme: as back up, when their own fixed-gear bicycles are stolen. The limited terrain available to Barclays Cycle Hire members doesn't bother them. They don't deal in suburbs. More and more now, the edges are melting, collapsing into human landfill. Nobody out there can afford a statement bike. Clerkenwell, Soho, the mainline stations, that covers it. The only certainties in being a paid-up Silicon Roundabout regular are: theft and road accidents. Every podist I questioned admitted that they would have a bike stolen once or twice a year – and suffer a bone-crushing shunt of some kind within three years. They were such cheerful fatalists. I liked them very much, in their difference.

Ben Judah, in *This is London: Life and Death in the World City* (2016), discovers that the young people of the severed railway suburbs aspire to come in, to join the pod. 'The sexually frustrated children of Neasden want to be close to Shoreditch not the M40 to the Cotswolds. They want to be central, they want to cycle – they want the city.'

Rowntree's most recent loss came when his professionally manacled machine was sawn in half. The noise of a bolt-cutter, whipped out from beneath a long coat, snapping through kryptonite, is like a gunshot.

And his latest accident? A broken shoulder bone, courtesy of an unmarked pothole. Most tumbles are caused by the state of London roads, or the intoxication (booze, dope, fumes) of cyclists who believe that drink-driving laws don't apply to Big Society pedlars, princes of the City.

They are confused, encouraged with slogans – CLICK YOUR WAY TO IMPROVED WELLBEING, LOOKING OUT FOR VULNERABLE ROAD USERS, NUMBER OF GOLDSMITHS ROW CYCLISTS TODAY: 1,713 – and inhibited by fearsome headlines. DEAD CYCLIST IS ITALIAN PRINCE. LONDON CYCLE RACE DEATH. DEATH OF CYCLIST LEAVES FAMILY DESTROYED. CYCLIST CRUSHED OUTSIDE LUXURY DEPARTMENT STORE. FATHER-OF-THREE THIRD LONDON CYCLIST TO DIE IN A MONTH.

The elite of pod world – or so they consider – are the cycle couriers. I asked Matt Sherratt, an artist and former courier, how he survived. 'Forty is the watershed. When you're young, you are pretty sharp-witted. On a fixed-wheel bike you are part of the experience, you dart through the traffic. If there's a whole row of traffic, you're not going to stay in that row. You get out to the opposite side of the road. You will absolutely *rip* down the other side, the wrong way. You've got clear visibility, it's perfectly safe. It's safer to just jump the lights. You create an open space. You own it.'

Being a courier for someone like Metro, the photographic agency, gives you credibility and uniform: 'beautifully branded kit'. You are special, one of the cadre. A Spitfire pilot in petrol heaven. Special status, special accidents. In Australia, Matt went straight into the back of a station wagon at a zebra crossing, head first through the rear windscreen. He made it back to London, where he hit a pothole and detoured to hospital with a rack of broken ribs.

The older, cannier Jock McFadyen agreed: 'I never wear a helmet. I ride on the pavement. I never go on the road, except out of frustration. And I *always* go through red lights, always. And never sound a bell. Traffic lights don't have the intelligence to say there are no pedestrians. You do have confrontations with drivers. I've had to punch mirrors off.'

What Jock likes most about the bicycle is the simplicity of design. 'You can build a bike from scratch in an hour.' He owns forty-five of them. Most of his shunts, he acknowledges, have been his own fault. A late return from a gallery opening up west: Old Street, pissed as a brewery rat, sudden application of front brakes. And he's lying spreadeagled across the bonnet of a shocked motorist, licking the paint job. Jock approves the Boris bike scheme, without knowing too much about it, but appreciating, with his painterly eye, the blue Barclays logo on the silver ranks of docking stations in dull places.

Nobody told me that it was easier to dock a lunar transfer module than a Boris bike in Shoreditch Park. There were more white-painted ghost bikes wired to crash barriers than docking stations on Kingsland Road. These poignant installations, dressed with dead flowers, were not just a memorial to a rider crushed at the side of the road, but a *memento mori* for the days of the Provo white bicycles, in their hundreds, in Amsterdam: free of access, free to travel the whole city. And doomed to disappear into legend after their brief, resin-scented moment of exposure.

'Sign up, hop on, ride off': the Barclays mantra. But it was not quite as simple as that. Boris Johnson, with no false modesty, accepted credit for a light-bulb idea that had very little to do with him. Ken Livingstone had toyed with cycling initiatives and despatched indoctrinated cadres with orders to stage pit-stop clinics. 'A female or male instructor can train you or accompany you on your usual journey.'

In August 2007 Livingstone directed TfL (Every Journey Matters) to examine the feasibility of a cycle hire scheme. By February 2008, he was ready to copy the *Vélib* idea from Paris. The Lib Dems, keen to divert attention from their complacent assumption of the privileges (and the shame) of a shared administration, explained how this cycle hire business had always been *their* pet project, proposed by Lynne Featherstone in 2001 – and stalled, for years, by Mayor Livingstone.

What they were stealing, in a modest way (6,000 bicycles against 20,000 for Paris), was the pet project of JC Decaux, an entrepreneur with licence to stick posters over bus stops. Decaux, who was labelled by *Libération* as '*le roi du mobilier urbain*', must have felt at home plastering a city with ranks of branded docking stations. Lyons, Decaux's home base, trialled the scheme. It proved a sound investment. Paris followed (as did Vienna, Córdoba, Brussels). And, eventually, London.

But does it work? Sign up and you have the theoretical freedom of a choice segment of central London. The initial scheme favoured tourists tempted to explore Hyde Park and commuters coming from mainline stations. It did not favour journeys of exploration, *dérives*, twelve-hour projects. The first thirty minutes, once you've been processed and accepted, is free. A day's outing costs £50.

I sweated through the online application, bank details, credit checks, childhood nickname. And then, after several days, I was told that my membership was approved. By the time the key arrived, a sliver of hard plastic, I understood that I had volunteered for electronic tagging. Would this slender fob work any better than those swipe cards that refuse to let you into Premier Inn hotel rooms? Move across the city, using the key, and your presence is logged. I would be paying, by direct debit, for the privilege of trundling around the side streets of Bloomsbury as a mobile sandwich-board for a group of investment bankers.

On foot it takes me around twenty-five minutes to reach Liverpool Street Station. It took fifteen minutes to reach the nearest Barclays' bike. Of course, all that has changed in the new, post-Olympic, hipster Hackney. We've been let into London, with Overground connection and docking stations dominating Queensbridge Road and shadowing the length of the orbital railway.

Plodding out to the cycle nest in Falkirk Street in Hoxton, I pass two ghost bikes, one a Raleigh, very much like the model Albert Finney rode in *Saturday Night and Sunday Morning*. It's a mild November morning. There are 26 slots across the road from Hackney Community College: all of them empty. 'Private Property, No Loitering.'

I don't loiter, I push on to the next option, Shoreditch Park. Thirty bays, two bikes. I try my key and score a red light: refused. I try the second bike, zip. I return home and ring the helpline, with which I will become very familiar in the succeeding weeks. We go through the muzak interference, the threat that our conversation will be recorded for training purposes, and then I'm informed that my key is a dud. 'We're registering a fault. You've got an invalid filter.' A new key is promised.

By the time it arrives, I'm away from London. An email informs me that the week for which I have signed up is over, will I renew my membership? No point in complaining that I haven't cycled one yard. From the instant the useless key went into the slot in Shoreditch Park, red light or no red light, I was burning credit.

Hanging around malfunctioning docking stations, I chatted to other clients. Their cheerful acceptance of the glitches in the system astonished me. Convinced that they were striking a blow for the planet, the Hackney eco-warriors in hard hats were happy to suffer local inconvenience, and to trot briskly away in quest of a rack with usable cycles. One woman, now a determined pedestrian, told me how she found herself being charged for rides she'd never made, in places she had never been. The non-return charge is £300. Barclays carry an entire department to argue over unfair deductions.

I waited for a break in the cold weather, the optimum morning on which to revisit Hoxton. Now cycles are available, my key is accepted. I speed away towards Shoreditch Park. My plan was to test the system with a relay of short-haul journeys, always within the free half hour, anti-clockwise around a loop of docking stations, from Hoxton to Regent's Park, Holland Park to Vauxhall, to the Tower of London. I felt like a first-year student in the open university of urban studies.

The first hitch was a crater obstructing the roundabout at the top of Hoxton Market. They were busy improving the image of construction again. The chasm was part of Hackney's £22 million investment in the streets (and Volker Highways). Detour completed, my heavy bike grudged into its Shoreditch Park slot. The light showed green. I moved down the line to inspect the three available mounts. Red light, key refused: the whole station was out.

Other Barclays' clients were sprinting off, competitively, in all directions. Boris was certainly doing his bit for the health of Londoners by initiating a marathon relay between docking stations. And keeping amateurs off roads where they faced almost certain injury and possible death.

Thirty-four accidents were reported for the Barclays Cycle scheme between 30th July and 30th September in 2010. A woman was knocked from her bike by one of the transporters used in the restocking process. A man was crushed against the kerb by a lorry. And a 7-year-old boy narrowly escaped injury when a docking station, butted by a car, fell on top of him. David Ellis, a photographer from Stoke Newington, was dragged under the wheels of a Barclays' trailer. He said that the transporters constituted a serious hazard to road users, being wider than the electric vehicles that tow them.

Marching down the canal to Danbury Street, the next station on my Barclays map, I passed one of the new caffeine refuelling facilities: Tow Path, a slot in the wall with a spread of outdoor tables. Freelance (unemployed) advertising photographers and digital wranglers, having dropped off their infants in schools and nurseries, parked their bikes for an ethical shot of brown powder from Colombia.

'San Francisco, the 90s. The rumblings of a coffee culture revolution. The smell of fresh-roasted coffee in the air. Fast forward to East

London, today…'

House-husbands scan the harvested packets while they wait, and wait, to put in their orders. Communal tables shudder with the fragmented phone-traffic of intercontinental breakfast meetings.

'So. I'll do my own publishing thing. Hoxton, yes. Absolutely. If I can source the right *size* of desk.'

'We've got very positive news about the price increase. Our French distributor tells us we are free to talk about branded products. We also talked a bit about almonds.'

'It's relatively difficult to fix a price definition ceiling on the competition. Plus margins of course.'

'Before college the other kids were getting rucksacks and walking around the Third fucking World. I went straight to Wall Street.'

'There are no zeros in banking. You work for us, you stay on it thirty-nine hours straight.'

At Danbury Street, on the flank of Islington, my key is refused: three times. A passing Boris initiate explains that if there are cycles left among the empty slots, it means they don't work. They are waiting on the trailer.

When I am denied again at Macclesfield Road, I ring in. It seems that because Shoreditch Park is out of order the return of my bike hasn't registered, and therefore no other docking station will accept my custom. Meanwhile the clock is ticking on my tariff. I've signed up and paid for two weeks, managed five minutes on a Boris bike, and walked for several hours. My intended Barclays circuit had become just another futile foot slog between docking stations. *Please don't call it cyclogeography.*

Chadwell Street: 18 slots, 0 bikes. River Street: 11 slots, 1 bike. Percy Street: 23 slots, 2 bikes. Guildford Street: 23 slots, 7 bikes. Margery Street: 19 slots, 1 bike. St John Street: 17 slots, 1 bike. Finsbury Library: 29 slots, 5 bikes.

And then, success, West Smithfield Rotunda, right outside St Bartholomew's Hospital: 25 slots, 24 bikes.

Are Barclays' clients superstitious about mounting up in such close proximity to a blood-soaked establishment; the place where

Dr Watson met Sherlock Holmes for the first time, when the great detective was busy beating a corpse? And where the Benedict Cumberbatch TV reboot appeared to take a suicide plunge from the roof? Maybe the doctors had their own bikes. And patients who survived operations and who were tipped out on the street in a state of post-traumatic shock were too weak to pedal home.

Internet reviews of the hospital were the usual blend of peevish and gushing: five star to no star. 'We are on an exciting journey to improve the quality of our service.' St Bartholomew's, just now, is particularly keen to solicit body parts from black and ethnic minority communities. 'Our daily mission is bringing excellence to life. To meet our ambition of excellence, it's crucial to recognise where we've come from and where we're headed.'

When I eventually found a station prepared to take my key, I enjoyed the weight and solemnity of the Boris bike. I decided to combine, on a day of snow showers, the song cycle and the bicycle. I made a meandering progress through the City of London, docking and redocking, as I searched out the hidden sites for the 'Surround Me' installations by Susan Philipsz. With minimal traffic and few humans, the bike came into its own. Philipsz's unaccompanied voice was a thrilling and melancholy confirmation of my mood.

Labyrinthine alleys I explored on foot were closed to me. I found that Boris bikes were a burden on icy steps. But that illusion of freedom, the way the machine could be dumped when you tired of it, the simplicity of the gears, was seductive. I signed up for a year's membership. I became a positive affirmation statistic. And then I forgot the whole business and returned to walking as usual, without the requirement of planning my journeys from one Barclays' oasis to the next. The brand faded, changed colour from blue to red, and shifted sponsorship to Santander. But the creeping colonisation of selected outer zones continued. You could tell just where you stood in the property market by measuring your proximity to an Overground station and a rack of Santander bicycles.

Certain cyclists of independent spirit, poets, philosophers, sociologists of the road, found their way to my door, to dispute my thesis: that there had to be something intrinsically wrong with any policy advocated by an agreement between local and national politicians. I was impressed by the height, demeanour, and name of Jürgen Ghebrezgiabiher, a man in uxorious love with his machine, which was an extension of his personality in the way described by Flann O'Brien. Jürgen translated impossible poets (myself included) and researched urbanists who converted their bicycles into delivery vehicles for bread or books or people. He wrote about his sadness at being forced out of London by economic necessity. He pedalled away, listening to the click of the 'prayer wheel of the cycle'. A monkish European scholar returning to the monastery of a Leipzig bike shop, puncture repairs and spindly poems.

Jürgen sent me an email recommending a film by Cynthia Beatt called *The Invisible Frame*, in which Tilda Swinton — who else? — rides along the vanished Berlin Wall. 'She's definitely not a cyclist,' Jürgen reported. 'Saddle too low. But there is a floating walker's air about her. There are long passages that seem to have been reeled on spools of film that come undone again.'

Jon Day, academic and author, was another initiate who taught me how to respect the warrior qualities of couriers who drove themselves to the point of 'annihilating exhaustion' by their fugue-like sprints across London.

'By night I dreamt of half-remembered topographies,' Day wrote in *Cyclogeography: Journeys of a London Bicycle Courier*. 'Hypnogogic jerks, those juddery twitches that occur on the edges of deep sleep, were smoothed out into circular pedal-strokes of the legs.' Every grain and flaw, every minute particular of the road is mapped on the consciousness of the cyclist. The streets of the City, Holborn, Clerkenwell, Bloomsbury, Soho, become a virtual velodrome to the fixed-gear bikes of the courier. The career is short-lived, an intense and exposed negotiation with place.

'I have known more couriers to have committed suicide than to have died on the road,' Day said. He had discovered a way of hiding

135

in full sight, becoming part of the slipstream. 'It was the perfect way of bearing witness.' Day traced the burning fuse of the London riots of 2011 from the saddle. But his own future was uncertain. After the age of forty, many couriers become controllers or cabbies.

Before Jon remounted to continue his researches by interrogating the land artist and committed cyclist, Richard Long, I recommended a favourite ride, in the wake of the artist/photographer Nigel Henderson, down the elevated track of the Northern Sewage Outfall to Beckton Alp. Day was game. It might give him a paragraph for his book. 'I climbed the weaving path that winds up the hill to its highest point and clambered through a gap… where a couple were kissing in the shadow of a fence across which several large crosses of St George had been painted. They didn't welcome the intrusion, and so I slipped away, back along the pipe, back into the city.'

After the scandal of Boris Johnson's Brexit miscalculation and his public penance as a Foreign Secretary doomed for a certain term to walk the night, while his foul crimes are burnt and purged by the barbs of disgusted European counterparts, London expected better from the latest incumbent, the diminutive and sure-footed Sadiq Khan. The new mayor followed tradition by instantly setting himself up against his own party boss and his immediate predecessor. He was a smiling audition for the opposition leadership that should fall vacant within a couple of years.

As Mayor Johnson cancelled Ken Livingstone's grand project of a bridge at Beckton linking the two sections of the suburban highway, the North and South Circular roads, so Sadiq gestured at kicking the wretched Garden Bridge into development limbo. A futile gesture? Nothing stands in the path of the vision of Joanna Lumley, London's twenty-fourth most influential person (according to a poll in the *Evening Standard*). Then, having perfected the art of making unobjectionable proposals and quietly forgetting them, he reconsidered. He also gave the green light for 'Barcelona-on-Thames' at Barking Riverside, a development pitch to trump the shattered communities of New Labour's Thames Gateway and the spiked Estuary airport of Boris Johnson.

The next gambit was the cycle rebrand. As Boris bullied his name on to the blue Barclays' bikes, so Khan decided to personalise the red Santander fleet. He came up with the wheeze of commissioning a set of the 'most comfortable and manoeuvrable' machines. Smaller wheels, lower frame, new gear hub: much better suited to the twenty-first-century metropolitan (of slighter size). An £80 million contract has been signed with Serco to maintain and distribute a generation of 'Sadiq cycles'. They will be made in Stratford-upon-Avon. All the boxes have been ticked.

The potter Grayson Perry, who is everywhere now, the articulate and engaging ambassador for the arts in London, told *ES Magazine* that his 'biggest extravagance' was a £15,000 dress in brocade silk with big ceramic buttons. Asked what he collected, he replied: 'Bicycles. I still have my specialised M2 Stuntjumper which I won in a mountain bike race in the late 1990s.'

Perry used to mudlark on scrambling bikes around Beckton Alp with Jock McFadyen. But the most unlikely duo of cyclists I have ever witnessed were spotted in the sad Haggerston precinct known as the 'Triangle'; a constantly revised retail strip lost between conflicted blocks of flats, close to where I have lived since 1968. In all those years, I don't remember noticing a single Hasidic man on this wind-blown corner of hopeless commercial optimism and failed council initiatives. Now there were two, ginger-bearded, bespectacled, with cartwheel hats and long black coats. They were wobbling bravely on what I took to be their first paid Santander bike experience.

They stuck to the pavements, tilted by a cruel wind rushing around new-build railway flats as they tried to corner into Clarissa Street. The senior man, who must have been in his mid-twenties, was more confident. He surged ahead at something close to walking pace, weighing up properties, taking the measure of new territory, and hectoring his younger companion, who held back, unsure if he could manage the awful trick of dismounting. Better, he felt, to keep going at all costs, hanging on to a hat that threatened to take off in the direction of Hoxton.

The crisis arrived when they reached the canal. The older man wanted to push east. The younger didn't fancy the proximity of water. The Bridge Academy was decanting its knots of liberated pupils. Shaven-headed artists, rehoused from the demolished flats, south of the canal, were exercising their animals. Bringing them back to piss against familiar posts. Haggerston technos were heading home, enmeshed in one-way conversations. It was like watching a pair of nervous Shetland ponies trot out on to a motorway. It was mayhem. The twin cyclists stalled, swerved, lost their connection. It looked for a moment as if they would fling their machines into the duckweed. They headed for the nearest docking station. I have yet to see an Orthodox woman on a Santander bike. Or a bicycle of any kind. In Haggerston or in Stamford Hill.

TWO SWIMMING POOLS OR, *SHARD*ENFREUDE

'I have howled at the foot of the glass tower.'
David Jones

Not many guests arrive at Shangri-La, the cloud-shrouded lamasery/ hotel that occupies the mid-section (levels 35–52) of the London Bridge prong known as the Shard, by way of a 149 bus out of Haggerston. And on the day of a ritual Underground strike that has to be explained to bemused tourists as they squeeze through automated barriers while encumbered by caravans of luggage. The dingy old railway terminus, established long before any blue-sky copywriter thought of calling it a 'hub', has been struggling for months, with many services discontinued and major elements hidden behind fences, while slick corporate mouthpieces attempt to justify the station's fortunate position as a satellite of London's tallest building. Collateral compost. Eye candy.

*Shard*enfreude. It assaults you: vanity in the form of architecture. Desert stuff in the wrong place. Money laundering as applied art. Another unexplained oligarch's museum of entropy for the riverbank. A giant dagger serving no real purpose: an exclamation point on the Google map of an abolished city once called London.

The great Cockney-Welsh poet David Jones, with his maternal lineage in Rotherhithe, abandoned a sequence called 'The Book of Balaam's Ass' when satire stuttered in a place he called the 'Zone'; a location somewhere between the ground where he trained for the First War trenches and our stretched metropolis. 'I have been on my guard not to condemn the unfamiliar,' he wrote. But the poet's trembling fingers, searching for discourse with the angular structures of 1930s modernism, can find no answering touch.

'I have said to the perfected steel: be my sister, and to the glassy towers: Bend your beauty to my desire.'

Trumpish towers require no plebian contact or approval. Quite the reverse. Their eros is dominance, warping the will of witnesses. And this is what is now labelled: LANDSCAPED PUBLIC REALM. Police vans, engines idling, are a perpetual presence. Sullen security operatives, worried for their continued employment, stare at us as if we were responsible for those terrible uniforms, the boredom, the pitiful wages. A railway station with a shopping concourse is an invitation to outrage. A negative space in which to be penned while you wait for the confirmation that today's trains are never going to arrive.

London Bridge station is a commuter isthmus accessed by Shard-approved tunnels as dark and soul-sucking as a labyrinth with no centre. The Minotaur is on gardening leave. There should be a tame monster, a fanged Farage, in a bluster of disgusted saloon-bar rant, like one of those hermits kept in follies by eighteenth-century landowners. The cycle sponsor JC Decaux has got his name on vast overhead screens, brighter than destination boards, pumping out a rinse of interchangeable news-porn and advertisements. Hurricanes, earthquakes, snatched children, stagnant football and UKIP resignations. BUY X-MEN: APOCALYPSE. YOUR HOME MAY BE REPOSSESSED.

The era of station hotels has passed, those convenient one-nighters at Charing Cross or Victoria before a continental adventure. Now London Bridge, like its neighbour, Guy's Hospital, is a confused veteran tasked with living up to the occult geometry of this brash invader: Renzo Piano's spectacular glass sail, the Qatar-funded investment silo of the Shard. Travellers seethe in a convulsive mob while they wait to be processed on inadequate platforms. To paying metronauts (£25.95 per ascent), basking on the exposed viewing deck, the people far below are so many ants. Upgrade to a £33.95 ticket and you get a glass of house champagne to add sparkle to your temporary elevation from the streets of London.

I came here that day to swim in the highest pool in Europe, fifty-two floors above the station. The surface of the infinity pond shivered with eel-flicker reflections like a Fun House mirror out of the Orson Welles film, *The Lady from Shanghai*. Ripple mosaics were memory transfers of recreational exercisers who were now taking their ease on couches and wetting plump lips with complimentary goblets of fruit-flavoured iced water. The pool was a quotation labouring to attain a modicum of reality. It was less like David Hockney's frozen Los Angeles splash than Richard Wilson's site-specific installation, *20:50*; his tank of sump oil miraculously transubstantiated into this brilliant new substance, a liquid thicker than jelly but lighter than air. The pool at the Shard is a blue carpet across which you cannot walk without sinking. A slap of wet light leaking into a vaporous cloud-scape, out there, just beyond floor-to-ceiling triple-glazed windows, across which tiny planes and large helicopters are creeping.

The silenced choppers are not so much a threat as a specialised form of surveillance: protection against base jumpers, eco abseilers and urban exploration collectives. They patrol like outriders at a royal

141

funeral. When you are swimming at the same altitude as a helicopter, the sight offers a reassurance that represses the recollection of those rare collisions with construction cranes hidden in fog.

The circling police helicopters of late afternoon, making their rounds of Hackney's estates and threatened public housing, are another thing. They are low and loud, blades set to maximum volume. An assertion of power. A jolt of homeopathic paranoia. They have cruised down the Lea Valley from Lippitt's Hill Camp at High Beach, a base right beside the poet John Clare's Epping Forest asylum, and they'll be back again tomorrow.

Sukhdev Sandhu, who flew with the sky cops for his book *Night Haunts* (2006), calls the experience 'the panoptic sublime'. The helicopters cost half a million pounds each, a sum that pays for a lot of clatter. Sandhu reveals that 'high-power lenses and thermal imagers allow them to… look through the windows of Canary Wharf and spot canoodling office workers from eight miles away'.

Ballard. Hitchcock. English vices. Punishment pleasures. *Rear Window* meets *High-Rise*.

Lotus-eaters of the Shard, drifting in a slow-motion ballet that seems to take effect only at forty or fifty floors above the agitated shuffle of London Bridge, are on show. And they know it. As they stare out, trying to identify specific buildings or districts, state-sanctioned voyeurs are gazing right back. The down force of the helicopter blades does not agitate the blue water. As we float in our infinity tank, we are immune to the acoustic footprints of the city, the sighs and grunts of the trains, the bone-shuddering din of the guardians in the sky.

'They do use sound as a weapon,' Sandhu says. But what wonders do the helicopter jockeys record to justify their hefty budget? 'You can see everyone's swimming pools.'

The Shangri-La pool, about the size of a cricket strip, shared that uncanny Richard Wilson gift for turning the fixed world on its head: floor as ceiling, window as wall, liquid as solid. Wilson has spoken of creating 'a Tardis-like space, where the internal volume is greater than its physical boundaries'. The idea for *20:50* came to the artist when he was resting beside a swimming pool in the Algarve. He knew that he wanted to place the viewer 'at the mid-point of a symmetrical visual plane'. His oil bath was promoted, from a pioneer gallery, close to London Fields, to an oak-panelled chamber in the decommissioned County Hall, across the Thames from the Houses of Parliament.

The Wilson tank, like the one into which I was about to plunge, was a concept pool, around which visitors moved like catwalk models and talked in whispers. There was the unspoken fear of baptism into some malign sect, part Trump, part Swedenborg, part DC Comics, for which the Shangri-La supplicants with their iced water communions, their bitter splashes of espresso, were as yet unprepared. Blind angels of the city. Floating upside down over the clouds, the smoke and sweat of labour. What if this tower was all a trick, an illusion, and we plunged straight into the sewers?

Was this brilliant blue lozenge really the highest swim in Europe? What about the nineteen floors (53–72) of 'exclusive residences' rumoured to be on offer from £30 to £50 million a pop? One of the more outrageous selling points is a promised 'clear day' vision of the North Sea fishing fleet, forty-four miles downriver from the pyramid lighthouse. Some of the private baths on the upper decks look competition-sized in promotional photographs. Wet rooms are like clearings in a tropical forest. There are marble foot basins in which you'd be tempted to take a few strokes. But the essence of the infinity pool as the lid and crown of the Shangri-La, the detail that sets it apart from that cocktail-bar tub on the modest elevation of the private members' club at Shoreditch House, is the way it merges seamlessly with its surroundings. At Shangri-La ticket prices, the *least* a swimmer can expect is the illusion of breaststroking on a kindly thermal above the lesser towers and steeples of London. Like a saint in some quattrocento triptych.

The integrity of the view is broken by squared columns and the metal frames of window panels dividing the spread of the city far below into a series of moving pictures. Pictures from which the privileged swimmer, or the sybarite with orange-flavoured iced water, is detached. Infinity, as a concept, is better appreciated fifty-two floors down, back on the street, waiting for the 149 bus. Here, the tapering mass of the Shard, a blue grid on a grey day, intimidates. It's like staring against the sun down an endless railway track or the roped lane of an Olympic pool stretching towards glory. A thuggish wind buffets and bends humbled clients sheltering against a wall while they wait for the Edmonton bus to ease forward, to let them on. The driver is busy texting.

Renzo Piano talks about London's river and the way his signature tower must breathe like a sail. The architect has reduced all that *weight* – construction traffic, tedious budget meetings, hoses spitting out concrete, drills, controlled explosions – to a tensile skein of captured light with the virtual city tattooed on its skin. He sketches this conceit on a napkin in a fancy Berlin restaurant. His patron approves. Piano has the life-enhanced, skinny-bearded, dressed-down charm that can be read as a form of integrity: the Jeremy Corbyn schtick.

When Piano presented the defaced napkin to the original Shard developer, Irvine Sellar, it was a Picasso moment. A free lunch paid in full. The doodle became a sanctified relic, framed and featured in proud documentaries. The Italian, a remote viewer of London's historic fabric, was never inhibited by modesty. He allowed that St Paul's, as realised by Christopher Wren, was 'a radical intervention'. The domed church expressed 'the spirit of change and inventiveness that drives great cities'. It was even, in its primitive way, a precursor to the Shard. 'I believe that the new tower will not disturb its stateliness,' Piano said. 'They are breathing the same air, sharing the same atmosphere; they are nurtured at the same source.'

It is certainly true that, gazing up from the 149 bus stop beside London Bridge station, the outline of the backlit needle of the Shard makes teasing reference to the slender steeple of Hawksmoor's Christ Church, soaring above the Georgian roofs of Spitalfields. But Piano's tower is non-denominational, a steeple without a church. The prong advocates no doctrine beyond its own presence. 'Symbols are dangerous', Piano stated. The Shard plays at being unfinished, open to the winds. It offers itself as a hostage to copywriters. It invites promiscuous similes. 'Like a sixteenth-century pinnacle or the mast top of a very tall ship.' It absorbs unfocused horizontal energics, to become a new kind of city; secure, supplied with shops, offices, restaurants and residential pods. The Shard is an Umbrian hill town hidden inside a medicine cabinet of mirrors.

I swam at the golden hour. There were softly-spoken barriers and checkpoints at every stage of my ascent towards the high pool. You come off the street, away from the fumes of stalled buses, the repressed waves of anger and frustration, and into this otherness of uniformed security that is both courteous and judgemental. You are bowed through to the metal cabinet where inappropriate baggage is checked for explosives. At the reception desk, thirty-four floors up, you must present your passport. The right credit status, the digital information that moves you to the new level, is never accessible on screen. The induction process acts like a Zen filter, fine-tuning anxiety and inoculating the unwary before the next stage of enlightenment in this attempt at a Tibetan lamasery out of James Hilton's *Lost Horizon*. A copy of Hilton's 1933 romance, newly printed in Singapore and cased in a leather binder, is left beside every kingsize bed. Immense picture books furnish the ledges of the reception area: *Theme Hotels, Beijing, Impressionism*.

Many of the investors waiting patiently for admittance to the restaurant, like dazed motorway supplicants at a Happy Eater, are Chinese. News of the market blip on the Shanghai Composite Index has not inhibited them. In fact, the Shangri-La feels like an upmarket Chinese dormitory. I knew that flats in Dalston Lane developments and Olympicopolis were being bought, offplan, twelve at a time, by Beijing investors who never intended to set foot in them. They preferred the Shard with its easy access to the Thames and the major heritage sites where they posed, in full rig, for wedding photographs. Treating London as a set, a designer shopping village, they were at home. We were the tourists.

As Jeremy Prynne points out in his *Paris Review* interview, the Mao Zedong style of Marxism is no longer 'part of the intellectual world of the Chinese'. And Western cultural *bricoleurs* of the Sixties, such as the Jean-Luc Godard of *La Chinoise*, have moved on to fresh fields. Although it is still possible, I like to believe, that hardcore Maoist cadres have chosen to destroy capitalism from the inside, by buying London and leaving it empty.

Those who successfully pass through their electronic induction at Shangri-La enter a low-lit and flatteringly mirrored lift. It is a confessional booth for narcissists, the quilted anteroom for an audience with a heretic pope. No fellow traveller will meet your eye. The usual laundry removers and cleaners are never seen. There is none of the brittle bonhomie of a Premier Inn; excursionists sharing the achievement of making it safely to ground in a shuddering tin box. In the Shard, if you have the right card to swipe, you are one of us. Business-class transit to the pool in the sky.

At the end of a baffled corridor, beyond the viewpoint bar where many are gathered to see and be seen, and the almost deserted gym with a single female cyclist, is another checkpoint to be negotiated before the powerful door guarding the pool swings open. Areas at both ends are dressed with sofas, small round tables, and minor sculptural mistakes that will never be noticed. An attendant informs me that the pool must close to swimmers at 8pm, when a disguised panel, like the door in a condemned cell, will slide back to give access to the overspill from Gong, the 'cinnabar inspired', dragon-red cocktail bar and champagne lounge.

The man in the clean white T-shirt, working a broom, preparing the gleaming floor for twilight drinkers, is happy to exchange pleasantries about the pool, the view and his own exposure to these things. But he is not permitted, at any time, early or after hours, to enter the sacred water. He is polite about my enquiry, but it makes no sense. Reflex affirmation defines his occupation. 'Yes, sir. Of course. Whatever you say.' Industrial action takes the form of handing me a fluffy towel. And commending the temperature of the water, chill taken off, nothing too soupy or soporific: perfectly calculated for out of the body bliss.

Can I carry off the decadence? With sentimental memories of rusty Welsh rivulets in the mining valleys and municipal chlorine tanks in refrigerated tile sheds. The abandoned lidos of a long life-time stretch back through the polio-defying 1950s to coal-powdered, Bristol Channel beaches still being cleared of barbed wire and mines.

There is no resistance in this water. A few easy strokes carry me, buoyant with borrowed status, to the turn. Floating is a natural response. I paddle to the window. The 'infinity pool' illusion, the dissolution of the membrane between interior and exterior, is inter-rupted by the rounded lip on which you can hook an elbow while you fail to come to terms with the enormity of the view.

The gutters that framed public swimming pools were known as 'scum troughs'. The architect Alfred WS Cross, in *Public Baths and Wash-Houses – a treatise on their planning, design, arrangement and fitting*, published in 1906, described how a glazed stoneware scum trough could double as a grab-rail and a device for collecting 'floating impu-rities' from the agitated surface. The trough at the deep end should be a few inches lower than the troughs along the sides and at the shallow end. I remembered those impurities very well, sodden cigarette stubs and corn plasters seesawing gently in a tired yellow wash.

Before I spoiled the surface, the Shangri-La pool was immaculate. The water was that profound ocean-blue achieved at Hastings in Swan Lake, the inches-deep concrete pond with the plastic swan pedalos, by extreme chemical means. Here it was a trick of underwater spotlights and shimmering aquamarine tesserae separated by thin white threads: to mimic the effect of Caribbean sand. The water was so pure that it wasn't like water at all. It reminded me of the elixir in which they keep tropical fish at Charterhouse Aquatics, beneath the arches of the London Overground railway in Haggerston. 'Surface impurities' are mopped up and eliminated by motors disguised as sponges or clumps of weed. In the Shangri-La pool there are no floating impurities of any kind. Apart from myself. My shape, my noise.

This is the place to sell your soul. A floatation tank of total sen-sory abandonment. I relish every second I am allowed to spend in this magical substance. I plough from end to end, under the low, wave-patterned ceiling, passing through the lines of dark bars from the shadows of supporting pillars, as a red sun drops behind the picture windows of the espresso lounge.

I climb out, chastened by my failure to properly engage with the panoramic sweep of our grey-white boneyard city. Watchers are watching watchers from other high windows and viewing galleries. Riverview flats are performance suites for tourists circumnavigating the tenth floor of the Tate Modern extension. Somebody has left a large, wet, lipstick kiss over Southwark. A red mouth is chewing up the blocks that are not yet fully engorged towers. It is swallowing cranes like so many broken toothpicks. Down there on Borough High Street, I can identify the outline of St George the Martyr, a church with its heritage role to play, as shelter for the excluded nocturnal wanderers of *Little Dorrit*.

A couple of days before my encounter with the mysteries of Shangri-La, I was invited to inspect another swimming pool, a little closer to home, at Whiston Road. In February 2000 a notice of temporary closure, for reasons of health and safety, was fixed to the padlocked doors of Haggerston Baths. I remember my annoyance, towel roll under arm, clutch of ice at the heart, after too many previous confirmations of just how accommodating that 'temporary' qualification could be. Schoolchildren arriving for their weekly session were turned away. They would never return. The site of their school, Laburnum, would be teleported into the contemporary world as a launch platform for the Bridge Academy (A Bridge to Your Future), which opened for business in 2007. The Academy is sponsored by UBS (Together we can find an Answer), a financial services operation based in Switzerland. As the world's largest manager of private wealth assets, UBS (Your Goal, Our Solution) suffered heavy losses during the subprime mortgage crisis. But the Academy (A Bridge to Your Future) thrives. And affects everything around it.

A former Laburnam pupil, a City accountant called Erol Kagan, who still lives in the area, felt the pain when his old school was demolished. 'One day it was there and the next it wasn't. I saw a bell tower standing in the rubble. I don't know how it got there, or where it went.'

The Bridge Academy (A Bridge to Your Future), like the Shard, is an alien invader inflated by entitlement. The Shard is about being taller than anything else in London, but mean as a lancet, while the Bridge Academy (A Bridge to Your Future) is a bulbous plank-ribbed nest, an infolded mass crushed into a space barely capable of tolerating its presumption. The central section is under permanent plastic wraps. It looks, from the far side of the Regent's Canal, like a garden toy that nobody can figure out how to assemble.

Erol Kagan recalled his visits to the local pool. 'As a kid I used to go for a wash to Haggerston Baths. Now they're closed, locked up. No baths, no laundry, no gym. No swimming. The building looks derelict. They have let it decay.'

Health and safety issues have kept the Whiston Road building in limbo for fifteen years; enchanted in a suspension of cobwebs, rusted shower units and slipper baths dressed in a shroud of fine grey dust. Through dim corridors, ghosts search for the pre-war EXIT sign and a directional finger stencilled on cold white tiles.

Coming east in 1968 and moving into a terraced property on the other side of the canal, Haggerston Baths became a feature of my life. Neighbourhood loyalties evolved around certain pubs and convenient bathhouses. On weeks when there were no opportunities to visit the flats of better-provided friends, we luxuriated in the deep tubs at Whiston Road. Soap and towel supplied. Or so I choose, in deep folds of sentiment, to recall. Thinking perhaps of vagrant episodes in mainline stations, breakfast at Victoria and on to the Tate and the river.

There were 91 individual slipper baths and a 60-stall washhouse. But there was no topping up of bathwater, no time to read a book. You hauled yourself out before the attendant rapped on your door. Suicides in Hackney tubs were not unknown. Haggerston Baths, with its soft red brick laid in English bonds, its Portland stone dressing, was a marker for the territory, from the 90-foot chimney stack for coal-fired boilers to the golden galleon that caught the wind as a weathervane. This craft was a trusted symbol of locality by which those staggering home from a cluster of pubs could safely navigate. Ships on swimming pool weathervanes and pub signs confirmed London's claim to be a world port. But the tarnished galleon on Whiston Road was empty, its immigrants dispersed. Thrown into the indifferent sea.

The story of Haggerston Baths is covered in a generously illustrated book by Dr Ian Gordon and Simon Inglis: *Great Lengths: The historic indoor swimming pools of Britain* (2009). Delving into archive, travelling the length of the country, the authors demonstrate how provision of swimming pools made a very real difference to the quality of life in impoverished inner city and industrial areas. But utopianism went out of fashion, that era of green-lung parks and chilly lidos. All such fripperies were swept aside by the *realpolitik* of Thatcher and the millennial boosterism of Blair and the New Labour spinners.

Alfred Cross, who argued in his 1906 treatise for the employment of specialist architects rather than borough engineers, won the commission for Haggerston Baths. The foundation stone was laid on 18th March 1903. The official opening was on 25th June 1904. Simon Inglis tells us how EJ Wakeling, vice-chairman of the Shoreditch Baths and Wash Houses Committee, enlivened the occasion by plunging into the pool and swimming a 100-foot length underwater. Alderman Wakeling's name, along with those of the builders and the architect, can still be read, in chipped and partly erased form on a stone tablet.

Haggerston Baths, this prime specimen of Edwardian baroque, is suffering; windows are sealed with black panels, points of potential access are defaced with razor wire and surveillance cameras. Warnings have been placed in six languages. The furnace-bright orange of the brickwork, in its pomp like the confident colour of London Overground, is dirty, dulled by neglect. The imperial swagger of heraldic carvings, lions and unicorns above the separate entrances for males and females, is diminished. Between a set of twinned Roman Ionic columns there is still a recessed central loggia for dignitaries to acknowledge the cheers of the crowd. But no crowds are coming.

Purple fuses of buddleia burst through the protective fence on the mockingly named SWIMMERS LANE (PRIVATE ROAD). The school-kids who were turned away at the time of the temporary closure are now in their mid-twenties. And they have never swum another stroke in this building. The Bridge Academy (A Bridge to Your Future) has no pool. But it does control the football pitches and tennis courts of Haggerston Park. They have bought public realm.

At the time of the Haggerston Baths closure, the estimated cost of renovation was £300,000. Small change in the light of future projects, but Hackney didn't have it. The council were in a hole and looking for deals with private developers. So they did what they have always done best, they obfuscated. They were economical with the truth and spendthrift with mendacity. They allowed pool campaigners to take the heat out of protest by putting their energies into proposals and alternative solutions. Promises were dangled and withdrawn. There was a lottery-heavy grand project on the horizon in Stoke Newington, the catastrophically mismanaged Clissold Leisure Centre.

'The wrong building at the wrong time in the wrong place,' Ken Worpole, of the Clissold Users Group, told the critic Jonathan Glancey. The architects were based in Manchester. It was a pattern repeated so many times, through Hackney education and social services: the appointment of high-salaried advisers from elsewhere, shadowy corporate multitaskers on maxi salaries. There was a bias towards smothering the nuisance of locality in public meetings and consultations. The proposed Clissold Leisure Centre, a smart CGI pitch in the post-architectural airport style that fits hospital, Ideas Store or new university, didn't work. The building leaked: from fancy roof, from glass walls retaining fetid water, from cracks in the squash courts, from warped floors. The budget was haemophiliac. It bled out. Clissold Leisure Centre opened, closed for major remediation, opened again.

While the millions stacked up, Haggerston Baths paid the price. By the time health and safety issues had been sufficiently resolved to allow Hackney to hand the amenity in Whiston Road over to an agent who solicited expressions of interest from developers – 'for uses including: leisure, hotel, office, educational, institutional, retail, restaurant (subject to planning)' – the estimated cost of reopening the Edwardian pool was £30 million (and counting).

A rare opportunity to investigate the forbidden interior of Haggerston Baths presented itself, when a phone call offered me the chance – 'right now, leave the house immediately' – to join a party of dark suits and hardhats who were weighing up the commercial possibilities. Bill Parry-Davies, local solicitor, jazzman, fisherman, activist and keen swimmer, was labouring to restore the Haggerston pool to life. He put together a consortium. He contacted the richest people he knew, the ones with collections they might need space to exhibit and the ones with dreams of cutting-edge bars and restaurants. In fact: anyone with a streak of enlightened altruism prepared to dig deep to 'burnish their reputation'. They calculated, so he told me, that it would take the redevelopment of the laundry area as a thirty-six-storey block of offices and private residences to pay for a pool. This wasn't about profit or vanity, tapping the *zeitgeist*; the plotters expressed a theoretical interest in making the pool available to all. It was never enough to swoon over architectural detail: brass handrails, teak changing cubicles, boxed-in steel arches separated by curved plaster panels. The revived pool would have to pay its way. The customer base would come, beyond heritage buffs, from the colonies of new-build flats along railway and canal; the red-bicycle tribes of Santander, the pre-coffee contortionists of Haggerston Park with their personal trainers.

Parry-Davies appreciated the fact that the original pool and its coal-fired Lancashire boilers occupied too much space. Plans were drawn up to drop the pool to a lower level, to do clever things to make it as adaptable as a post-Olympic stadium. One way or another, if the proposal succeeded, the pool would be re-opened to the public. To those committed individuals who had carried on the fight for fifteen years.

It's like breaking into an Egyptian tomb: catacomb corridors insinuate in every direction, dusty stairs rise towards hidden Howard Carter chambers, cobwebbed offices and storage spaces. There are utilitarian grey tubs, the remnant of the second-class female baths, calling up archival footage of suburban lunatic asylums with cold-water hoses. The swimming pool is drained and the three high windows towards which I used to swim in my laboured crawl, as through a flooded cathedral, before breaststroking back, were covered over. Natural light is excluded in favour of sanctioned municipal entropy. Haggerston Baths is another of those decommissioned non-places kept in a persistent vegetative state, like the gothic sprawl of the neighbouring Queen Elizabeth Hospital for Children in Hackney Road. While spiders knit their sticky nets. And shivering phantoms stand before empty mirrors in tiled washrooms where thick taps leak coal dust.

Location-promiscuous film crews exploit the creep of suspended animation, the unreachable lives, the echoing emptiness of cellars and toilet stalls, for YouTube bits invoking Tarkovsky, for fashion shoots and music promos. It is only reasonable that tribes of squatters, sensitive to the spirit of derelict places, occupy buildings dedicated to social improvement – from which society has been ruthlessly excluded. Haggerston Baths, on this hardhat tour, is so far from how it struck me on my last visit before the padlocked doors and the fateful announcement that I began to mistrust my own memory. Did I ever bathe here? Am I confusing episodes with other bathhouses in other parts of London or Dublin? Research suggests that the male slipper baths were removed between 1962 and 1964 to make way for a gym.

We never entered through the twinned doors, male and female, on Whiston Road. The front elevation, in a style known as 'Wren Revival', was too grand for the traffic ditch the road had become. Paying customers climbed a few steps to a new entrance on the west side, aware of the hissing steam from the laundry, the looming chimney stack. I came with my children. They learned to swim, with bribes for achieved distances, and years of self-confident feats of diving and underwater retrieval ahead. The clapped-out changing rooms and dribbling showers took nothing away from the experience of a community asset within a short stroll of our house. On wet afternoons, when I didn't fancy walking, I detoured to Haggerston Baths for an equally valid immersion in the matter of London. Amniotic reverie. Drift. Reverse evolution. I met people I hadn't seen in years, time-managers between episodes of childcare, enthusiasts with relish for a resource that had outlasted its permissions. Those meandering lengths, before the era of roped-off fast lanes, were a chlorine meditation, puckering the skin and opening the swimmer to an enhanced connection with locality. This building, along with associated libraries, hospitals, street markets, struggled to justify its continued existence in the coming era of leisure as a billable outcome.

It was immediately evident to the Parry-Davies reconnaissance party that Edwardian gothic had been improved by twenty-first-century defacements by the expelled squatters. The drained pool, some of its tiles chipped out, was rimmed with comic book skulls, acid-house signatures, tribal tags and post-political slogans. Quorums of hardhats, fingers to lips, contemplated the enormity of the renovation. Chilled speech bubbles leaked from their mouths. Street codes of the vanished denizens of the last London.

Windows were veiled in gauze. Furniture and machine parts from the earlier regime were adapted for use by the freeloading clients of this beat hotel. Dark passages were snowed in white powder. Cellars with massive, rusting boilers offered a covert terrain as an alternative to the conspicuous visibility of the Shard. Comments were not filed on tactfully provided cards. They were chalked, sprayed or scraped on the walls. DEATH SEX IS FOR LIFE NOT JUST FOR XMAS! LSD. LIZARD NATION. A PLACE WHERE SKATERS, JUNKIES & ARTISTS CAN EXCELL IN. Schematic heads look like Polaroid passports for Charles Manson. This was a building in which it was easy to lose your shadow. A carbolic depository for unclaimed memories. A museum in which time festered.

The party of potential rescuers split up. In hushed groups, they nodded over some trophied talisman from another era. Their whispers carved the heavy silence. They left footprints in the dust. It would be a great thing to bring the pool back to life, but it would not be *this* pool. And the tribes who had occupied the sealed and suspended building were dispersed and disbanded. There was no legislation to sanction their trespass. The outcry for new housing was the necessity of keeping builders and property developers in business. I wondered if the economic dip in China would have some benefit for the London property market, all those empty tower blocks in Stratford, the speculative purchases. Parry-Davies explained that it would have the opposite effect. With the stock market in trouble, the Chinese would want more bricks and mortar in a safe and welcoming city.

Anna sat up all night in our Shard suite looking at London. There would never be another chance. A few hours camped on the fifty-second floor was the holiday I'd been promising for ten years. I stood beside her waiting for the sun to rise over Rotherhithe, and remembering how it felt to be trapped, with no idea what was going on, on the road far below, in the madness of the great spike's launch.

A firework orgy of bands, champagne and Hollywood searchlight beams announced a new order for new money. Old London had fallen. The transient mob was ecstatic. We were gridlocked in a small car on Borough High Street, trying to get back to Hackney, after an ill-advised excursion to a bookshop in Denmark Hill. There is a toll for crossing the river. The Shard was a lighthouse flashing a brash runway of fiscal opportunity deep into Kent.

Underdressed young people, decanted from pubs and offices, were choking the narrow pavements. This was a VE night tribute bonanza for all the wars they'd missed or experienced on iPad. Royalty should have been down here, joining the conga, incognito, mingling with the lowlife mob, like Prince Hal in Eastcheap. The crowd were genuflecting, raising their arms in spontaneous salute of strange lights in the sky. The Martian tripods had landed! And turned to ice.

Some came running, trying to get closer to the incident: the wailing ambulances, the cordon of police forced out of their cars. A meteor was arcing to its own fiery destruction or ours. Ever since a hosepipe ban was announced, the heavens had opened: sheets of barcode rain. Tonight, after acceptable sacrifices, the sky gods relented. A steady London drizzle, no thunder and lightning.

Our car leaked. My feet squelched on the pedals. Girls in short white raincoats and young men, stripped to the waist, raced through the throng. Boris bikes ploughed into the festive crowd like Boudicca's chariots. Basque anarchists smashed beer bottles and shoved them under the wheels of stretch limos packed with hen parties from Bromley. Cab drivers guillotined their electric windows to curse the stupidity of the human race. As coke-couriers heading for the City jumped out and dodged into the mob, to frustrate racing meters, redline fares. It was a night of obscenities.

On London Bridge, couples were splayed in the road, simulating, or actually performing, acts of frenzied coitus, excused by the communal delirium of the occasion. Japanese visitors in slick retro styles from Brick Lane crossed and recrossed the metal river of stalled traffic to frame the best selfies. They called out in high, excited voices. Fist-phones became torches, burning brands. This was a frost fair or a public execution. The last London as a Vauxhall Pleasure Gardens grope sponsored by oligarchs and arms dealers. A flash mob, texting and tweeting, experienced the show in boosted miniature. Connoisseurs of alternate realities.

'It's got nothing on Blackpool Illuminations,' Anna said, displaying a prejudice for her birthplace. But this was more like Rimbaud's *Illuminations*. Total derangement of the senses. *Pendant que les fonds publics s'écoulent en fêtes de fraternité, il sonne une cloche de feu rose dans les nuages.*

Bells of fire ringing in the clouds. New spectres of modernity, only modern 'because all standards of taste have been avoided'. Last London of a stillborn millennium. Railways. Hotels. River. *L'acropole officielle outré les conceptions de la barbarie moderne les plus colossales.* Wealthy passerines framed in their high windows are shot down by this street boy and his lover.

The City of London police are blinded by a blizzard of cameras and illuminated phones. In those fondly-recalled Thatcher days of primitive surveillance systems, I was regularly pulled for the crime of photographing the recording systems that were photographing me. Tonight the checkpoint bullies, drooping under the weight of weap-onry, are subdued, overwhelmed, shuffling along with eyes down, as if prospecting for dropped coins. The cops are behaving like bounc-ers on overtime. They are grabbing minor celebs by the collar and throwing them into the Shard to dress the party at the end of time.

Hemmed in by the crush – abandoned cars, psychosexual perver-sity on all sides, screams, blood, wine, hysterical laughter – I thought I could catch dissenting voices coming from the Resonance FM sweatbox studio on Borough High Street, where they kept windows open to make interviews sound more authentic, with ambient street noise and the odd ambulance shrieking towards Guy's. We were stuck in our pod right alongside that unnecessary management sign: STOP WALKING, START WORKING.

The car radio was still alive, part of the raging acoustic surf below the *Götterdämmerung* of coloured lights splintering Renzo Piano's giant sail. BBC Radio 4's arts correspondent was attempting to glamorise this circus of the damned with an eyewitness report. Like Ed Murrow among the smoking rubble of a dockside warehouse.

'I'm standing under a great *wall* of glass. If like me you suffer from vertigo, stay away. Only faith is keeping this thing up there.'

Then he cued the Peter Ackroyd pre-record. Mellifluous, and with a becoming lisp, Ackroyd made his pitch. 'Admirable! This aspiring, grandiose, almost greedy building aptly fulfils the conditions of London's growth.'

Cancerous. Contagious. Out of control.

The Shard was an inverted *V for Vendetta* symbol dwarfing cathedral, hospital and station. The ice dagger was an astral flightpath narrowing to some remote and scarcely imaginable point: the furthest horizon of the possible.

In my nearside driving mirror I watched as bands of green leaked across the light-polluted sky. Ackroyd, who exploited this district in his first novel, *The Great Fire of London*, was well qualified to mark the moment. In 1982 he had written: 'Tim turned towards the river, as if for relief. But it had become brilliant and fiery, taking on the shape and quickness of the flame… Eventually, legends were to grow around it. It was popularly believed to have been a visitation, a prophecy of more terrible things to come.'

After the publication of his novel *Hawksmoor* in 1985, Ackroyd took Melvyn Bragg (and an accompanying TV crew) to inspect the white stone pyramid in the grounds of St Anne's in Limehouse. The Shard was only the latest clone of that coded memorial, now pushed to the point of absurdity. The launch party at London Bridge celebrated the promotion of an antiquated Masonic symbol into the dizzying post-truth world. And the neutralising, by public exposure, of London's occult geometry. Towers along the banks of the Thames formed strange geometric figures, random signifiers of a culture that it will take a thousand years to interpret.

The consortium responsible for the Shard (once known as the Commerzbank Tower) included, at various stages, the Qatar National Bank, the Qatari Islamic Bank, the Halabi Family Trust, the Nationwide Building Society, and the London-Jewish entrepreneur Irvine Sellar. The New Labour deputy prime minister John Prescott pronounced himself entirely satisfied with the latest imposition on

the skyline: 'The proposed tower is of the highest architectural quality.' Stability of structure, post 9/11, was the clinching argument in
the pitch. And there will be no Westfield Olympicopolis casino here.
Shia-compliant financing forbids it.

I returned to the periphery of the Shard with Bradley L Garrett,
author of *Explore Everything: Place-Hacking the City* (2013). I asked
him to show me how he avoided the £25.95 elevator surcharge
by breaking into the construction site. And running, undetected, up
seventy floors of the central concrete core, before clambering out on
the counterweight of a giant crane to snap a few selfies. To experience the ultimate vision of the sentient city, where everything flows;
railways are rivers, and rivers are pulsing veins and arteries. There are
no people. The only sound is the wind. The Shard is most itself when
it is registered from the one place where it can't be seen, from the
pinnacle of the sail.

I thought, on a previous expedition, how unlikely and irrelevant to
the matter of London the spike of the Shard appeared from grassed
mounds where planners are scheming a 900-metre-long elevated
park on railway sidings between Peckham Rye and Queens Road
Peckham. If I hadn't stayed for a night in Shangri-La, I wouldn't have
believed that, at about the point where the cloud base circumcised
the thrust of the glass tower, people were swimming their leisurely
lengths, and basking in their divorce from the complexities of the
world outside the window.

The Shard is an implanted flaw in the eye. It moves as we move,
available to dominate every London entry point, to endstop every
vista. Even the fee-paying advertisers of Santander bikes are carrying
the brand. It is imprinted on the red mud-panel, along with Anish
Kapoor's ArcelorMittal Olympicopolis helter-skelter. London icons
all. Photographs we are no longer permitted to take. Target architecture. Structures made to be blown apart.

We leaned on the bridge above the escalators linking London
Bridge station and St Thomas Street. It wasn't quite how Garrett
remembered it. He was preoccupied by new projects; a novel of

UFOs, ley lines and a 3,000 mile US road trip to hot springs and abandoned mines. And then, closer to home, by guerrilla initiatives in response to the housing situation in London. We compared notes about the catalogue of unoccupied buildings, locked, boarded up, and cast into development limbo. Asylums. Cholera hospitals. Public baths. Schools. Redundant factories. Discontinued industries. Abandoned shopping malls not yet converted to messianic African religions. How many unsponsored wildflower meadows could be found behind corrugated-iron fences? Secret spaces not worth the cost and hassle of security.

The best time to infiltrate a site, so Garrett said, was shortly before the topping-out ceremony. His associates had no problem with the Shard. They watched the watchman as he left his hut. And they walked straight in through the open door and across to the central staircase.

It takes longer now, as a site worker or jobbing designer, to get to the levels designated as offices (04–28), than it took Garrett and his urban explorer crew to run up the ladder to the stars. I asked one architect about her experiences fitting out a floor for a company selling desk space. It was quite usual, she said, to wait thirty minutes for a lift. The empty space on which she worked was partitioned into theoretical cubicles and sub-divisions. Some clients want nothing more than that Shard address. They employ a person with a low boredom threshold to sit at a desk, while they never leave the safety of the suburbs. Others run their affairs from Shanghai or Malaysia or Estonia. You can phone through and be connected, as if to a human standing at the window. The office floor is quite deserted, a work in progress. Like an absence on an ordinary failing high street waiting to become a charity shop. But Irvine Sellar continues to endorse the vision of the Shard as 'a place where people live, work, enjoy themselves'. Renzo Piano wants 'intensified' urban experience, a 24-hour vertical city without suburban stretchmarks.

Bradley Garrett found an exposed ledge, on the rim of the troposphere, on which to commemorate his intrusion. For blogworld publication, notoriety, arrest and trial.

***

The solution to the housing crisis that Garrett and his friends are working on sounds very simple: put up shacks and hideaways in places so obvious that nobody will notice them. Robert Macfarlane, who lodged in a hut assembled by urban explorers wearing orange hi-viz overalls during the fuss of the London Marathon, called his windowless shelter an 'urban bothy'.

The crew survey the territory as thoroughly as the developers with whom they are in open competition. They smuggle plywood constructions under concrete stairs, in those awkward angles left over by architects who haven't had time to find an elegant solution to a problem. There are bivouacs, where people are free to rest, write, eat, sleep, disguised by black paint and a padlock. They look like any other workman's hut, within the dead zones of some of the most secure and spooked enclaves in the City of London. With so much random construction work in progress, who will notice another hide or yurt shaped from standard building-site materials? There is an invisible army of occupation, an informal network providing free accommodation without direct confrontation, without the battles faced by squatters or Occupy campers alongside St Paul's. The hut I visited with Bradley Garrett was still in play when I passed two months later.

Now, as I move around, I notice more and more of these unlicensed shelters, often parasitical on the chaos of development. Huts in places where you expect to find them. All you need is a sticker for VolkerHighways (Considerate Constructors). Plywood boxes assembled around potential basement excavations that will never be undertaken. There *are* answers to the housing crisis: the crisis is money and manipulation, artificially boosted prices. Profit. Equity. Inheritance. The city is emptying into investment shells and towers engineered from stolen credit cards.

The Garrett huts have no windows. They are Reichian orgone accumulators bombarding you with atoms. Good spaces in which to hibernate, or crash, but hard for living. The empty towers control view. Up there on the fifty-second floor, you can't help witnessing the incoming waves of the future. As Mike Davis said, in the Preface to the 2006 reissue of *City of Quartz*, he anticipated: 'Moments, ripe with paradox and non-linearity, when previously separate currents of history suddenly converge with profoundly unpredictable results.'

When I took an early swim after my night in Shangri-La, the only other participants loosed themselves, very tentatively, from couches where they might have spent the hours of darkness. They seemed to be rounding off a heavy night and not greeting the rising sun over Tower Bridge and Canary Wharf. The man who looked like a slightly hungover and less twinkly Russell Brand – and who might well have been him – watched his companion, a slim girl in a black bikini, enter the water. To test it, over a couple of lengths, on his behalf.

I waited my turn. I tried to calculate where the shadow of the Shard would fall. *And I knew that place.* I had walked there with Bradley Garrett, telling him about how I'd been challenged by security, on the slithery grey surface outside our seat of local governance, City Hall, for the crime of talking to a recording device in public. Which struck me as a severe reaction, when the high walkways of City Hall, with the backdrop of the river, were nothing but scenic platforms for recorded interviews. It was an extraordinary evening when Boris Johnson did not present himself, shovelling back his golden fringe, on the 6.30pm London news. My interviewer put away his kit. He didn't have the energy to argue his case. He told me that his father, who had been in haberdashery, was once called to make a sales pitch to Irvine Sellar in his Carnaby Street incarnation, before the great entrepreneur found his *métier* in property. Sellar received him lying full-length on a couch, like a Roman provincial governor waiting for the next peeled grape.

If the Shard collapsed and fell in a straight line, I calculated that it would fracture the new cancer block of Guy's Hospital and spread its splinters as far as a park with a singular atmosphere. Restoration work was in progress and there was, currently, no access to Angel Path. But the freshly pointed wall, propped up by locally-sourced tombstones, had a heritage plaque recalling the site of the Marshalsea, the debtors' prison.

The collegiate atmosphere of this sinister den, with its respectable quarters for the well-connected and slum conditions for those who could pay nothing, was vividly described by Charles Dickens in *Little Dorrit*. And painstakingly recreated, at the height of the Thatcherite period, by Christine Edzard in a two-part film version. Now the park has been rescued from its obscurity and rebranded as the 'Crossbones' Garden of Remembrance.

The Marshalsea was way ahead of its time, a privatised operation. Its failings were the failings we are hearing about on every news bulletin. The governors and turnkeys bought their positions and turned them to profit. Starving prisoners died in conditions of hideous overcrowding. Courts of enquiry stalled, leading to new trials and larger fees for the lawyers. What was prophetic about the scheme was the understanding that even debt, even the most wretched depths of human hopelessness, can be spun and presented as a workable solution. Taking those miscreants with no respect for the sanctity of fiscal obligation, the natural rights of property, off the street. And out of sight. Giving their care to the smartest bidder, the least worst option.

Rock gardens made from rubble were neatly bordered by the curved tops of nameless gravestones. There were poignant clusters of aniseed herbs and sharp-leaved stonecrops. And paths of crushed green glass crafted to invoke the bed of a mountain stream. Under the shade of an enormous London plane tree, and pillowed by a set of torpedo tombs, a number of rough-sleepers were cocooned in body bags, folded arms covering hurt eyes against daylight. Surrounded on all sides by high buildings and improved brickwork, the Marshalsea still functioned like the open yard of the prison. Groups of men, in hushed conversation, occupied different benches.

It was the prong of the Shard, looming over the cranes of lesser construction sites, that looked anachronistic and absurd. When Renzo Piano's folly shatters and is replaced by something bigger and brighter, the wooden benches and the people perched on them will still be here.

VOICE OF THE HUTS

The last London is a lost London, a city of fracture and disappearance. I set out early one morning, with notebook and pocket camera, to map the emerging *favela* of huts. I mean those secret places – riverside shacks, containers, empty packing cases – where urban explorer collectives have established their hides. Two things became clear very quickly. There were many more of these alternative free-Airbnb accommodations than I'd previously suspected. And they weren't all operated by Bradley L Garrett and his crew. The germ of the idea was out there now and it was spreading fast, facilitated by technologies I scorned or misunderstood: fractal worlds beyond the reach of my Nokia duncephone.

My crudely assembled chart, very much like the one I produced, many years ago, for the alignment of Hawksmoor churches, was outflanked before it began. All this stuff was already available on YouTube and a dozen apps. Streamed with ads for Santander bikes, MYRUN TECHNOGYM (the intelligent home treadmill) and WALK LONDON MAYFAIR VELVET STUDDED LOAFERS. I spotted one cod-psychogeographical plan of Hackney, contrived from mystical pentagrams and triangles, emblazoned on the rear flank of a silver hire car, right over the petrol-flap.

How to tell pirate shacks from the legitimate ones that appeared in new places every morning? On the flat roofs of developments frozen in limbo. In the front gardens of Victorian houses divided into units where neighbours are strangers. On wasteground that might once have been school allotments. How to separate the cabins of urban explorers from those of council-sanctioned, road-digging invaders? This was the beauty of the scheme: *the huts were identical*.

Everywhere I looked, potential hideaways were revealed. I marked down four definites and three possibles in the City, in close proximity to anonymous block-buildings from the 1950s or '60s, their survival dependent on Secret State affiliations: phone-tapping operations, redirection of post, immigration filters sifting the dubious identity papers of money-market cooks and cleaners. The windows of these buildings were dirty and unreadable, entrances dim and protected by policed barriers. Angles of approach were covered by banks of surveillance cameras. But an orange jumpsuit and a yellow hardhat gave the hut-builders a free pass. For recreation, they climbed to the top of the latest towers and swung in the breeze from giant cranes, watching drones swirl and mob in intricate patterns like starlings coming to roost.

Seven crosses in the City, three in Bethnal Green, two in Shoreditch and eleven in Hackney. The squatted nexus around Corbridge Crescent, the railway-bridge camp, the narrowboats with pirate flags, felt like a good place to start. But it was all too obvious. There were shelters. There were squats. And anarchists with busy stencils: IF YOU WORK FOR A LIVING, WHY DO YOU *KILL* YOURSELF WORKING. RIP. But no visible or invisible stopover shacks. The canalside container suburb was so tight that I passed a young black man raging at the locked gate, tapping his security code, yelling and whistling, to gain access to his expensive shared desk.

A WISE MAN TURNS CHANCE INTO GOOD FORTUNE. So the artist (or collective) known as RIP sprayed on the wall beside the Empress Coaches yard. WHATEVER YOU'RE THINKING THINK BIGGER. Local developers obviously agreed with this sentiment. They were about to tear down the gothic ruin to give us something much bigger and louder. On the other bank of the canal, in Andrews Road, THE SECRET SOCIETY OF SUPER VILLAINS AND ARTISTS left their boast in full view, around a skull and crossbones design. This corner of the neighbourhood was resolute in its determination to be part of a graphic novel.

As Jarett Kobek points out in *i hate the internet* (2016), comic books are the loam from which a world-devouring monster grew. For many of the new Londoners there is no other point of reference, no better authority than this self-cannibalising reductive form. 'The business practices of the American comic-book industry have colonised Twenty-First Century life. They are the tune to which we all dance,' Kobek wrote. 'The internet, and the multinational conglomerates which rule it, have reduced everyone to the worst possible fate. We have become nothing more than comic-book artists, churning out content for enormous monoliths that refuse to pay us the value of our work.'

And in just this way, the anarchists of Corbridge Crescent have processed village entropy into one giant comic book. Urban wanderers, flâneurs with tenure, private income or book commissions, feel free to sample, copy or blog these scripted walls and back alleys, on a daily basis. Sometimes collections of spraygun murals and stencilled graffiti, made over months, are turned into indie publications with laminated covers: hip graphic novellas stolen from the work of anonymous others, with no permission fees to be paid. The theft of content fits neatly inside Kobek's model of comic-book capitalism.

THE ALBION SAILS ON COURSE. Black script on white wall. The spill-zone around Corbridge Crescent, the painted devil heads and hybrid monsters, the bare-breasted pin-ups from naughtier times mouthing Situationist slogans, are captured and made fit for purpose by film crews and television set-dressers, lighting technicians and catering caravans, responding to dissent as: *exploitable edge*.

LOADED WITH/ MEMORIES/ I WAS NOT AFRAID/ TO SET OFF/ AN ADVENTURE/ ANY MORE.

14 November 2016: the words I copied into my notebook yesterday are painted over with white undercoat, so that professionals can create rebellion suitable for television. For example: a Warholist head of Che Guevara – CHE GAY – inflated to cover an entire wall, with fake yelps about eating the rich to replace the groundwork of RIP and the Secret Society of Super Villains and Artists. NO PIGS.

The coaches from the garage, *Empress of London*, have to be relocated, clogging up streets where parking has been suspended, giving the council a double hit: the charge on residents, who are not getting what they paid for, and the levy on the film company. Win, win! Health and Safety demands that the production commandeers an ambulance, to be kept in the yard of the emptied coach park, in case one of the precious stars trips on a wrecked staircase in the preserved ruin.

The outlaw in his shack on the ledge by the canal sleeps through the entire fuss. He learnt his lesson after the first Immigration Enforcement raid. Now his shelter looks like the detritus of a lumberyard. Like the reassembled aftermath of a Cornelia Parker explosion. To mark the approach of Halloween and the yawning of graves, a young boy cycles uncertainly to school, in the wake of his mother, wearing a silver skull-mask. Welcome to comic world, Hackney. At the base of the image swamp we find the sinister clown: child-catcher, grinning molester. The public joke, the big-haired politician who dissolves into the Joker © DC Comics. 'The principal products of the comic-book industry,' Jarett Kobek said, 'were 32-page monthly pamphlets containing drawings of gargantuan-breasted women… Most of the industry's output was subtle pornography for the mentally backward.'

Extinguish fire with petrol. One of the latest Andrews Road de-facements is a poster: SILENT BILL MUSE WANTED. Silence against the noise of imagery? The meditation of a hooded man sitting all day on a bench? Or another who dreams the fading city through all the hours of daylight in an Arsenal-branded sleeping bag? 'Be silent in that solitude,' said Edgar Allan Poe. Let them come. The restless spirits of the dead are 'in death around thee'.

My cartographic tour became a quest for silence, somewhere to kill the cortical hum, the tapping and pecking of boney digits on digital screens. I had been transcribing the broken monologues of Overground clients in transit, as they ignored the passing scene, ignored their fellow passengers, and asked for money or time or forgiveness. *So? Really?* Now I noticed that other playlets, one-sided dialogues were being broadcast from the ticket halls and conversation courts along the interconnected necklace of Ginger Line stations. At Shoreditch, for example, or Highbury and Islington. But not at Haggerston (the plaintive cry of the beggar: *Sparechangeforfoodplease*). Or at Whitechapel (drowned by Crossrail development).

At Highbury I was confronted in the 'profound dull tunnel' leading to the escalator by a regiment of First War infantrymen marching in silence like ghosts who had found their way home from the trenches in time for vote for a hard Brexit. Their hoarded silence, I later discovered, was an artwork. More Walter Owen – whose strange novella, *The Cross of Carl*, describes the journey of a Tommy, left for dead after a minor skirmish, being transported by rail to sidings where he will be rendered into pig meat – than Wilfred Owen. 'I knew that sullen hall.'

Tin hats progress, unremarked, through a scatter of Highbury commuters ranting on mobile phones. Like a launch party at which everybody is talking loudly and insanely to themselves. And ignoring the product on the walls: those enlarged photographs from the Other World of vagrants, boy soldiers, motel light bulbs, universal graffiti.

The entrance hall at Whitechapel is disputed territory, trapped between systems, haunted by spectres of sickness and poverty, haunted by progress. Phone babble would be a discourtesy. A ravaged young woman calling herself 'Bets' puts the bite on me, while we wait for a delayed District Line connection. Unasked, she describes herself as a smack addict, off for six weeks, trying somehow to make it to the safety of Soho, without hitting Liverpool Street, from which she has been excluded. She lived within the Underground system, the heat, the shelter, but she never mastered its complexities.

Bets struggled to pull a blanket from her ratty bag. She chewed the blackened quick of her nails. Her teeth were ruined. She said that she wanted the toilet, but then she always felt like that, and wouldn't bother just now. Her mouth was white and flecked. 'I won't come too close,' she said, cupping a hand for coins. The train was held for a signal. She moved off down the quiet carriage.

Climb the foothills of privilege if you want respite from the starling-chitter of cell phones. Highgate is good. Putting in time before visiting my dentist, I inspect the bookshelves of the Oxfam shop. And listen to the conversation at the till.

'I saw *V for Vendetta* last night. DVD. Two pounds. Alan Moore.'

'No.'

'*Watchmen*? You *must* know Alan Moore? *From Hell*? Jack the Ripper. Johnny Depp.'

'No.'

'John Hurt. He was Winston Smith in *1984*. And now he's a minister in *V for Vendetta*. England is a dystopian dictatorship. Alan Moore. Two pounds. I watched it again last night. I'll bring the DVD in tomorrow.'

I retreated to Waterlow Park and thought about writers and tennis, Martin Amis and Julian Barnes knocking it about in the days of their friendship. Nobody playing today. Not even that phantom patpat of the deserted courts of Maryon Park in *Blow-Up*. Highgate honours the silence of the bridled Coleridge. The granite head of Karl Marx. The cushioned footfall of Hush Puppies on the pavement between Oxfam and off-licence. I used to explore reforgotten fiction in the basement of Fisher & Sperr. Now the antiquarian bookshop is an animal clinic. Highgate is a good place for the upmarket dog trade.

'What do you do, if you don't mind me asking?' The fit young South African dentist probed.

'Writer.'

'Have I read any of them? What are they about?'

'London.'

'Plenty of history there.'

'I saw Julian Barnes coming uphill, right outside your place, in a blue shirt with blue jacket. The writer.'

'Don't know the name. Is he good?'

On the wall, where my former dentist used to keep his Turner landscapes and views of Edinburgh, the new man has an Olympic artwork with an upbeat message. As he drilled, I thought about my father's patient who believed that elements of the Secret State had implanted radio transmissions in his teeth. He was a conscientious objector in the Second War. Brought to London to face a tribunal, a paid assassin pushed him in front of a train. He survived, but sustained damage to his foot that left him with a lifetime battling for compensation. When his strength gave out and he died, he willed my father the foot. It was delivered in a hinged black box like a pygmy coffin.

The noise that I couldn't shake off, in teeth, ears, bones, was the soundscrape of dialogue transcribed in spaces outside and alongside stations. *No worries, no worries then.*

***

THEY'LL BE LIKE REALLY *REALLY* HAPPY. SHE ADMITS TO BEING A LEZ. BUT THEY'RE SUCH A GREAT COUPLE. MONEY, REALITY. WORLD, HALLUCINATION. IF I HAD A MANIFESTO, I'D HIRE CORBYN TO CARRY IT THROUGH. HE CAN'T BE SHIFTED. HE'S A FORCE OF NATURE. HE'LL WIPE OUT THE LABOUR PARTY. THEY'LL BE LIKE REALLY *REALLY* HAPPY. I'M NOT RINGING TO BE A FACEBOOK FRIEND. BUT TELL HIM THIS IS WAR. I'M NOT BLAMING YOU. HE CALLS *ME* ON MY MOBILE. HIS NUMBER IS SPECIAL. *MY* NUMBER IS SPECIAL. I'M IN THE TRAIN STATION, SHOREDITCH. THEY'LL BE LIKE REALLY *REALLY* HAPPY. CALL YOU BACK. YOU STOOD UP AND WALKED OUT? THAT WAS GOING TO BE A SUCH GOOD STORY. WAS IT ON FILM 4? THEY'RE ALL REPEATS. DO NOTHING, HE SAID. THINK NOTHING. THIS IS WAR. HIRE CORBYN. HE'LL WIPE OUT THE LABOUR PARTY. WAS IT ON FILM 4? MONEY, REALITY. SECONDHAND BOOKS, LIKE *MILITARY*? GROSS. KEEP APPLYING, THAT'S GOOD. EVERYONE'S REALLY INTO THAT AESTHETIC NOW. HE'S A FORCE OF NATURE. THE DOCTOR IS SICK TODAY. SHE'S UP AND DOWN. SHE NEEDS TO HAVE RESTART, BASICALLY. I'M GONNA SERIOUSLY PICK THIS GUY'S BRAINS, THEN FUCK HIM OVER. YOU KNOW THEY'RE REVISING THE FOX HUNTING LAWS ON MONDAY. ASK FOR A REFUND ON THE TOILET. I'M NOT BLAMING YOU. IT'S BEEN A VERY SWEET YEAR. I FEEL WORSE THAN YESTERDAY. CALL YOU BACK. I CAN'T FIND THE LETTER WITH THE DATE FOR WHEN YOU PEOPLE ARE COMING. CALL ME BACK. WHERE WOULD YOU LIKE TO GO FOR YOUR HONEYMOON? RAPID CITY, IOWA? TECHNICAL DOCUMENTS, NOT SEA LEVEL OR VALUE BASED. THEY'LL BE REALLY *REALLY* HAPPY. SHE ADMITS TO BEING A LEZ. I LEFT HALF THE HOUSE IN TRUST.

I'M ON MY WAY TO THE OVAL. I HAVEN'T GOT ANY OF
THE 5%, OVER AND ABOVE. I'D LIKE THAT BACKDATED,
TO BE HONEST. HIRE CORBYN. IT'S LIKE DJs AND THAT,
BUT IT'S ALSO LIKE A PHOTOGRAPHY EXHIBITION.
FUCKING WEIRD. LIKE SEX ON YOUR WEDDING NIGHT.
BORIS IS BEHIND ALL OF THIS. I'VE BEEN GOING TO THIS
OPTICIAN IN COVENT GARDEN. THEY DO GENUINE
VINTAGE MODELS. THEY DO SILVER ON THE LENSES.
I'M READING GASGOYNE'S *A VAGRANT*. WHEN I GET
HOME IT'S LIKE RELIGIOUS STUDIES. HIRE CORBYN.
THIS IS WAR. I'M NOT BLAMING YOU.

WALKING

THE MILKY WAY (TO CROYDON)

'We can walk between two places and in so doing establish a link
between them, bring them into a warmth of contact, like introducing
two friends.'
Thomas A Clark

It *could* have been, but he thought not. Ambiguity of distance and fallible memory. Right books, wrong set to contain them? Right rucksack,
for sure. Stephen gave me that story. And the photograph on page 55
of the Penguin paperback of *Austerlitz* was something approaching
an actual icon now. 'A sign or representation that stands for its object
by virtue of a resemblance or analogy to it.' An honoured relic too.
Sanctified by its biography, the pilgrimages it had made across Europe,
and the journeys it had not made, and would never make, across the
Alps from Italy into Germany; a legend confirmed or embellished in
print, all the way back to the moment of purchase on Charing Cross
Road, in a shop that is no longer there. The conjunction, in earlier
times, of bookshops, used and new, and suppliers of rucksacks and
raincapes, was sympathetic. Which came first, the canvas receptacle
or the books that would fill it? In the end, Stephen said, after many
years of good service, and that appearance still undamaged in Sebald's
Austerlitz, books were the undoing of the rucksack.

Stephen Watts, poet and translator, was returning from Lithuania,
coming in on the Stansted Express, where his documents had been
scrutinised and his luggage checked, to Liverpool Street station. The
place where we met before our first walk through Whitechapel and
Mile End, and where he waited to greet Sebald as he stepped from the
Norwich train, to begin one of those meandering expeditions that

informed and animated the novel-in-progress. Held at the barrier, trying to force the bulging rucksack through its blind mechanical opposition, the strap broke. Lithuania had been a treasure trove of poetry and folk history, the food and substance of future projects. Stephen loaded the pouch to capacity: it burst, spilled. It could never again be suspended, as it is in *Austerlitz*, from a hook on the wall of the Toynbee Studios on Commercial Street. The post-Lithuanian rucksack, the one I photographed in the Jewish burial ground at Alderney Road, was repaired with strong twine, shepherd's twine, looped around the padded leather collar. The twine was milky white and could have been woven from strands of Stephen's untrammelled hair. The rucksack had become as much its captured representation as its physical self. But it was still in service, still being exploited in other stories. The leather collar was gouged with marks of travel, compulsive nomadism.

But the photograph of the bookman's cave, from page 43 of *Austerlitz*, was not, as I had imagined, the workshop and library of Stephen Watts, from his nest at Toynbee Studios. Rachel Lichtenstein, in her memory-expedition *On Brick Lane*, calls Stephen's hideaway an 'office'. An office precariously perched above the abyss of poverty. A mendicant scholar's cell supported by columns of books, files of research, set-aside essays, epic poems in progress, translations bringing to life voices of migration, angelic glimpses. 'Why don't you sell some of your books?' Lichtenstein asks. Registering the horror on Stephen's face. 'He looked even thinner than usual and seemed exhausted.' Familiar ghosts attend their conversation in a neighbourhood curry house. The Yiddish poet Avram Stencl. The historian and teacher Bill Fishman. And of course Sebald: 'who had recently died'. They move on to Stephen's office. Climbing weary stairs, Rachel follows Stephen in expectation of encountering a chamber as haunted as the weavers' garret of the recluse David Rodinsky, above the Princelet Street synagogue (now a Museum of Immigration). 'The walls are covered in bookshelves that reach to the ceiling and heave with thousands of volumes, including poetry books in different languages. The floor is alive with orange peel, tea bags, towers of polystyrene cups and stained coffee filters, which Stephen sees as sunflowers. An ever-growing collection of stones, bone and pieces of worn wood retrieved during his many walks is scattered among the debris… Somewhere, buried in the centre of all this, is the ancient computer where Stephen sits and writes.'

The elements are generic. They are found in the snapshot Sebald positioned in *Austerlitz*, where the unoccupied room is surrounded by a sympathetic border of words. Surveillance reports on truth. Stephen, hesitating, placed that photograph of the office at UEA in Norwich, the lair of the German scholar. But he couldn't be sure.

'I would usually spend an hour or so sitting with him in his crowded study, which was like a stockroom of books and papers with hardly any space left for himself, let alone his students, among stacks piled high on the floor and the overloaded shelves,' Sebald wrote. He was conjuring Stephen's retreat or his own, and trapping them both, and readers seduced by the tale, into a close inspection of the photograph – which, because it is so firmly fixed in time, serves to anchor the play of fantasy. It sits like a darkened window into a past that never quite came into being.

But Stephen was not to be located. Since he published *Republic of Dogs / Republic of Birds* in 2016, he had vanished from view. We had our rituals and our paths crossed from time to time. There are risks, as I was well aware, in resurrecting abandoned manuscripts, books that decided, somewhere in their travels, not to permit completion or publication. The prose-poem of doubling, pulling focus between North Uist in the Outer Hebrides, the Western Isles of the early 1970s, and the pre-Docklands Isle of Dogs in the late '70s, establishes a seductively unstable force field. Flashbacks. Eidetic insults. The recovery of a text composed in the late 1980s and misplaced until 2012, before being translated into laptop in 2013, and finally published by the independent Hackney press, Test Centre.

I have it on my desk. I handle it. Book visible, poet erased. 'There is no edge to this city that extends all the way to the sea.' Stephen hymns migration, the drift of transhumance with the changing seasons, mountain pasture to river valley. He finds his place in Whitechapel because of that history of bruised settlement, first breath, recovery

and recuperation, outside the walls, real or imagined, of the established city. Where money is always pushing at the boundary fence,
hungry for more, more of everything.

We plotted a walk from Shadwell, where Stephen had lived for
more than thirty-five years in a council flat, to West Croydon, the end
of the southern spur of the London Overground line. A metal ladder
down which fire, fanned by digital communication, had rushed at
the time of the riots in 2011. West Croydon, the emerging city of
towers, was where Stephen's maternal grandfather, Sebastian Longhi,
kept his Creamery, his café and ice-cream parlour, across from the
station. A democratic resource, Stephen liked to think, a place to sit,
take serious coffee, discuss the day. Much like the little breakfast bar,
close to the Thames, close to a set of steps running down to the foreshore, where Stephen walked on good mornings, to open his emails,
to read and work. He kept that nuisance out of his home. In this
interval of retreat and reverie, before the engagements and collisions
of the day, the poet watched cormorants – as, perched on rotten tripods and moorings, they kept their own watch 'over the dead docks'.
He tried to remember what that Russian had written. 'The grasses
in the streets of the city were the first runner-sprouts that would end
up covering even the interstices of contemporary space.' There was
a primer in his pocket on the burning of books, the 'firing of the libraries of the Republic'. Dried leaves of the libraries of the world are
gathered in one small Spitalfields cabin. Correspondences. Versions
from Irish Gaelic, Hungarian, Russian, Icelandic. 'Live archaeology
of my mouth.' Stephen was the true keeper, the last witness.

In those final years, they had often discussed the notion of a walk
from Stephen's grandfather's Italian village, across the mountains, to
Sebald's village on the German side. They studied maps and projected
routes, huts where it was possible to lodge. The unwritten poems and
the potential books hovered and worried like birds in the room.
'Cutting a section across the Alps / or a section through a glacier's
brain,' Stephen called it in a memorial poem for his friend. 'From
Precasaglio / in the Alta Valcamonica to Wertach in the Allgäu.' He
paces his stacked office, staggering and mewling, and he hears Sebald

speak in that deep Bavarian growl: 'They are ever returning to us, the dead.'

The walk will be made alone, the poet hopes. But it will no longer be *the* walk. The words will be made alone.

Stephen protected himself, treating electronic communications networks with suspicion, handling email traffic with metaphorically gloved hands. Therefore, it was said, and his publishers confirmed it, he was not an easy man to find. My emails were unanswered. The poet, who could be relied on to appear, hovering and attentive, at readings, lectures, independent film shows, wasn't there. He wasn't well. He was barely strong enough to make it down to Cable Street for the launch of his own book at Wilton's Music Hall. He had been giving blood or bone marrow or body parts to a relative, so rumour went. There had been a terrible family tragedy. It was not the moment to pursue the notion of a walk down the Ginger Line to West Croydon.

The difficulty was that Stephen's identity had merged somehow with that of a character in Sebald's novel, *Austerlitz*. 'It was almost impossible to talk of anything personal, as neither of us knew where the other came from... He clutched the worn spectacle case he always held in his left hand so tightly that you could see the white of his knuckles beneath the skin.' Did he walk with Max through the Isle of Dogs to the Greenwich Foot Tunnel? Or did he write his terse account from something I told him? Stephen had forgotten. And then there was the version Rachel Lichtenstein crafted for *On Brick Lane*. Stephen Watts as secular saint, troubled among a ballast of books. The poems that have still to be translated. 'There is a tidal wave of sound and memory running down that street.' In his portrait, snapped by Rachel, Stephen is smiling.

One afternoon I walked to Whitechapel to see if Stephen had been visiting his office. But Whitechapel was no longer there. The whole sweep on the south side of the Spitalfields Market, apart from a tragic façade propped up as a mocking quotation, was gone. Dust. Grit. You could taste it in your mouth all the way back to Hanbury Street. And without the brewery to wash away the hurt. Heritage tourists, style scavengers and City overspill occupied the narrow pavements in puddles of noise and whelping chatter. The concrete slab of the multi-storey car park built over the site of the final Ripper murder in White's Row was a nightmare eddy of oil and filth. But this view across the open ground, towards Hawksmoor's Christ Church, had not been available in generations. And would soon be obliterated by the latest thrust of aspirational towers. Already the field of rubble was enclosed with a green fence suitable for CGI promises and upbeat slogans. Toynbee Hall was part of the outwash, a pit, a destructive upgrade.

Miraculously, the studios at the side were still in play. I was fearful that Stephen's myth had been swept away with the old bricks. Did he have the willpower to husband this latest insult and turn it to advantage? I left him a letter, with no more expectation than stuffing the paper into a bottle and throwing it overboard. A couple of weeks later I received a reply. 'I'm just back from Romanian villages… but I appreciate your flexibility & the pencil.' A date was set. Postponed. Set again. We would meet at Shadwell Station on 24th October at 8am.

Half-an-hour early, on a bracingly crisp morning, and making a slow circuit while I took my bearings, I spotted Stephen, tumbled from his warm bed, hair streaming behind him, trying to keep up as he rushed down the culturally diverse and conflicted street in quest of coffee. The curator Gareth Evans called the poet's work 'fiercely engaged internationalist writing invaluable to our understanding of the Crisis'. Crisis with a capital C. Stephen's long stride was enveloped in windblown wrappings of free newsprint flagging up the closure of the Calais camp. And demanding the first wisps of fire, scarlet splashes across the grey. CALAIS EXODUS. TEMPERS FLARE AS THOUSANDS OF MIGRANTS LEAVE 'JUNGLE' CAMP. *Flare. Jungle. Exodus.* Old Testament apocalypse. *Scuffles. Fires lit. Tear gas. Shantytown. Flashpoint.* Full-page picture spread: a single, white, 'British volunteer' struggling to hold back the mass of young black men pushing against a barrier. BANKER KILLED TWO WOMEN

AND FILMED TORTURE: PAGE 22.

Out of hot underground tunnels, dead newspapers. They drop, un-read, from the hands of travellers. Every railway cave down here is an active concern: MEAT BAZAAR, FISH BAZAAR, VEGETABLE BAZAAR. A reward is being offered for the recovery of a female, five-year-old, Russian Blue cat called Marta, chipped and registered in Lithuania. The arches of the Docklands Light Railway – Shadwell is the point of transit – have been converted into sponsored windows: TO LEARN AS MUCH AS TO TEACH. The doctored art pho-tograph, making its allotted space into stained-glass, is a portion of English field with the tracings of a white line showing us the direc-tion of travel. Like a theft from Richard Long and the land artists of the Sixties and Seventies. The only legitimate journey is into the past.

Stephen sets off at a clip. I admire his shiny black walking shoes, acquired from a shop in Aldgate: light enough and stylish enough without making a fashion statement. We will retrace my *London Overground* route, station by station, to Surrey Quays, and then pick up the West Croydon tributary. With black linen book bag to replace the famous *Austerlitz* rucksack, and bareheaded, grey leisure top and poet's trailing red scarf, Stephen leads us past his own building, the bicycle on the balcony. A narrow pier from which he has witnessed the world and its changes. The view is tranquil, he reckons, the back-waters of a maligned neighbourhood. 'I did not stand on my balcony in London for thirty-five years,' he says, 'watching the children grow to their delinquence.'

There is an established path of desire, it is part of his being now, and I have stumbled on it from time to time, carrying the alert pil-grim to the Thames at Wapping. Flowering plants have been hacked out of the beds beside the path to make way for barriers of thorn and close-knitted municipal greenery. The ventilation shafts for the Overground tunnel remind me of Shetland brochs. Stephen has the gift of registering plural landscapes in a singular time. 'Because to breathe is to be forever on the move.'

The night before our expedition I met Peter Bush, a former

colleague of Sebald at UEA and a great friend of Stephen Watts. He asked me to send his love to the poet. Bush was a translator of French, Portuguese, Spanish and Catalan. As a gesture of solidarity he was on hand at a promotional event for *Bookshops* by Jorge Carrión. His services were unrequired, Carrión was fluent in global anecdotes, and in love with the particulars of bookshops everywhere. At the meal afterwards, Bush remembered Sebald with affection and respect. But the German professor was not, it seems, an easy person to know. There was always the mystery of his craft: where does it come from and what is the secret? Beyond the particular space occupied by a man carrying out his duties, living his life, driving between campus and the Old Rectory in a Norfolk village.

Stephen said that, perhaps, it's possible, he didn't want to conjecture, there was a palpable tension between Sebald's professional life and the impulse, or more than an impulse, to write. That privacy. That perversion. That magic when the alchemy works and the printed page feels like a recovery from an illuminated testament that was already there. 'We are each of us republics with many trapped voices inside,' he said. The struggle he felt in Sebald, the pressure, was a recognition of the stress in his own life, between poetry, the trapped voices, and the necessity to complete applications, fill in forms, present himself: to engage with the mundane world. Peter Bush, coming at the question from another angle, intimated that Sebald was happy with the job, his duties, because, every third year, he would have a paid sabbatical; a certain balance could be sustained. As we walked towards the river, Stephen pondered the question. And decided that the 'free' year was a time for travel, European train journeys, walks, Belgium, Switzerland, Corsica. A time to rehearse a character that might, at some unspecified point in the future, convert experience, reading and photographs, into an improved version of himself and paradoxes he had yet to unravel.

Before lectures, Bush told me, he would often find Sebald, who spurned required university computer systems, running and re-running video footage, newsreels, archive, Fritz Lang, Murnau. The spectre of Dr Mabuse was stalking the corridors of the academic asylum. 'The most interesting attempts to transcend the received limitations of fiction were made in the literature of continental Europe,' Sebald said, as he set out to investigate 'new models and hybrids' that factored a climate sympathetic to his own work: Beckett, Perec, Canetti, Walser and Kafka.

Just once, Bush was invited to dinner at the Old Rectory. Sebald cooked with produce from his garden. His wife was not present. 'They led separate lives. They were both German, strong personalities.' Stephen did not agree. 'I saw them as very close, bonded over a long period. But following their own paths, obviously.'

The German department was absorbed, in one of those management rethinks, into Literature and Creative Writing. Sebald told Bush that if anyone was to be appointed as poet of place, the essential voice of UEA, it should be Stephen Watts. The one whose Whitechapel vision, derived from Hölderlin by way of Michael Hamburger, and rising above the houses, came through the car radio, causing him to swerve, all those years ago, on the road to Poringland. 'What rough circle in our language has / brought us back to here?'

Stephen believed that the radio message was something like what happens in Cocteau's film *Orphée*: the blocked poet being contacted from beyond the mirror of death by oracular phrases that cut through conditioned behaviour patterns. Broken reception. Interference. Radio was the medium of wartime resistance, bizarre coded phrases initiating action. In 1985, while crossing the Alps, Sebald underwent a liberating spiritual crisis. 'He seems to have lost some sense of himself only to discover himself anew, in prose and poetic prose.'

Stephen's poem began: 'Lord in dream I was lifted out of London.' And now, on this mild morning, that was precisely what we intended: under the river and over the hills to Croydon. Floating on memories and conceits.

Sebald, Stephen tells us, 'was not one to walk in company'. He made an exception for the Whitechapel poet. They drifted in slow circuits, like damaged artists in a French asylum, around the perimeter fence at UEA. They discussed the expedition from Precasaglio to Wertach. Sebald walked with his camera and Stephen with the urge to retrace the migration of his grandfather from that village in the Alta Val Camonica to Soho and Croydon. Croydon, as the poet spoke of it, took on the aspect of a site of authentic pilgrimage. For me, it was simply the end of the line. It was where London Overground gave up the ghost. Where London abdicated. Gotham City towers, sliding off the screen and on to the street, were the most lurid manifestation of the future as a giant comic book. When you arrived at West Croydon by train, the air you struggled to force into your lungs was different. Croydon was a botched experiment, inspired by the anti-metropolitan bias of Margaret Thatcher, in turning the city inside out. Leaving proud but peeling stucco cemeteries like Chelsea and Kensington empty, while hard-nosed business shifted to the bleeding edge, closer to airports that must grow and spread until they made London, as Ballard always contended, a mere satellite of no consequence; a cobweb museum of ridiculous monuments and equestrian statues of forgotten military butchers.

Croydon was the Shining City at the end of our desire line, *La Voie Lactée*: the heretic's Santiago de Compostela. For Stephen it was where he could pay his respects to his mother's family, to the economic migration and resettlement of his grandfather. It was the abolished European café where the conversation continued, in many languages at once; an early model for the place by the Thames where he took his coffee and opened his laptop. For me, there was a chemical element I had yet to identify, something better than riot and fire. Croydon was over the hill from West Norwood, where I had lodged in my first London stay, when I was attending the Brixton film school. Croydon was the destination of choice for Norwood shopping expeditions, or so I was told by my landlady; never Oxford Street, too many foreigners.

If Stephen was quiet as we walked, he was not subdued. He had taken off his hiking boots to creep through a stranger's house, fingering the curtains, stroking the books, admiring the plants. 'I wasn't physically tired,' he said, 'more mentally (or spiritually).' The span and scale of unforgiving suburbs, clean avenues without pubs or shops or evidence of any activity beyond sleep, drained him.

Balanced on high stools in La Cigale, close to Surrey Quays station, coffee secured, we were approaching the point where the West Croydon spur of the Overground breaks away from the circuit previously walked with Andrew Kötting. La Cigale was always a Kötting favourite, and now it was one of mine. A good place to reflect and talk. The atmosphere was Italian and therefore appropriate to our sentimental journey – hissing coffee machines, panini, cannolo – but the name was French? Locust, cicada. The buzz of morning conversation, the rustling of newspapers.

Stephen talked about his grandfather's boyhood, about transhumance, a theme that engaged him. How the young shepherd followed the flock down from the mountains to the Po Valley. And then London. And how we were all nomads, it was our natural condition. He felt it, when I saw him before we left Shadwell, as he rushed out along the newspaper-strewn pavement in the direction of Watney Market: stalls where nomads set out their wares for other nomads camping in alien tower blocks. In 1904, Stephen's grandfather was 'second-head waiter' at Caruso's Italian Coffee Parlour in Greek Street.

I told the poet how struck I had been by a film, viewed a few days before our walk, in which the painter Renchi Bicknell, who had accompanied me on a trek around the M25 in 1999, played the part of his great-grand-uncle Clarence. Renchi doesn't have to utter, but his mimed performance is much more than an impersonation. Authentically bearded and costumed, and grasping a thick staff, he climbs with purpose, hopping from boulder to boulder across swift-flowing mountain streams, to pause at the edge of the forest, while the crew frame the shot of a panting hare. Renchi lies down, charcoal in hand, to make accurate copies of the rock engravings in the Vallée des Merveilles. And he paints, afresh, the watercolours Clarence produced of the region's rare and spectacular flora.

As Stephen's grandfather retreated from the mountains to make his way through the maze of London, Clarence Bicknell, the privately wealthy high churchman who made nature his god, came to Bordighera on the Italian Riviera and then into the Val Fontanalba and the land of the pre-historic rock engravings. His fortune devolved from his father, the great whale-oil magnate, Elhanan Bicknell, friend and patron of Turner: the man who gifted London with its soft and shimmering light. And reeking reminders of where that light came from. Clarence, the thirteenth child of Elhanan, was a man of many parts; botanist, archaeologist and champion of Esperanto. He died in his summer home at Casterino, close to the Franco-Italian border. He left a large enough collection of drawings of alpine flowers and rock carvings, stones, bones, butterflies to found a museum. There is a photograph of the old man – about Renchi's age, eyes narrowed against the pinch of sharp sunlight – in a deckchair, up in the mountains, pondering the sketch of rock markings he holds open across his lap. Like Esperanto, the movement of the pictographs are in a universal language that nobody remembers how to use.

But I do remember, vividly, discussing these things with Renchi, up on the North Downs, on a section of the Pilgrim's Way, on a hot summer morning, overlooking torrents of traffic on the M25. And how, in our lives, we can go no further than to reprise work laid out by our great-grand-uncles or great-grandfathers. Renchi, physically, accepted the imprint of Clarence, as well as a portion of his questing spirit. I avoided the beard and the watch-chain of Arthur Sinclair, my Scottish great-grandfather, the one who wrote a book about his travels in Peru, but the rhythms of my prose, wherever they came from, echoed his. Maps of improbable destinations have been pressed into our hands. Never satisfied, we pass that burden on. We have to make our own treaties with the knowledge that we are sponsored by remote and much diminished dividends of colonialism.

We were soon confronted by recent rocks, in which Stephen showed little interest. The granite boulders of New Cross, some carved or scratched, formed circles derived from no obvious belief system, beyond casual affiliation with the Overground railway. Low punishment benches, made to deter rough-sleepers, were arranged around the boulders. Stephen notices a handpainted sign outside a junkyard: FOR SALE. ICE CREAM MACHINE. And he takes it as confirmation that we are still on the right track for the Croydon Creamery.

Almost as soon as we left La Cigale, we found the first immigrant enterprise, a failed Italian roadhouse aimed at a cancelled highway: VILLA ROMANA. BAR & RESTAURANT. FOR SALE. White lettering on green. Red plants dying slowly in decorative pots. A battleship-grey corner building, with a tired awning, slapped against blue-balconied flats. Railway money is flowing another way, into an anonymous new-build, flat-roofed structure with picture windows.

The strip of park shadowing the railway led us to a deserted New Cross estate with shuttered shops and low-level flats. In one of the designated play-zones, carpeted with squashy grey rubber to deflect harm, was a fountain of wilted flowers and cellophane wraps. Silver night-lights. Pink ribbons. Messages and black hearts scrawled on cardboard. Stephen walked away. He knew only too well what this portended and he had no desire to absorb, exploit or express prurient interest in an all too common tragedy.

SUNDAY 3rd APRIL 2016. # MDOT'S WORLD// 8.14pm. AGED 17. YOU ARE STILL MY WORLD EVENTHOUGH YOUR GONE.

Myron 'MDOT' Isaac-Yarde, 'aspiring musician' and popular rapper, was stabbed after an altercation with a number of disaffected estate youths. He died in hospital. Witnesses did not interfere: 'It's just gangs. People don't have a little row anymore, they get out knives.'

Joane Dean, who lived in New Cross for more than ten years, said: 'We were supposed to get community centres but all we have is a pile of rubble.'

In Fordham Park, they have totem poles quoting the area's distant maritime history. And yet more scattered rocks. The Overground station at New Cross Gate is a dangerous orange colour. Like a nuclear tanning bed they forgot to turn off. The naked vitality of the traffic-snarled street, with its choking fumes, its shivering junk-wrecks bonelessly folded in fastfood doorways against the nudge and knock of hustling pedestrians, is a relief from imposed-from-above schemes and crass municipal art. Only serving to remind us of what is missing, the art of risk, spat in the teeth of disapproval.

In lockstep with Clarence Bicknell and Sebastian Longhi, we climb again, following the flight of the rocks and taking our own rubbings of the broad pavements, the uniform ribbons of settlement: up Jerningham Road towards Telegraph Hill Park, where pulsing messages travel out over the spread of London. The drumbeat of our footsteps. The folding and unfolding of a map that makes no sense. The futile attempt to re-establish contact with the theoretical river of the railway, somewhere down below: Brockley, Honor Oak Park, by way of Pepys Road and Avignon Road.

Our first encounter of the day is with a woman tidying a children's playpark. She sets us on the right track. It is said, though she does not say it, that Queen Elizabeth I, Gloriana, sat in the shade of the sovereign oak on Honour Hill on May Day, 1602. The last year of her life. The Overground line, flowing south, has meadows of death on both banks: Nunhead, Brockley, Camberwell New Cemetery.

The trail of Italian restaurants and Creameries has run dry. Honor Oak is fronted by Colonel Sanders and his battery chickens: 'It's finger-lickin' good.' For the first time, as we close on Denmark Hill, someone – an Indian man, app-confused, smartly besuited, in a big hurry – asks *us* for directions, the quickest way to the station. I know this place, the crossroads, the Horniman Museum. It was where my son, my daughter-in-law and granddaughter lived, behind temperamental electronic gates, in a new property, across from the station and backed up, rather too intimately, against a lively pub. Which was why they moved out, and on to the south coast. They couldn't afford a larger, quieter place in this rising Overground settlement.

When I paused to take a photograph of record, the gates swung open and a young mother, pushing an infant in a buggy, walked towards the house where my son and his family had made their London life. It was convenient, except at weekends and holidays, when this stretch of the line often folded in favour of Crossrail excavations, to take advantage of the railway link with Haggerston.

We discussed the status and vintage of Il Mirto, purveyors of 'Italian Deli & Ice Cream', and decided to accept the place, hung with trapezoid panettone boxes, displays of regional cheeses, olive oil, Prosecco, into the canon. London's suburban stations are village halts supported and supplied by migrants from Alpine regions, from Sicily and Trieste. Sebastian Longhi, having served his time in Greek Street, followed the railtracks to their source in Croydon. Stephen has written of his mother as a child suspended in a photograph: 'peeping round from / behind the ice-cream vendor's barrow as / if she knew what was to come'. Croydon was such a distant elsewhere. They returned every Thursday – half-day at the Creamery? – to Soho, to stay in touch with the gossip, and for 'fresh pasta and spinach'. Their rinse of dialect was polished with use. It echoes in Stephen's head. He always comes back, after one of his energy-sapping fugue walks, to his Shadwell cave in the 'degenerate regeneration zone'.

In Sydenham, before we swung away to the west, we passed a pub theatre featuring *The Silence of Snow: The Life of Patrick Hamilton*. No English writer has earned his place in the bar of a roadhouse, breaking from some doomed drive to kill time, more than Hamilton. Stephen didn't know the name. I recommended *Hangover Square* and *Twenty Thousand Streets under the Sky*. By this stage of the day, it felt as if we had walked most of them. Unredeemed boozers from earlier times held their precarious ground between cemeteries, allotment slopes and the competing railways that branched off in every direction. Mark Farrelly's play is set in the clinic where Hamilton underwent brutal sessions of electro-convulsive therapy, jolts of electricity into an already ruined nervous system. The broken novelist sits in the lounge waiting on his summons to the next hit. 'The silence of snow,' Farelly tells us, was Hamilton's metaphor for loneliness.

Penge West, Anerley: exotic names. But is this London? It's tempting, on the platform at Anerley, with tracks stretching to the horizon in both directions, to place an ear against the cold rail, to pick up faint whispers from Shadwell and Haggerston. Out of our knowledge, the afternoon is turning; whoever we are now supposed to be, we are not those innocent walkers who began the day with clear eyes and great expectations. The tide is on the turn. Black windows in spiked houses flare with aftershocks left over from the mistreatment of Patrick Hamilton. Ice cream for a scorched tongue. Stuffed bears are being crucified in railway parks.

Perched on top of two green plastic bags, set aside for recycling, is a wooden tribal fetish, a mask. African, Melanesian? I can't be sure. Long slender painted wood with curving brows and prominent grooved nose. Thick lips form a flat base on which the mask could stand. Other jazzier masks, from an acid festival of the dead, are sprayed on the station wall. Teardrops of blood. Spanish lace around blank eyes. Costumes for mediation between the world of the almost living and the living dead, the ancestors. Our unseen accompanists on the wrong side of the river.

I wedged the mask in my rucksack, from where it watched over the way we had already walked, whatever lay safely behind us. And

I only hope there is not a significant gap in some display case in the Horniman Museum. My act of piracy reminds me of the cultural appropriations of Picasso's mask-heads of the Cubist period, 1907–1909. *Les Demoiselles d'Avignon*, those brothel furies, become the respectable suburban matrons of Avignon Road SE4.

When I try to photograph Stephen, now moist enough to remove his grey top to reveal a maroon fisherman's knit, against an autumnal blaze of Virginia creeper, my Nokia duncephone starts to tweet: Anna in Borough High Street. She has taken my advice and is about to ring on the door of the clinic. Since she went deaf in her right ear, her sense of smell has become acute. Now she is staggering, not just from lack of balance, but from the reek of competitive fastfoods wafting down the ancient pilgrims' track. I was sure that the treatment would succeed, our long day's march must have secured that favour from the gods. I imagined Anna's olfactory sensitivity accessing the jagged saws cutting through fat and bone in the sawdust operating theatre of St Thomas's hospital tower and the puddles of beer and piss from medical students and market men, and the rotting mush of unsold vegetables carted in from Kent, and hot dung splattering from heavy horses on the road to Canterbury.

In Love Lane it started to go wrong. Stephen thought he remembered coming out here to visit an Italian translator, who soon left for Oxford. Everything fitted, for a few yards, and then it didn't. Love Lane belonged in the City, in Southwark, among the stews and dives. It had no claim on Anerley. Nor did the postman who sent us off, in a spirit of mischief, in completely the wrong direction. Over railways and tram tracks (destined for Croydon). Into cemeteries, allotments, country parks. All the extra miles and big skies we needed to coddle Stephen's preoccupied silence. The gathering up of his poetic persona from a maelstrom of sense impressions, splintered anecdotes, granite boulders and commissioned totem poles. He didn't want to pause on the approach to Norwood Junction, the final fold of my *London Colour Street Atlas*. The cafés were wrong or insufficiently Italian. It could be that he didn't eat before sundown.

One coffee with a dose of sugar at La Cigale carried him through the day. Soon we would lose ourselves, it would be *terra incognita*. Penge Road, the A213 heading south, was solidly Afro-Caribbean. And in play: noisy, street-feeding, fly-posted, familiar. *Occupied*. Railway connected. Awash with blue bags and polystyrene cartons and all of the traces of active existence banished from those deadly dormitory avenues.

There is no obvious station café. Its place has been taken by a blistered hulk with blind windows: JR IMMIGRATION LTD. PROVIDING IMMIGRATION SOLUTIONS WORLDWIDE. The foot tunnel under the railway, through to the clocktower, has been dressed with photo-impressions of the journey we have just made or are about to make; a slow-cinema panning shot through which Stephen and I, as today's token pedestrians, are obliged to provide the action.

Stephen gave the impression that he never ate. He took daylight food on sufferance. He had his own coffee places and there were certain ceremonies and obligations that went with them. It was a part of his relationship with Sebald that they met and indulged at McDonald's, near Liverpool Street. *A cup of tea.* With such fastidious men, I can imagine a single cup shared between them. The refreshment was taken so that Sebald could express his solidarity with ordinary people 'who had little other option'. In his turn, at the end of a long ramble through the cemeteries and spectral terraces of Whitechapel, Stephen induced an unenthusiastic Sebald to join him for a curry at the Dhaka Biryani House in Mile End.

It is my contention that poems are Stephen's food, his breath, his existence. Sometimes they are walks, stately dances around the memory of an honoured person, relative or friend. They are written tastes and smells; the drama of notable meals recollected in tranquillity. 'Fresh pasta & spinach... another coffee... cabbages, aubergines, lemons, pears... orange peppers and okra... plantains and sweet potatoes... bread... mushrooms and moss... polenta and a fistful of cloves... lemon in lentil... unbone the ilish-fish... slabbed carp with blinded eyes, raw dog-fish... aniseed loaves looped on poles to dry.' Scents and anticipations of flavour melt in the mouth, in word-recipes, as thought forms. The ideal kitchen is the space where the dead go through their preparations for the meals of childhood. Nomad poems of hungry migration down endless roads.

We were off the map but inside the pull of Croydon. THE PICCOLO – 'A little piece of Italy in SE25!' – SANDWICH & PASTA BAR, CAPPUCCINO & ESPRESSO COFFEE. Norwood Junction. Blue and white oilcloth tables. Quartered mirrors. Movie star portraits from another era. Big hair and ambitious bosoms for Mediterranean women. Lounge-lizard men with loose black ties and white shirts. The proprietor was not Italian, nor easy to place: Mongolia, Kazakhstan? One of Stephen's globe-straddling nomads come to rest, and opening his tent to display his produce on the fringes of what the poet was now calling the 'Southern City'.

A rather peculiar and ripe-smelling ecumenical curry, with Vietnamese aspirations, was bubbling away as the special of the day and the proprietor was pushing it. Timidly, we settled for variants on the early-afternoon breakfast and more coffee. Or I did. Stephen, feasting on remembered herbs, the wild garlic of Irish tracks, settled for tea. Fingers interlocked, elbows on table, he prepared me for a detour to his grandfather's grave by telling me something more of his family background.

Stephen's father was English, northern and in local government. He came south to Wallingford, where he met his wife, an Italian, through mutual friends. The poet's own life-voyage carried him downriver to Shadwell, Thames cormorants, a sniff of the Estuary and the open sea.

After Sebastian Longhi's premature death, Stephen's grandmother left the Croydon Creamery and relocated to a quieter place. 'Wisteria and summer jasmine melted their scents in that yard.' Those scents are memories that do not fade. Stephen's quest is to recover the ground of his mother's childhood. And from that, the rest. 'The body leaves the body with such suddenness, such speed.'

On the oilcloth table he unrolled a stiff scroll: the monochrome record of Coloma Convent School in Tavistock Road; now migrated, he suspects. He points out his mother among the regimented ranks of trimmed pudding-basin hair, the starched white collars. Daughters of god in the charge of nuns. Polishing his spectacles to scan those ranks of serious faces, Stephen succeeds in identifying his mother as a young girl, against bare winter trees. Hundreds of stilled faces. Hundreds of white collars shining out of the fog of time.

'Somewhere after the platform at Anerley,' Stephen said, 'we lost forty minutes. It's gone. Did you notice that all the clocks have different times now?'

Coming off the map has liberated us. The person I describe, sitting in Il Piccolo with a mug of coffee, is not the person who wandered around Shadwell, waiting for Stephen Watts. Each episode is a fresh invention, drawing on what went before. By the time we step into the public library to see if they have a plan for the road into Croydon, we are in a quite different story. There is no self outside the written self. And the mysterious fugues that happen between incidents deemed worthy of report.

Before we find the station, there is the sealed church and the burial ground. IN LOVING MEMORY OF SEBASTIAN LONGHI. DIED 4th DECEMBER 1924. AGED 51 YEARS. ALSO NINA, HIS DEVOTED WIFE. Grey stone. A cross on a three-step pedestal. Nicely tended grounds. A scatter of red-brown leaves. The company of other Italians. The poet pauses, photocopied section of map from the library in his hand. His jersey complementing the colour field with a splash of blood-dark red. We detoured to Tavistock Road, unwinding the scroll, and testing the photograph of the massed girls against various backdrops, but nothing quite fitted. The southern city had excommunicated its past, in favour of a rash of speculative towers, the latest ones with blade-like prows. Small winds ramped the chasms, as Stephen tried to identify the bureaucratic blockhouse where immigrants have to apply for their necessary papers and confirm their resident status for another few weeks.

SAME DAY SIGNS: a swaying tin notice in orange against an orange wall, anticipations of the Ginger Line station. QUALITY SIGNS. BUILDERS SIGNS ONLY £12. UNION ROAD.

In St James's Memorial Garden where we paced the paths looking for traces of the removed Coloma Convent girls, a reward was being offered for a LOST BLACK 7" TABLET MOBILEPHONE. Frowning, blue biro-cap in mouth, Stephen made notes in his ledger and took down website addresses.

Beyond West Croydon station, and a precinct of deleted shops with pop-art Mexican gods in red and white on black shutters, we found the row of crafted buildings with decorative brickwork, tall curved windows and Masonic symbols, where the Creamery had offered refreshment to travellers. Current traders were resolutely downmarket in yellows and pinks: BEAUTY QUEEN, BODY & HAIR PRODUCTS, NEW FASHION LOOKS, HATS, HANDBAGS, LUGGAGE, JEWELLERY, T-SHIRTS, FANATIC CLOTHING. Retail dyslexia.

No fanatics were kitting up, just then, for a run to town. But plenty of rucksacks, less noble than the *Austerlitz* example carried by Stephen Watts, swung in the doorway.

The poet headed off, to find a library in which to pursue his researches. Or to experience another fugue, lost time in a lost place, out of which a pattern of words might emerge. Some of the poems, Stephen said, were related to the Alpine rock drawings. His method was a form of rubbing against the resistance of place. Poems could also favour the essence of pictographs, involuntary movements of the hand.

I took the Haggerston train. It was less digitally agitated out here, better insulated with abandoned newsprint. In late August 1912, the 37-year-old composer Samuel Coleridge-Taylor collapsed at West Croydon Station. Overworked and fretted by financial worries, he succumbed to pneumonia. He died a few days later and is remembered by a heritage plaque on his house in St Leonards Road. Coleridge-Taylor's mother was an Englishwoman, Alice Hare Martin. His father, Dr Daniel Taylor, was a Creole from Sierra Leone, of mixed European and African descent. The boy was brought up in Croydon, before studying the violin at the Royal College of Music. Touring the USA, Samuel became interested in his father's lineage, the connection with African-American slaves freed after the Civil War. A modest man with a fondness for pale waistcoats, floppy bow ties, and the occasional thin moustache, the composer liked to collaborate with poets. He left an unfinished opera, *Thelma*, themed around deceit, magic and retribution. Recovered from a manuscript in the British Library, *Thelma* was given its world premiere in Croydon in February 2012. The composer was buried in Wallington.

Back home, I was delighted to find that Anna's problem had been completely cured in Borough High Street. Now she could hear rather more than she wanted about our walk. So there were minor disadvantages to consider. The world was suddenly loud and close. The dogs. The drunks. The door.

I laid the tribal mask from Forest Hill on my desk. It was a relief map of the journey we had made: uphill along the ridge of the nose, then into the maw of Croydon. Reversed, the mask became a leaking boat, holes for the eyes. With my fingers I could feel the strokes of the chisel or blade, the force of the original maker.

DOWNRIVER

'He explained to me that night in Paris that madness is a geographical
location inside the self.'
Kay Boyle

Making landfall at Gravesend – like the dying Native American
princess Pocahontas – and wobbling up the raked walkway in a stiff
breeze, I have to duck very sharply to avoid the menacing swoop
of a tethered crow. This is a malignant spirit in an evil wind, in a
defeated place loud with absence. On such a day and at such an hour,
I'm on the lookout for symbols and portents. The funeral rites of
Lady Thatcher, the great leader, permafrost warrior and motorway
ribbon-cutter, celestially upgraded from her complimentary suite at
the Ritz, began as our ferry, the *Duchess M*, butted out, crosscurrent,
from the container stacks of Tilbury Riverside (Maritime). The vessel was transporting an elderly couple, huddling close against the
breeze, and one distracted, finger-scrolling young man. The service
was too useful to survive on such modest pickings without the financial support of the revived Port of Tilbury. Back in August 2007,
the Lower Thames and Medway Passenger Boat Company Limited,
owners and operators of the *Duchess M*, were fined £18,000 (with
£9,000 costs) for transporting more passengers than their certifica-
tion allowed: 90 Essex-fleeing migrants were crammed aboard. Here
was a metaphor for much that was to follow.

Gravesend feels like the kind of place where people without papers, without credit, are forced to wait. An English Calais where
fig trees thrive on the heat left in the walls of abandoned riverside industries. An old established port, downgraded into a camp

of refuge or imprisonment, hoping for regeneration from some outside agency. Or total clearance. Bulldozers. Plexiglas hit squads. Journalists. Celebrity squalor tourists. There is such a morbid history, you can smell it in the air: entrapment, putting on time, being caught between tides, fleeing from one post-colonial horror, but unrequired in the, as yet imaginary, better place.

'The air was dark above Gravesend, and farther back still seemed condensed into a mournful gloom, brooding motionless over the biggest, and the greatest, town on earth.'

Joseph Conrad coming across the river from his retreat in Stanford-le-Hope: *Heart of Darkness*.

'We looked on, waiting patiently — there was nothing else to do till the end of the flood.'

Marlow, the one who has 'followed the sea', seems to be channelling its voice, becoming voice as light fades. He drones on with the authority of the river itself, through the smoke and sediment of a nightmare dusk, about the impulse to capture, dominate and improve. 'They grabbed what they could get for the sake of what was to be got. It was just robbery with violence, aggravated murder on a grand scale, and men going at it blind – as is very proper for those who tackle a darkness.'

The Gravesend Heritage Quarter, with its ironwork security gates, is in receipt of bad news. A care-in-the-community reservation for a community that does not care. Not one jot. They are otherwise engaged in strategies of survivalism. The charity shops are shut. It would be a charity to send their contents upstream to the landfill dunes of Rainham. The nail parlours are spurned. And the *Ground Zero* cocktail bar is bereft of punters willing to suspend their distaste for the tactless title in order to raise a frosted glass to the memory of the golden-maned Boudicca of their pushy neighbour, Dartford.

Dartford is where Margaret Thatcher, like Mick Jagger and Keith Richards, launched her career as a world-stage performance artist. A mummified icon of Britishness. Yes, *icon*. Abstracted symbol. Lipstick automaton. Sleepless and hyper-energised on regular hits of intravenous Scottish firewater. With age, Thatcher and Keith Richards recalibrated their Deptford years with fat biographies and autobiographies; bad behaviour – pissing on petrol station forecourts or sinking the *Belgrano* – ameliorated by extreme wealth. Both, if we buy the spin, have been gentled; drooling not spitting now. But while the Stones are still working hard in support of their properties and investment portfolios, Lady Thatcher's twilight was infolding and static: as she struggled to make her perceptions conform to the world as she remembered it. *Lear*-anguish well ahead of the intersexual grandeur of her political opponent Glenda Jackson's assault on the role in the production directed by Deborah Warner at the Old Vic in 2016. Lady Thatcher was no Vegetative Buddha, sofa-bound, waiting and witnessing: the epitome of her time and place, her city. She became instead a destination to be visited, afternoon tea taken, like a famous rock or lighthouse. In her statuesque final act, more mask than meat, Thatcher was revealed as a fallible old woman whose sharpest recollections were of childhood, the tight Grantham years of strict Methodism and endless homework, before she lost her essential self in becoming a voice-coached projection. 'O let me not be mad, not mad, sweet heaven!'

A mantle of sullen silence had fallen over land and river. The elderly couple, propped on a hard bench, resting, enjoying their £2 concessionary ride across the broad Thames, offered no response to this moment of national bereavement. The funerary procession by limousine and gun-carriage, out of Westminster to St Paul's Cathedral, had the appearance, on news updates streaming unwitnessed into the cafés and pubs of Gravesend, of a triumphalist reunion for veterans of the Battle of Orgreave, at the British Steel coking plant in 1984. A reunion attended, in true Brit fashion, by a stubborn knot of anarchists and committed leftists willing to confirm the special status of the dead woman by turning their backs on her. Without consultation or consensus, we were all chipping in to cover the millions required for this solemn state occasion, the public acknowledgement that a career politician could symbolise the best of the nation: conviction, courage, shellacked coiffure and limitless, unapologetic self-interest. What is good for business is good for Britain. Good for me and mine. For all. For all of *us*.

This was, as the clatter of media types, up at dawn, primped and powder-patted, insisted, an arguable proposition. In borrowed black, they stalked the perimeter of St Paul's Cathedral – where the Occupy protesters had been permitted, for a brief time, to pitch their tents, without nuisance to paying customers or the secure moneyman behind their barricades in Paternoster Square.

One by one, or in contrasting couples – Ken Clarke and Shirley Williams – funeral attendees were interrogated about the Legacy. Rarely can such an *Alice in Wonderland* charivari of stereotypes have been assembled. Some of them, like David and Samantha Cameron, were quite obviously having a good time, social smiles and quips and politic handholding. The front pews were a woodpeckerish nip-nip of Judas kisses, blood enemies pouting stiff lips towards cold cheeks. They were all there: from the inherited formaldehyde dignity of senior royalty to the public faces of smug and comfortably suited former cabinet colleagues, along to be sure that the Lady is really in the box. To broken bullies blinking back tears under an unruly thatch of eyebrow. To the shameless court of right-opinionated entertainers still at large. To ennobled perjurers, medal-snaffling athletes with drug exemptions, well-connected arms dealers, coup plotters, City bagmen, honourably wounded veterans, and such foreign dignitaries as could be persuaded to take a mini-break in one of springtime London's riverside towers.

This cartoon sketch, assembled from TV footage witnessed by cricking my neck in the fug of downriver cafés, is unfair. Exaggerated. And accurate. The spill of black, massed through Wren's state cathedral, had its own dignity. The melancholy of a congregation considering mortality and loss in an echoing vault. The guilt of survivors. The marking of years. The knowledge that they were contributing to a historically significant event. End of innocence.

But dead means dead.

The only obvious sensitivity in this circus – so unlike the private funerals of Attlee and most of Thatcher's predecessors as First Minister – was that the funerary flotilla kept off the Thames. Churchill could be invoked but not so directly challenged. Military honours for the painful losses of the Falklands adventure couldn't be promoted alongside Churchill's aristocratic bloodstock and martial history. And, in any case, the Palace would certainly have vetoed a return to the water for the Duke of Edinburgh, after the long, cold and wretched hours of the Diamond Jubilee river pageant and their effect on an aging prostate. On this day, above all others, the Thames was the safest place for dissenters, those who wanted to keep well away from the reverent silence of Westminster and the muffling of Big Ben.

In Gravesend, on the stroke of twelve, the clock-mechanism of St George's Church, where Pocahontas is buried, sounds the hour. Distant chimes, rippling across the cataleptic town, respond in a celebratory chorus. At the Towncentric Tourist Office, where they have decided to reboot the whole zone as 'Gravesham', the latest update from the funeral is so soft that the manager's radio makes no impression on the reveries of leaflet collectors. The main attraction of Gravesham seems to be its easy access to the Bluewater shopping hub in its excavated chalk quarry and the getaway Eurostar link at Ebbsfleet.

And what about the name of the ferryboat? The *Duchess M*, trundling backwards and forwards across the river, between the bustling international container port of Tilbury and the legacy-encumbered sump of Gravesend, is a subliminal tribute to Thatcher. Perhaps there is a nudge in the direction of Jacobean tragedy, John Webster's *The Duchess of Malfi*? 'She stains the time past, lights the time to come.' That black crow, savaging migrants as they step ashore, is revealed as a thing of tatty plastic, a loud fake, a deterrent. It shrieks in the wind, lacking claws and beak. Passengers heading for the pier even don't notice it.

If you travel against the flow of inrushing City workers, the mob decanted at Fenchurch Street Station, then a railway excursion to the Thames Estuary is a pleasant affair. I climb aboard for my return to Tilbury Town. A young woman, having let the crowd disperse, leaving a monstrous tidewrack of throwaway newspapers, jumbo coffee containers and breakfast-bar wrappers, finishes her complicated make-up routine and adjusts her tight skirt. The Thatcher funeral doesn't make the front page of *Metro*: PUTTING SEX BACK INTO BALLET.

I decided to pay my respects by time-travelling into the geography of Thatcher's pomp, the heartlands of resentment where she brewed and bottled the bad will of a disaffected populace – while doing her best to handbag the benefit-coddled, socialist sinkhole of metropolitan London. 'Drain the swamp!' Big-hair Trumpery learnt its first lessons about the post-truth culture here. Murdoch populism and a chorus of lynch mob slogans. 'Drain the swamp!' Thatcher was the revenge of the suburbs, delivered from a position of established privilege. She might have made an investment in a Dulwich retirement property, but she wouldn't sleep in it.

But I shared a guilty secret with Margaret Thatcher: the worst of times was also the best of times. Without her presence and personality and the way she brought the crisis of London into sharp focus, I would never have become a novelist. I was obliged to recognise that painful Oedipal conflict by attempting to revisit the romanticised estuary of my book *Downriver*. I carried a copy of the first edition with me on the train out of Fenchurch Street, the one with the reproduction of Ludwig Meidner's *Apocalyptic Landscape* of 1913 on the cover. This vision of a ruined city came before the bombs fell: dying sun, turbulent river and collapsing riverside towers. I planned to annotate succeeding chapters as I travelled through the day, pasting contemporary snapshots over the yellowing print of the original. On the blank page alongside the opening chapter, I tipped in an agency photograph found in a Buddhist charity shop in Bethnal Green: Jimmy Savile, bottle-blond hair and dark glasses, gold necklace and white tracksuit, presenting a grimacing Mrs Thatcher with a fistful of cheques, on the doorstep of Number 10. The chippy entertainer is delivering a humorous aside, reflex banter. Thatcher, unamused or not getting the joke, has her bulging eye on the cameras.

In the 1980s I began to explore the derelict deepwater docks of the Isle of Dogs and Silvertown (already being floated as a future Olympic site). Margaret Thatcher, in the person of the 'Widow', was a dark deity presiding over a dystopian version of England; channelling our worst impulses, our meanest prejudices, our fear of the alien. In those days the hoofprint of the beast was clearly visible on the ravaged edgelands between A13 and the river: discontinued industries, Rubik-cube towers in jazzy colours rising on the toxic compost of deregulated financial markets, primitive surveillance systems protecting speculative retail parks. First glimpses of future fashion statements: the electric-orange hi-viz jumpsuit. And the exhaustion of low-paid guards, often black, more prisoner than protector.

Thatcher was an abiding presence. Pervasive as the smell of the Thames: oil spill, river-rot and yellow mud. Along walls and embankments, rabid slogans and anti-Thatcher curses were large and scarlet. In hideaway pubs, inscribed photographs in polished frames signalled their allegiance to pre-Farage demagogues who could hold a pint.

Now, from the window of the empty train to Tilbury, there was nothing. Inside carriages where edgy clients kept their eyes open for ticket inspectors, I heard no mention of this day's funeral pageant. Thatcher's legacy was smeared over container stacks, retail parks and hollow estates under drooping pergolas of pylons, but the woman was forgotten.

Tilbury is as much a two-finger salute now as it was in 1988. But while Dock Road remains the essence of entropy, the rebranded Tilbury Railport, protected by high walls and security cameras, thrives in a rumble of lorries churning up dust. In windowless sheds specialising in Logistics. In red, brown and blue containers: HAMBURG SÜD, HANJIN, MOL. When I researched *Downriver*, I was enthused by local piracy, the hopeless scams of dealers in trashed electrical goods, small businesses trading in fire sales and offering cold-water dormitories to paperless transients. Tattered notices recalled the ghosts of unions exorcised along with the industries in which they once played a dominant role.

There used to be a junkshop flattering a Thatcherite fiction of the past, made up from chipped colonial artefacts and blatant fakes. Everything looked like an Arthur Daley smokescreen for whatever villainy went on in the backroom. There were mountains of washing machines dripping acid and being made ready, so I was told, for export to Nigeria. Armadas of stolen cars were sliced and reattached by Dr Frankenstein's scalpel. Otherwise, the only action came from bankrupt mini-cab firms offering the fastest way out.

Travellers' horses, chained and hobbled, cropped the rubbish-strewn fringes of the defunct railway. There was no sign of life in the Dockers' Social Club. The *Stallions* fastfood restaurant offered kebabs or burgers. A cash-for-gold pawnshop will remain closed for the foreseeable future. 'Sorry for the Pinconvenience' is a neat coinage. A trade sign for SUNLIGHT SOAP can still be deciphered.

Peckish now, I opted for a coffee in the Dock Café, where I hoped to pick up on Tilbury Town's response to the national day of mourning. This bright, clean facility was certainly an improvement on what

had been here before. The starred item was the Olympic Breakfast at
£5.80, with two eggs, two sausages, bacon, tomatoes, mushrooms,
beans, bubble and squeak. I settled for a cappuccino and a vegetarian
fry-up. The breakfast crowd were rigorously monocultural, razor-
cropped and upbeat in laundered leisurewear and new white trainers.
Very young children, the inheritors, ran about between tables, or sat
on them, dipping into the enticing mess on the plates.

'Watch out, mate. She's a little devil, that one. She'll nick your
toast,' one teenage mum warned. Too late.

The place was an amiable, extended-family crèche. If you transcribed some of the dialogue — as I did — it sounded bad, but the
tone, the spirited banter, neutralised the venom. Laughter drowned
phone-music and TV funeral news.

'I told her, you don't want to do that,' a jobbing builder reported.
Of his estranged partner. 'Then I whacked her across the front room.
Silly tart. I'd rather fuck my sister.'

Workers without work, or immediate prospects, plated up for the
morning. There were no obvious trickle-down benefits here from

the thriving dock zone. The café crowd did not represent a severed community as much as total decapitation. An in-the-shit-together endgame behind steamed up windows.

Just as I was about to leave, to make my way over the railway bridge and down to the river, a young woman staggered through the door, hugging a heavy tripod and an oversupplied bag of camera kit. She wore her name around her neck on red and white ribbon. My idea of sounding out Tilbury for sonar echoes of Thatcher was not so original. The new face was Angie Walker of BBC London News.

Angie was pleased, she confessed, to be invited to cover the funeral. She had hoped for a prime spot in Westminster, if not actually inside St Paul's – only to discover that they had banished her to Tilbury Town. This was a very long haul from her home in Windsor. And now that she was here, there was no *here*. She couldn't find anything open: not a docker, not a UKIP cheerleader, not a single card-carrying leftist willing to be sound-bitten. Delighted to have bumped into someone ready to talk, she offered me a coffee – before she realised that I was in the same dubious trade, trawling for exploitable copy. No patrons of the Dock Café had the faintest interest in Margaret Thatcher or London's remote and contentless television ceremonies. The dead politician meant as much to them – zilch – as royalty. Queen Elizabeth I, so they were told, schlepped down here to deliver a rousing speech to the troops at the time of some Spanish invasion. They didn't watch that one. They were relatively innocent of digital technology, the TV monitor had about as much appeal as a machine for zapping flies.

Tilbury Railport, on the far side of the tracks, was booming, but passenger transit from the far-flung reaches of Empire to London was over. All those railway platforms – plangent ruins at the time of my 1988 visit – were now enclosed, privatised, part of the container colony. In the three hours since I had left my house in Hackney, I found not one image of Margaret Thatcher, subversive or supporting: the glamorous granny of punk was without honour in her own country. The fabled Iron Lady was reduced to a rusting footnote in a culture that had abolished history. Or a tethered lamia in the form of a flapping black crow on the gangplank of a riverside ferry.

Gravesend has a witchfinding, female-fearing pedigree. Anne Neale, known as an 'ill-tongued' woman, was accused of witchcraft and sent for trial in 1675. It was discovered that she had 'several excrescences or buds on various parts of her body'. On closer examination, these minor blemishes exhibited signs of having been 'regularly sucked'. Or so I discovered in the neo-classical Town Hall, where choice anecdotes of place have been published in 'Discover Gravesham' pamphlets. Flicking through bullet-point highlights, it can be seen that the Poll Tax hearings of 1990 replayed former times when a Gravesend mob responded to inequitable tax demands by hauling fire-boats through the narrow streets. Two hundred persons, denying and repudiating Thatcher's Community Charge, were summonsed to appear before the Gravesend court. Thirteen presented themselves. An inherited antipathy to rules and regulations imposed from elsewhere was still strong.

The port of Sheerness, at the mouth of the Medway, is terminal. And it glories in that status. In atmosphere and aspiration, it is an assisted suicide trip. End of the Medway. End of connection with London. End of hope. Point of departure. The ideal landfall for an amnesiac in a black suit, found dripping-wet, and resolutely mute, wandering on a road by the shore. Had he fallen overboard? Had he come here to kill himself? Was he inventing a new identity, as he emerged from the water, like John Harmon in *Our Mutual Friend*? They called him 'Piano Man' and removed him to the Medway Maritime Hospital. Why Sheerness? Where better?

The undrowned man, the bridled alien in the black suit, had located Kent's nearest equivalent of the Kara Sea. A nuclear junkyard over which a red sun pulses like a dying bulb. The station is deserted. The depression of those railway platforms, between Gravesend and Sittingbourne, is critical. Solitary, pacing figures are wired for sound, instructions from elsewhere. Some of them hold up books like radiation shields. But they never turn a page. Convalescents, between hospitals, between refuges, are exposed to the unforgiving river. To regimented ranks of dwarf fruit trees. To migrant work-gang shadows in polytunnels. To evidence of collapsed degeneration projects.

It was like talking to the grateful dead. Climbing out of the train in Sheerness on a late afternoon in April is as close as it comes to understanding the postmortem visions of Emanuel Swedenborg. You can talk to the limping ghosts but they do not hear you. You are always the intruder, the thing to be stepped around on a return from the pub. Stepped around by the lucky ones who can still unstick themselves from their benches. Canvassed opinions, beachside, disclosed reflex responses to Margaret Thatcher's demise: admiration for her strength, discomfort over the council house sell-off and the Poll Tax.

Council Leader Andrew Bowles said: 'She turned the country around. It was going to the dogs.'

Down at the waterline, with casino-city Southend gloating across the Estuary mouth, the dogs have won. They swagger and shit on sand, dragging bent walkers against the slapping wet breeze, the sting of salt. Concrete steps leading down to the beach have been painted with bracing prophecies of doom.

BURIED IN THE BELLY OF ITS LIBERTY. YOU CAN SEE THE END OF THE WORLD FROM HERE. MARK THE WATER. BEYOND ALL HELP. GREET THE WALKERS IN THE MORNING.

Poetic fragments reference the American Liberty ship, *SS Richard Montgomery*, wrecked off the Nore, with 1,400 tonnes of explosives on board. They say that if the *Montgomery* goes up, the detonation will take out Sheerness. Three masts of the death ship are visible and sanctioned with a warning buoy. Afternoon strollers, overdrawing the last of their strength, come here to watch and wait. One man, stripped to the waist, is filling a blue plastic bucket with sand, and carrying it, time and again, to his car.

Those thermoplastic letters across the risers and treads of the stepped wall, impregnated with tiny glass spheres, will become more reflective as the sea and the weather do their worst and rub away their impertinence. The broken sentences do not have the innocence I wanted. They are of course an art commission.

The poet Ros Barber said, 'I've always wanted to do some sort of public graffiti – *sanctioned* graffiti.' Which is just what graffiti cannot be: it must bite, it should be anonymous. If it is not condemned to be washed away by indignant high-pressure hoses, it has failed. This latest intervention is a mediated response approved by the Medway Swale Estuary Partnership (MSEP), Arts Council England and Kent County Council. The architect Simon Barker, Design Advisor for Design Excellence in North Kent (DENK), worked with his team on the technicalities of getting the poet's words on the steps of the promenade. Nicola Barker, a committed haunter of liminal places, came to Sheppey looking for something else, the strangeness that became her novel *Wide Open*. 'I left – when I finally left – quite undone,' she said.

Patrick Wright, a graduate from the University of Kent who lived for a time in Hackney, and who investigated these places with me, when I was writing *Downriver* and he was assembling *A Journey through Ruins*, uncovered the hard facts behind Uwe Johnson's decision to relocate – after Berlin, Rome and New York City – to Sheerness. A mysterious career diversion for a respected European novelist and translator. Canetti took up residence in Hampstead. Céline, shrapnel splinters in skull, had his picaresque Soho nights. Sebald lived, worked and died, around Norwich. But *Sheerness*? The Medway port was altogether too much. It was several sets of ellipses too far… even for the deranged momentum, hopping on and off buses, hanging around dock gates, of Céline and his idiot crew.

In 1974, when I was cutting grass and picking up broken sherry bottles in Limehouse, Uwe Johnson put aside his *Jahrestage* project, after three published volumes, and found a terraced Victorian house on Marine Parade. Wright, in his pursuit of the German author, noticed that 'Sheerness was often stigmatised as a place of industrial dereliction and defeated people.' But that was its strength. The old Millwall, Thatcherite boast: 'Nobody likes us and we don't care.'

Cultural migration to the Isle of Sheppey now looks like a smart decision, carrying the questing and troubled author to the bitter edge of things. Silence, exile – and gallons of brown ale in the Seaview Hotel. Or, more probably, regular crates of decent wine delivered to his doorstep. Johnson's wife and daughter moved out to another property. He liked to stare at the sea. This was his return to the Baltic of despair. They say that, in his forties, the writer had the lightning-struck look of a premature pensioner. That polished, hairless skull. The close-set and unblinking eyes of a ferret. Spectacles, pipe and pen. Leather jacket, leather tie. The established Sheerness drinking classes were suspicious, then welcoming. Johnson was one of their own. He had made his choice: abdication, solitude, liquid witness. A nail through the tongue. 'Call me Charles,' he said.

Call him whatever he chooses. Call him the Estuary Ishmael. The great European novel, Johnson knew, was to be lived but not written. And lived at the end of its tether. On a small island, loosely affiliated to a larger island. Waiting to cut its cables. To sever all connection with the continent.

Occasional scholars found their way to Johnson's door. There were no satisfactory answers. He took his all day breakfast and put on solid English pounds. He sketched the particulars of economic and social collapse. He was one of the sitters, the stickers. The watchers who no longer fret or speak. He liked the way the English said 'thank you' when they bought a train ticket, in order to escape.

The novel Johnson never wrote – he had other business, he came to Sheerness to atrophy and die – was the Piano Man: a fugitive German by the name of Andreas Grassl. Grassl was another unexplained émigré. Another spoiled artist squeezing his art out of place. In hospital, Grassl banged away at the piano they provided and made some drawings. He was reluctant to engage with his interrogators. The story was nothing more than his sudden appearance, the enigmatic Kaspar Hauser of Sheppey, on the foreshore, in a wet black suit – and a fugue state, a vegetative pathology or performance. Tabloids represented Grassl as an asylum seeker, a threat; a useless economic migrant draining valuable health service resources. He made marks, unintelligible symbols in his sketchbook. After he produced one coherent image, a grand piano, they called him 'Piano Man'. And worked back from that: the fictional biography of an idiot savant, a busker, a spy. A lost soul washed ashore.

In the chapel of the maritime hospital, the paperless stranger obediently attacked his instrument, while the doctors made notes. If strangers approached, he would roll up into a ball and edge towards the nearest corner.

Tirez sur le Pianiste.

They wanted him to be Charles Aznavour in Truffaut's film, the saddest man on the planet. The classical musician busking in a zinc bar. Black suit, white shirt. They wanted that freeze-frame from Truffaut's first feature, *Les Quatres Cents Coups*, when the reform school escapee, Jean-Pierre Léaud, turns his back on innocence, the grey sea.

Charles Dickens, our most celebrated London walker, came to a halt down here. 'There are some out-of-the-way landing places on the Thames and the Medway, where I do most of my summer idling. Running water is favourable to day-dreams, and a strong tidal river is the best of running water for me.'

The weary author is suspended between sky and shore. He is watching 'without obligation', when a boy appears out of nowhere. Dickens calls him 'Spirit of the Fort'. He seems to speak out of the centre of the spreading circles from a stone flung into the river.

I return by way of Stratford International – which involves a compulsory detour through the labyrinth of the Westfield superstore. At last, at the conclusion of my Thames Estuary tour, I find images of Lady Thatcher: a strategic window display in Waterstones. *The Iron Lady* by John Campbell. *Thatcherism: A Graphic Guide.* Shoppers, marching to the beat of piped muzak, do not pause. Throwaway bundles of the *London Evening Standard*, with the flag-draped coffin, have been crammed into a silver bin, along with polystyrene coffee cups, crisp packets and energy drinks. The headline in the *Hackney Gazette*, as I plod home, is not Thatcher-related, even though it sounds as if it ought to be. It's local and ordinary, another tale of failing services, burdensome bureaucracy: BODY LOCKED IN MORGUE FOR WEEKS.

Such fortuitous ironies were always noticed by Patrick Wright. He had, as he demonstrated on the walks we took in the high Thatcherite days, an eye for the telling detail, the coming horror anticipated in the crack of a paving stone or a vanished telephone kiosk. *A Journey through Ruins*, conjured from a couple of hundred yards between his home on St Philip's Road and the Dalston Lane bus stop (or bus queue), reached out to the world at large. His polemic, or curse on the corruptions of locality, was dedicated to 'Lady Margaret Thatcher'. The woman who had done so much to inspire silenced poets and cultural historians.

Way back in 1991, Wright used the *Hackney Gazette*, as I did, for divination. In a report on the hubristic plans by a bankrupt council for a lavish upgrading of Hackney Town Hall, the Dalston pundit heard the elephantine shudder of much heavier footsteps, the apotheosis of Donald Trump. In the shameless marble floors and 'curved glass walls', Wright recognised an elective affinity with the retail atrium at Trump Tower on Fifth Avenue in New York City. He also recognised the moral vacuum at the heart of this 'King of Bullshit'. Trump was 'a smudged deadbeat left over from the Reagan era... and propped up in a temporary kind of way by ailing US and Japanese banks that couldn't afford to let him expire completely'. The Master Builder, the post-truth artist of the deal, was a perma-tanned bagpipe held in place by weight of hair. 'I don't do it for the money. I've got much more than I'll ever need.' All this trumpeting inflatable was waiting for was the invention of worldwide social media, slavish followers hungry for the latest jab of his thumb.

Insane ambitions, as Wright demonstrated, were hiding in full sight. Commentators sneered, it could never happen. 'If Trump was in the White House which, he was rash enough to hint in those undiminished days, he might well be before too long, he would follow the example of Presidents Reagan and Harding, and look for astrological anchorage in the stars.' The big man appreciated, like a true Mafioso, that 'you can trust family in a way that you can never trust anyone else.' You can rob a country blind and they'll still vote you into power, your kin and your billionaire cohorts. Wind the story right back and it 'eventually delivers us onto the steps of Hackney Town Hall'.

ABSOLUTELY BARKING

I met Chris Currell, our friendly neighbourhood estate agent (and art collector), outside the shell of Haggerston Baths, after the tour of inspection by potential investors rounded up by Bill Parry-Davies. Nothing, as yet, has come of that initiative. The building is still in secure limbo, while the improvers circle and calculate. And make their pitches to the council. And Swimmers Lane is still PRIVATE and battened at either end by slate artworks, minor megaliths of incomprehension.

Chris said that he'd seen me on the street – he was an early morning dog-walker – but we'd never stopped to chat. Then one morning, this brisk and personable operator appeared on my doorstep. We receive courtesy cards most days, instructing us to sell up, cash in, get out. I didn't expect a home visit from the man, a foot in the door. But this was merely social. One of the artists in whom Chris was interested was Ceri Richards. He owned a few good pieces. I had written something about Richards and the painter loomed large in my memoir, *Black Apples of Gower*. I was invited to view the Currell collection and to take part in a Hackney cultural soirée promoting the book. Such opportunities were rare. Conversation darted and flickered across all sorts of theoretical social divides. Stereotypes never conform to the narratives you lay on them. I knew that Anne Currell, CEO of Currell Residential, had been the inspiration for the conversion of the modernist nurses' wing of the German Hospital, off Graham Road, into private apartments. I had visited one of them. And witnessed how a new kind of community – artists and artisans with funds to invest – was emerging. I didn't appreciate that Anne had a special interest in this kind of property. She had been a nurse at St Bartholomew's Hospital for eight years, before the management situation deteriorated to the point where she felt that she had to change career, public service to private enterprise, by becoming a sales negotiator for Hotblack Desiato, the estate agents based on Upper Street, Islington. Currell Residential emerged from that beginning, before tracking money (and energy) to the east. Offices, hung with tapestries by Grayson Perry and others, were established on Kingsland Road and close to Victoria Park.

When I ran into Chris and his dog heading south towards Haggerston Park, he confirmed what I had already suspected: the future of our stretched city was Barking. Barking was the *where next* for the dispossessed of Hackney. Walthamstow, they said, was already played out. Tottenham still too edgy. Margate was discussed. Whitstable gone. And Dagenham – a personal favourite – only attracted more adventurous spirits like Bill Drummond. The Currell Group was opening a new office, pumping investment into granaries and warehouses on the banks of the Roding. The ancient abbey town of Barking was the future terminus of another spur of London Overground; diverting from the loop, the orbital circuit, at Gospel Oak. And therefore twinned neatly with Croydon. It was a walk I would, one day, have to take.

The new mayor Sadiq Khan, dissociating himself from Boris Johnson's follies, his grotesque overspend on the conversion of the Olympic Stadium, his Thames Estuary airport scheme, decided that Barking was the next Barcelona. Khan signalled his approval of the building of 10,000 new homes in a zone to be called 'Barking Riverside'. Here was another widely promoted edgeland conversion: questionable historic exoskeletons, decommissioned industries, stumps of retail opportunism and misconceived public art. And all of it feeding into an outwardly-mobile, river-sniffing reservation of promenades and wildlife reserves with a spanking new marina.

And this at the very moment when long-established operators and occupiers at the Gallions Point Marina at Beckton were being evicted by the Mayor of London's office, and granted seven days to remove all property, in order to facilitate a thrusting enterprise zone for 'international business'. A zone commensurate with the pretensions of the City Airport and ExCel Exhibition Centre.

'They will have to take my lifeless body out of here,' said Leigh-Jane Miller, who runs the doomed 'Moorings and Hard Standing' with her father, Eric.

I picked the right day for my Barking walk: 9th November 2016. Bulletins confirmed that Donald Trump was going to get it. Rain was strafing the pavements. And the news from Croydon was awful. Those tram lines I crossed with Stephen Watts, symbols of regeneration, led to a derailment, with seven deaths and many more injured. The driver took a sharp turn too fast. Previous warnings had been set aside.

Property development by way of railway fever has been around for a long time. In 1907 WC Berwick Sayers published an account of 'The Old Croydon Tram-Road, Canal, and Railway' in *The Home Counties Magazine*. A bill was passed in 1834 authorising the construction of the London to Birmingham Railway, along with a lesser bill promoted by the London and Croydon Railway Company. One of the provisions of the Croydon bill was that the company should purchase an unproductive canal and construct a line along its bed. It was always about speed and money and a brighter future when the work was done. Canals set aside for tramlines and trams for railways that could make the push to Brighton. Tooley Street to West Croydon: 'The London and Croydon Company did not pay very much attention to the comfort of its passengers. The carriages were invariably jolting four-wheelers, divided into three compartments, one first-class, two second.' These commuters, on their daily grind between city and suburb, regularly featured in crimes investigated by Sherlock Holmes.

The *Quarterly Review* of 1836, concerned about trains travelling at excessive speeds of twenty miles an hour, denounced the project as 'a visionary scheme unworthy of notice'. An experiment was made with an 'Atmospheric Railway', operating with a long cast-iron tube laid between the lines. One end of the tube was open to the air and the other was fitted to a pump. 'The speed attained on the atmospheric railway was enormous. From Forest Hill to Croydon, a distance of 5¼ miles was accomplished in 2 min. 47 sec., a speed exceeding 100 miles an hour, and on slopes this was much exceeded. Passengers have likened the sensation of travelling in the trains to that of falling from a height.' Croydon owed her status, Berwick Sayers concludes, to the railways that served her. '*Sanitate crescamus* – By health we grow great – is the motto of the town; but given a healthy site and people intelligent enough to develop it, we must look for the most powerful factors in making that healthy position known and accessible to the railways.'

Soon after we returned from our Ginger Line walk to the home of Stephen's grandfather, I read about a series of Halloween knife attacks in Croydon, leaving several men in hospital and one dead. Later there would be an unprovoked mob assault on a Kurdish refugee at a bus stop. But the most affecting news for me, and it came from so many sources, the range of this man's contacts was astonishing, was the death of the fabled rock guitarist, my former colleague in the used-book trade, Martin Stone.

Martin had roots in Croydon. He was a child of the South London suburbs. He did his time in the John Whitgift School for Boys. Doubtless, there is a scrolled photograph somewhere, like the one Stephen Watts produced, showing Martin, before the varieties of Fu-Manchu moustache, the beads and beret, as a scrubbed lad in a blazer (and customised Slim Jim tie). With contacts in the local folk scene, meeting Dave and Jo Ann Kelly, hanging out in pubs, clubs and dives, beginning to scope bookshops, junkshops, street markets, Martin swerved higher education for a gig with the *Croydon Advertiser*. 'I wanted to be Muddy Waters. Instead, I was covering the Women's Institute donkey derby for seven quid a week.'

The spirit of Martin was with me that trumped November day, as preordained drizzle washed the slopes of Parliament Hill: the tumulus, the omphalos and its invocation of a mythic democracy. Many of our conversations, as I drove the scholar-magician on another insane quest, were about ley lines, Albigensians; Golden Dawn conspiracies melting into parallel literatures of the lost and reforgotten. Every red-eyed expedition with Martin followed the same template: false trail, wrecked car, strip-search, Prevention of Terrorism challenge. White lines on tattered black briefcase. But it always turned out well in the end; another hit, another buried hoard to be evaluated and dispersed, converted into powdered energy – as Martin's nostrils flared, his nose ran, and those ancient unforgiving eyes lasered through walls. He laughed until he coughed. His smoky, kippered voice enchanted dealers and friends, as the anecdotes, never self-serving, spilled and spooled. Mr Stone was modest, but he knew his worth.

The man can't be contained in a couple of digressive paragraphs, he should be a book. But then he already is. My first novel, *White Chappell, Scarlet Tracings*, opened with Martin at the roadside, throwing up. 'Nicholas Lane, excarnate, hands on severely angled knees, stared out across the dim and featureless landscape...' Without Martin, there would have been no novel. The man never searched, he found. I could not have written a single paragraph without the conviction that certain characters – we are lucky if they cross our path, if we recognise them – are self-created, sliding through this life, many lives, linking unfinished or never-quite-composed stories. Before they drop back into the friable paper where earlier authors tried to fix them. Such men leave a magnesium flare in rumours that grow up around sightings. In gossip. In aborted 3am telephone calls. They are glimpsed in a Cecil Court shop, at a street protest in Paris, a poetry reading in Wales, on a train. In movement between provisional destinations. Their greatest gift is knowing when to disappear.

Martin had to be heavily sedated, coshed into a coma, before you could get him on a plane. He liked trains. He liked Amsterdam, Brussels, Paris. He toyed with the notion of setting himself up in the Midi: pink suit, drainpipe trousers, in the sunshine. Bringing his friends, Mike and Linda Moorcock, along for company, for book talk. Making music.

A true European, and no respecter of borders, Martin never abandoned that part of him that was Croydon. And that's what, newly dead, translated to a better country, he was telling me as I set out for Barking. The election of Donald Trump was the point beyond which he didn't want to travel. Trump's trumpeting, his meaningless visibility, his compulsive Tourette's tweeting, was the contrary of Martin's measured respect for the printed word and the structure of a sentence or musical phrase. The creatures of Trump's court were spooks of antisocial media, dripping poison into the veins of the internet. Martin was that person you can never contact, until he walks into your shop, and out of it into another universe. He was off-grid before there was a grid.

I picked up books from my shelves with Martin Stone's pencilled pricings, books that had survived all my cullings and clearouts. A first edition of *In Parenthesis* by David Jones in grey dustwrapper. I couldn't afford it at the time, now I couldn't afford to be without it. Jeremy Reed, a friend and admirer of the spectral dealer, told me how Martin supplied him with the rarities he required for works in progress. And how he wouldn't charge, or would seriously under-charge, a poet.

What else? A handsomely bound limited edition of *Axel* by Villiers de l'Isle-Adam. With a preface by WB Yeats. And a loosely inserted letter from Æ (George Russell). Such golden decadence: Martin laid his weekly treasures on a grubby cloth, for the vultures (myself among them) crowding his table. The bills and scribbles tucked among un-cut pages are still to be interpreted. 'The ceremony,' Yeats wrote, 'of some secret Order wherein my generation had been initiated.'

As had Martin. I never would be. I was left with the books, the physical objects. They came from the stall in Camden Passage, those two. The last slim volume was all I managed to retrieve when Martin, for a brief period, tried to be a shopkeeper, with premises conven-iently close to King's Cross station. He was never there. Frantic dealers paced outside all night, hoping to catch him if he stopped off to change suitcases.

The Secret of Mont-Ségur by Raymond Escholier and Maurice Gardelle: £5 (less discount). I haven't got around to reading it. 'After the war he was able to return, and piece by piece, from letters and diaries, from court records and by word of mouth, he put together the story of this girl and her ill-fated search for the treasure of the Cathars, the lost Gospel of St John, the Book of Love.' One day, perhaps. Andrew Kötting has a hut in the shadow of Mont-Ségur. This may be his project, Martin's posthumous gift. That's how it works. We move the books around. We facilitate, leaving the dealers with just enough to keep them on the road, telling their tales, dragging their suitcases.

'Who in their right mind would seek asylum in Croydon?' A good question from Shena Mackay in her 2003 novel, *Heligoland*. And my proof that books picked up at random – in this case, a groaning table outside a seafront shop in Hastings – can act as oracular support for a rackety superstructure. End-of-the-line Croydon, aspiring city of enterprise, balances end-of-the-line heritage sump Barking.

One of Mackay's characters, like Stephen Watts, feels the need, way ahead of the advent of alien-fearing, wall-building Trump, to visit Lunar House, the Home Office headquarters of the Immigration and Nationality Directive. An independent entity, at the limits of London's imagination, is where asylum seekers are condemned to queue and wait. 'Supplicants of various nationalities stand or crouch, supported by handmade placards pasted with photocopied documents and photographs. Every picture tells a story but nobody pauses to read. Inside, some fifteen miles of shelving sag beneath the weight of 200,000 case files bulging with a backlog of heartbreak, lies and truths lost in the translation.'

TRUMPPENCE: the electoral placards said. Fraudulent coinage. Like Bitcoins. And just as sinister. Chump change. Money that isn't money. The bouffant Don was in his pomp, the Hierophant from the Tarot deck, making a show of conciliatory interviews, before gathering his spooky cabal around him, those hardshell ladies and the scrubbed pro-life death addicts, and *really* letting rip. The boss Apprentice had nailed the big throne. The archive groper had his fat fingers, legitimately, in every pie. While Martin Stone, the invisible bookman with his candle of hermetic knowledge, was gone.

'Sham fight, strenuous competition and struggle of the search after riches and fortune,' said the key to the Tarot. 'A card of gold, gain, opulence. Reversed: litigation, disputes, trickery, contradiction.' Mirror of Donald. Mirror on the wall.

'The World's Most Popular Free Newspaper', *Metro*, had nothing to say about any of this. Trumped by royalty.

HARRY: YES, MEG *IS* MY GIRLFRIEND (NOW JUST LEAVE HER ALONE). LET ME SERVE LIFE IN THE UK: SEX KILLER BANKER'S PLEA TO HONG KONG COURT. GREAT WESTERN RAIL LINE COSTS SPIRAL TO £5.6bn. LEAVE'S 'LIES' NO WORSE THAN REMAIN'S. VIP SEX RING WITNESS WAS NOT CREDIBLE, POLICE ADMIT.

The Overground shuttle to Gospel Oak was as packed and steaming as the old freebie North London Line. There was an un-inhibited redistribution of dripping viral threads; full-frontal sputum exchanges, Grindr intimacies wet-coughed down the back of the neck. An excited Hoxton beard was calling his partner with urgent smartphone updates. 'I feel the world's kind of ended tonight, but whatever… Heh! Heh! Apocalyptic, *yes*! See you tonight if we're still here. Heh! Heh!'

Back with the Ginger Line, negotiating a rustle of chittering school-girls in green anoraks, parakeets jostling on wet stairs and mobbing narrow pavements, I broke away to align myself on Parliament Hill. Certain tramped paths were evident, but I could not take them. EO Gordon, in *Prehistoric London, Its Mounds and Circles* (1914), says: 'The Llandin – Parliament Hill – is the largest, loftiest and most imposing of the four prehistoric "Gorsedds of *Great Seats*" of the Metropolis.' London clay rising to sandy loam. A traditional place of assembly. 'On the north-eastern slope is a stone monument on which an in-scription states that here public speaking is allowed.' On the morning of Trump's triumph, we have no public. They are keeping to their beds. Even the dogs have been turned to stone. A petrified Labrador retriever guards a green shack known as The Mutt Hut ('because they're woof it'). Junked coffee beakers, among a quilt of rusty leaves, pretending to be mushrooms.

Laying a hand on the cold monument, I try to anticipate the Overground spur to Barking in the way that Martin Stone would thread bookshop to bookshop, to locked room, to private house, to su-icided collector, right across the city, across continents. He called it the 'Vine'. Pluck one fat grape and the next will make itself known. There is no Blackhorse Road without the *lived* experience of Harringay Green Lanes. A book hunt, like a deep-topography *détournement*, is about continuity, harvesting contour lines, paying adequate attention to signs and signatures. If Barking, or Barking Riverside, is indeed the golden reservation on the River Roding, it must reveal itself, in homeopathic doses, as I follow the curve of the silent railway.

What did the promoters of this El Dorado of the A13 promise?

> The Barking Boathouse is a unique riverside arts venue, at the heart of the emerging Ice House Quarter, featuring exhibition/ café space, the terrace and riverside studios. A beautiful location for a fashion or film shoot, or simply a place to chill out and relax by the river. Discounts available for certain entrepreneurial 'start ups' or emerging creative talent. This is an area of historic and cultural significance, being home to Barking Abbey (Ruins), Abbey Green, Town Quay (Short Blue Fishing Heritage) and the historic Granary and Malthouse Buildings.

They had the history (in tatters) and they were getting the railway. Tim Burrows, in the *Guardian*, said: 'Barking Riverside has a decent case for being the most isolated place to live in London.' A great location for mystics and desert saints. Why spoil it by letting the world in, the expelled of Hackney? The Riverside promoters, trying to attract settlers to this desolate colony on the site of a former power station, dangled the promise of a tram link to the centre of Barking.

The rain was unrelenting. Main roads were clogged with a sclerotic agitation of fume-exhaling vans and cars dodging wet cyclists, some of them cushioned by a matching set of helmeted babes, looking like polychromatic airbags, on their way to the crèche, the holding pen. But once you stepped across the ribbon of commuter traffic, progress was steady. Here was a comfortable land, with artisan coffee outlets, gentle ascents and windows in which poets left capitalised messages.

HAPPINESS: AND WHAT YOU DO WITH WHAT YOU'VE GOT / CAN CHANGE THE WAY YOU FEEL / JUST DO YOUR BEST AND SMILE A LOT / YOU'LL KEEP AN EVEN KEEL.

On Junction Road a plaster chef, with deeply furrowed brow, did his best to stay upbeat, raising a thumb against the weather, the cars denied access to the southbound A1, and a cyclone of bad news from across the Atlantic. I narrowly avoided being rammed into the window of a barber shop by a skidding invalid carriage piloted by a woman in blue wellington boots whose sightline was completely obscured by a rainbow-defaced pink umbrella.

Where aspirant Scottish politicians, especially those fortunate enough to live in London, bag their Highland Munros, mountains over 3,000 feet, I collected rain-smeared snapshots of non-functioning London Overground stations. Upper Holloway was a holding pen of secure fences and orange Trumpsuits of aggrieved workers waiting on wet-weather gear approved by Health and Safety. Hands in pockets, bearded and booted, they smoked roll-ups on the pavement, blocking passage to a notice boasting (against all evidence) that shops and businesses are open as usual. If you can get to them around the perpetual Crossrail burrowing. The Overground is a dead track, all the way to Barking. IMPROVEMENTS UNDER WAY. COMPLETION BY FEBRUARY 2017. Meanwhile: detours, bus promises.

The London Overground branch from Gospel Oak to Barking was conceptual, a theoretical boost to property values: there were no actual trains. The long delay in service felt like class action, as if Hampstead liberals from the moral high ground were not yet prepared to cohabit with darkest Essex. The line was 'closed for improvements' in June 2016 and these improvements would not be delivered before February 2017. If it all went well. (And it didn't.) If there were no more problems. (And there were.) The upgrade was budgeted at £130 million. Overhead cables could not be fitted to incorrectly designed masts. Piledrivers smashed through sewage pipes in Walthamstow. Construction materials were not delivered on time, while gangs were kept waiting. TfL (Every Journey Matters) asked for a grovelling apology from Network Rail (Delivering for our Customers). Network Rail (Delivering for our Customers) feuded with the Department of Transport (Putting Passengers First). The Department of Transport (Putting Passengers First) demanded a public enquiry. And another million in compensation. They are all minded to initiate a robust plan and a major review, with pretty blue bottles of spring water, artisan coffee and ethically sourced bread rolls, into what went wrong. And how many more meetings and discussions, claims and counter claims, should be held to carry the work forward, to make life better for all of us.

Sadiq Khan, our Mayor, said that unless £32 billion was provided by Government for Crossrail 2 (Connecting Jobs, Homes and Opportunities), London would grind to a halt. Long queues, desperate to save a few minutes in getting to Birmingham, would spill on to the streets around Euston and gridlock Underground platforms.

On Fairbridge Road, now soaring in value, thanks to its Overground proximity, I barely recognise the house that Chris Petit managed to flog before it slid down the embankment onto the tracks. This was where we edited – or brewed coffee, fetched chocolate biscuits, while Emma Matthews edited – two films for Channel 4. Chris spent much of the day, when he wasn't reshooting my flickering 8mm footage from the bare wall, or shaking his head and sighing over the latest assemblage, on the phone to estate agents, solicitors, potential purchasers. He said that his career was about making the right moves in the property market, squeezing a book or at worst a script out of every address in his drift across North London. Fairbridge Road was as close to Hackney as he wanted to come. Peter Stanford, visiting the director on behalf of the *Independent on Sunday*, described the house as: 'an oddly utilitarian home in an industrial unit.'

I photographed the revised borderline bunker in its metallic grey finish, with the container-stack makeover that Petit would certainly approve. The property right alongside his former studio was now CARWORKS GARAGE: SERVICE, REPAIR, BRAKES, MOT. Petit plotted a Warhol factory, shutters closed against daylight, commissions flooding in. But the Fairbridge Road address soon declined into an embassy of inconvenience in which the filmmaker, unravelling CIA conspiracies or making complicated connections to Nazi bankers, became a self-immolated Julian Asange with rescued charity-shop jackets and piercing eyes. An Edward Snowden, services rendered, banged up in Moscow, staring at a railway going nowhere.

'He is a man,' Stanford wrote, 'who enjoys living in the seedier parts of London, who is fascinated as a filmmaker by people on the cultural margins, and who is pessimistic about the direction his industry is taking… Petit is very much the observer, charting worlds of which he himself is not a part.'

The carpet boys on the other side of the road, the chancers who provided Chris with many hours of innocent entertainment, as they ducked and dived, were still in the game. The director used to watch from behind his shutters with the detached gaze of a hungrier Maigret, small cigar instead of pipe. Chronologically arranged shelves of Simenon first editions offered a clue, probably false, to Petit's bleak philosophy of life. But the rest of the opportunistic retail concerns of earlier times, and the parking spots favoured by dealers, were swept away for a delicatessen. A stencilled Jesus, baring his breast to reveal a scarlet anarchist tattoo, holds a finger to his lips. Say nothing. Feel nothing. Move on.

★★★

Crouch Hill was a drowning village, soon to be given the kiss of life by the orange Trumpsuits standing motionless on the steps behind the inevitable blue fence. A suspended station as a staging post to nowhere. The most striking feature is a heritage dairy, with scenes of waggoners and milkmaids in a bucolic England: GRAZING, MILKING, COOLING. PRESENT DAY DELIVERY. Under the city, Welsh cows. Economic migrants.

There are vans of bored electricians, putting on time, lodged on every bridge across the railway. I have no difficulty in following the tracks, even without the wail of trains. One of the bridges on Stapleton Hall Road is a beautiful mass of Pre-Raphaelite ivy and creepers, the vegetable world swallowing the arch of old brick.

On Sunday, 16th July 1944, a V-1 flying bomb hit Granville Road, killing fifteen people. 'Their purpose was terror,' says the Peace Garden board. Two young girls, ribbons in their hair, movements synchronised, are dancing on a bald strip of grass in the front garden of a prefab.

By the time I found myself on Endymion Road, I had lost my sense of direction entirely; railways were criss-crossing on the flank of Finsbury Park. Was this the *Endymion* of Keats? 'Of all the unhealthy and o'er-darkened ways / Made for our searching.' Or a novel of railway mania and Chartism by Benjamin Disraeli? Martin Stone could have hunted down first editions with surprising dedications, annotations, inserted letters, mysteries creating further mysteries to keep the story alive. Register that reflex smile of amusement, the cigarette wedged in corner of mouth; the ash caught in his hand and pocketed, as he slides the latest find into his bag and runs for the last train. 'Ghosts, adieu!'

I am striding uphill towards Manor Park. It is coming apart. My interior compass is shot. I have to reverse, realign with the future railway at Harringay Green Lanes. Time to get out of the drizzle for a coffee in a Turkish place, where the elevated TV has my neck cracking for more and worse Trumpery. The screen glows like a wall

at a safe distance from the centre, was founded in 1890 to deal with the sweats and tremors of an unhealthy city. It was expanded two years later, after a scarlet fever epidemic, as a colony of wooden huts. During the First World War, St Ann's was requisitioned as a Base Hospital for the American Expeditionary Force. Wards were painted in a restful shade of green and provided with high beds suitable for strong men from Denver, Colorado. Therapeutic plantings were undertaken by a former employee of Kew Gardens.

As the London population increased and incomers moved into the area, the number of available beds went down. In 1951 there were 756. In 1964, 606. In 1984, 320. In 1993, 246. By April 2001 the freehold ownership and management of the site had been transferred to the Barnet, Enfield and Haringey Mental Health NHS Trust. Many of the buildings were empty, others in partial use. Patients had to learn to navigate the tactful spread of the fever hospital.

A church with a forbidding wooden door has changed allegiance: MOSQUE ENTRANCE IS FROM SUFFOLK ROAD. Where the future Ginger Line, rebranding old tracks, crosses St Ann's Road, my path is challenged by a much more important route, the Cycle Superhighway. There are few bicycles out here in the dozing suburbs, but distances are flagged in cycle-time. And appropriate cycle destinations: STOKE NEWINGTON 8 mins, THE CITY 25 mins. The City feels like a very remote prospect, a fever dream, removed by the miles required to neutralise contagion. Biological and moral.

Emerging on Stamford Hill High Road and swinging north is a shift into the past, the deep past of the Great North Road, the way out; first intimations of elsewhere, the excursionism of Izaak Walton on a quest for pleasure, the English pastoral of milkmaids and fishing inns, and the mad tramping of John Clare – and alongside that a rind of memory running back to Stoke Newington, Hackney and the City, our earlier selves, in 1969, walking in the crowd to White Hart Lane, to pay a few coins to stand and watch Tottenham Hotspur confront the hated Leeds United of Bremner and Giles on a sheet of snow. And the noise of splintering glass and the excitement of riot travelling faster than the progress of the railway hidden behind blue boards, set off by the curdled yellow of a parked ambulance with a flashing blue light. Travelling like fire.

After Green Lanes, Turkish enterprise, men talking on the pavement outside wedding shops and restaurants, the faces labouring with bags on the pavements were mostly black. New communities want to adapt the failing structures of old places. The St Ann's Redevelopment Trust (StART) aspires to build affordable homes on the site of the hospital, where two-thirds of the land is being sold. Architects commissioned by StART are drawing up plans. 'It is at this point,' said the *Tottenham Community Press*, 'that communities must take it into their own hands to tackle the crisis head-on.'

In North Tottenham regeneration takes the form of demolishing 1,800 homes. Community groups, as ever, battle to defend the theory and practice of council housing. Estates are wiped from history. And Haringey Council promises (post-truth): 'Once the Development Vehicle is established in 2017 we will work closely with residents to deliver new homes.' Meanwhile, demolitions and expulsions continue, shifting cargoes of human landfill to the outer Essex limits, to other counties, dying resorts, Peterborough. 'It is a tough road they walk, at times lonely,' writes Adjoa Wiredu, editor of the community paper.

I met Adjoa, a bright and committed young woman, with a proper sense of the absurdity of bringing a conversation about demolition, social engineering and street art into such a place, in a cellar across the road from Haggerston Overground station: Ginger Line coffee (for me), with an immaculately delivered artisan flourish in the froth. Well worth the wait, while the barista talks *sourcing* with his disciple. Bare bricks, wooden tables and forms, post-industrial chic, laboratory lighting. Music pitched a decibel below the level of walkout annoyance.

Adjoa is a mature student at the University of Kent. She grew up on a Tottenham estate, before relocating upstream to Chiswick. She couldn't believe that this was still London. The release of a certain kind of pressure was extreme. She floated. She moved in a

231

different way. Then she returned. Her work, in a more sophisticated digital form, was much like my own: image-gleaning, wandering, assembling, sticking to the territory. Where would it go? What did it mean? I couldn't help her. I never learned when or where to stop, every small advance was another digression. London was overloaded, collapsing under the weight of memory.

LIFE IN THE UK TEST. ENGLISH LANGUAGE CENTRE. GENERAL ENGLISH. ACADEMIC ENGLISH. BUSINESS ENGLISH. LIFE IN THE UK COURSE. With reserved parking for JJ Rhatigan & Company.

An impressive High Road building dedicated to processing applications, getting you through the barbed wire of bureaucracy. LEARN ENGLISH IN QUARTER OF THE TIME.

This used to be the desperate freelance poet's trade, teaching English as a second language in Tottenham and Walthamstow. But times have changed, the language game is now a high street business, a funded operation. An investment. With more clients every season.

I'm on the curve of Broad Lane to Ferry Lane and feeling the pull of the marshes, an oily breeze, smelling of burnt rags and comfrey, from ruffled reservoirs. The Tottenham Hale Retail Park, colonising a strategic bend in the road, thickens that sensation of being trapped in the gutter of the map, heading into some off-highway wilderness with fresh brown fields to exploit. Subsequent research discovered that visitors to the Retail Park stayed, on average, between twenty minutes and an hour. Some, intimidated by security barriers, looked as if they had taken up permanent residence, camping in skips, feeding on throwouts. Others, presumably, were permitted one glance at the promised land before being bounced.

A skeletal sail, or single wing torn from a giant corvine, guards the entrance. It is badged like the denim jacket of Peter Blake with come-ons for Argos, Next, Costa Coffee, Halfords (where insurers allow you to choose a replacement for a stolen bike), JD, Poundworld, O2, Carphone Warehouse, Burger King, Carpet Right, Lidl, TK Maxx, Currys PC World, B&Q, and all those enterprises so attractive to rioters.

Parked at the perimeter of this potential excitement is a double-decker bus with open doors. The bodywork is embellished with a smiling black girl and an encouraging slogan: MEETYOURFUTURE. More Trumpery has been laid on for this day of days. The stalled Tottenham Hale transport could be the Teflon Don's campaign vehicle: HIRE AN APPRENTICE. They did. And we must live with the reality TV consequences. DIGITAL FUTURES. CREATIVE EQUALS.

A post-architectural malapropism of stunted tower blocks in play-dough colours, buttressed by failing shops and offensive artworks, has been left to expire on the hard shoulder like radioactive roadkill. Ferry Lane is such an evocative name. I stopped, from time to time, at the Ferry Boat Inn on my way from a single room in Hampstead to my classes at the South-West Essex Technical College and School of Art in Walthamstow; back in the Sixties, my first real London job. Ferry Lane was a broad causeway. Essex was another country guarded by water.

'Get on with it,' Martin said. 'The light is running out.'

'Hang on. One more thing. And it's important.'

On winter days in Camden Passage, you feared for Martin's physical wellbeing. You could hear his bones chime in the wind. The pale glow of a cigarette was his only source of warmth. His nose dripped steadily. Those emphatic, medieval eyebrows were lightly frosted. But a charm I couldn't define – courtesy of address, aborted rock-legend status – drew them all in: top-dollar dealers from Covent Garden, Savile Row and California, paper-addicted postmen, actors, punks, public eccentrics, Jimmy Page, Michael Moorcock, Marianne Faithfull, Barry Humphries, mildewed weirdo collectors of single titles, shy Irish builders with a thing for William Faulkner and a rubber-band roll of cash-money, smooth villains, chipped saints, mystics, undead 1890s decadents, old men of the suburbs, married women, infants setting themselves up to deal in Baedeker guidebooks. He fulfilled some strange need: the outsider/insider with the keys to the celestial library.

'Are we *ever* going to make Barking? I feel like I've laid my neck on all the sleepers between here and Gospel Oak.'

Martin knew that there were no bookshops in Barking Riverside. And nothing wretched enough to qualify as junk.

'Wait,' I insisted. 'I can't let my gross bit about that railside development looking like roadkill pass without qualification. I've just realised that Mark Duggan was invited to step from the boxed-in car and shot, Operation Trident, at that precise spot, Ferry Lane. He was coming back over the causeway from Walthamstow, in possession of a recently acquired BBM Bruni Model 92 handgun, a blank-firing replica. After that everything is up in the air. The police treated the minicab driver with their usual courtesy, spreadeagled in the dirt, sworn at. "Don't look, don't look," they kept shouting. The gun migrated, in some never explained way, over a fence into the long grass. Don't look. Don't see. Don't remember. Don't tell. The event, right here, was the trigger, the source and fountain of the Tottenham riots.'

Walthamstow was much changed and I had to push on, hard, to make my late-morning appointment. On Blackhorse Road I registered an entire window of the Oxfam shop given over to martial glorification: war memoirs, zap-a-Nazi comics, neutralised weaponry. Lifting a camera was a provocation. A station beggar at Walthamstow Queen's Road lurched towards me. 'I just want to ask a question, one simple fucking question. *One* question.' With peripheral vision, I had already watched him track an Asian woman, loaded down with shopping from the market; he circled her, physically blocking and nudging as she tried to pick up the pace. 'One fucking question. *One* question.'

This was a bad moment. After Trump, the dispiriting trudge in the slipstream of an inoperative railway, the killing of Mark Duggan, a return to the sorrows of Walthamstow, and my sense of hopelessness in confronting opposed factions in a city stretched to breaking point, with the gated quarters of the entitled surrounded by homeless madmen raging for pennies, dredged up unsuspected reserves of bile. I had a question of my own as the substance-abusing self-medicator snarled and spat.

'Do you want me to drive the point of my umbrella into the juice of your eyeball?'

The psychopathology was alarming. And it could have happened. Hard-Brexit London was defined by such out-of-character atrocities. A previously mild-mannered, quietly inebriated underground film-maker, affronted on an all-night bus by ordinary chip-chucking juveniles, stabbed one of them in the thigh. To salve this redline metropolitan fever, I walked very slowly and deliberately through the High Street Market. An Asian shopkeeper was cursing an African woman who tried to bargain for a dog's bath in pink plastic. He punched the bottom repeatedly to prove its strength. She smiled and waited. She had won. He wrestled the tray from her grasp, spitting on the notes she held out. She waited. He took them and wiped them with a rag, before they went into his pocket. He raged as she walked away.

At the Palmerston Road crossing, where FEVAR GRAFFITI is asserting his copyright, there is a grinning skull and crossbones with the inscription LONDON BAD. This badness has eaten into my soul. I blamed it on the umbrella, which I had not unfurled, even at the most biblical passages of the morning deluge. I dislike umbrellas, seeing them, even now, as symbols of a prefect's authority in an English public school. Umbrellas are a discourtesy and a menace. Their bearers and brandishers walk around, insulated in little domed shelters, private tents, poking out the eyes of innocent pedestrians. What is so wrong with getting wet?

Perhaps the umbrella had a voice of its own? I clicked along, taking pleasure from driving the metallic point into London dirt, using it as a ski pole. Scratching curses. There is no comfort to be found in charitable exchanges, given or withheld. Sentiment had me digging into my pockets for gentlemen of the road with an oblique way of asking, as if they were doing you a favour with a generous spray of whisky breath. Which, in a sense, they were, by invoking Mayhew and Dickens. Beckett's tramping scarecrows. But I was prejudiced against appeals, from a pavement nest, based around the ownership of some subdued dog. Or the cruel professionalism of the doped and sagging infant. Otherwise, donations were offered according to the mood of the moment: awkwardness and regret, whichever way it went.

Shame always. Waifs on platforms. Crazy girls who catch you in an Overground compartment with speed-freak nonsense about evil lovers, expulsion from Shadwell flats, cancer taxis to hospitals. Too much detail. Even when true. Too much to absorb. No dole of silver coins for chippy operators – SPARECHANGEFORFOODPLEASE – staking out new Ginger Line halts with beakers and chat. And no sponsorship for the robotic ones who thank you and bless your day with such wounding irony.

On Hoe Street there is one of those redbrick, many-windowed properties set well back, assertively so, from the vulgar business of the road. Behind iron gates: CAMELOT PROTECTS BY OCCUPATION. Meaning: keep out. Meaning: no occupation by foreign anarchists or housing collectives. This building is already squatted by security. It's big and it's empty – and there used to be room around the back for the Portakabins in which classes were held. I saw out my final days as a jobbing Liberal Studies teacher in those kabins. The chaotic freelance miseducation – in which I learnt much more from the students than I had to offer in return – was being upgraded to Polytechnic status; more management-speak, a better class of forms to fill in. I was never paid on time, in any case; there was always a suspect date, a misplaced hour on my pink form. The choice was stark: fulltime accountable employment or labouring in the badlands of opportunism around Stratford. Within a couple of months, I was paying my dues, marked on a grubby yellow card, to the Transport and General Workers Union at Chobham Farm. What I remember now was the journey across the marshes, and how I had to park the battered old Mini facing downhill in Hampstead, hoping the engine would fire before I reached the bottom.

On High Road Leyton, COMMUNITY PLACE (which looks like another lost cinema) has become an outlet for Ladbrokes. If I was a betting man, I'd put good money on John Rogers appearing, with a grin of welcome, before I hit the future Overground halt at Leyton Midland Road. John was my late-morning appointment. And he was reliable. Even with an off-colour son, now home alone, taking a day out of school. And having to deal with a major white goods delivery. John Rogers was the animating spirit of Leytonstone. When he was in attendance, streets from which I felt a double alienation (theirs and mine) came to life.

It's not just the rusty beard, the high dome, the earring he should be wearing (but isn't): John is Elizabethan, a film-poet, writer/walker from a better time. He has a history of alternative stand-up, alliances with Russell Brand and the deep-topographer Nick Papadimitriou. A history of persistent engagement in the politics of protest, being there, bearing witness. Keeping the record. And posting it. He was good company on a second circuit of London Overground; a series of excursions fitted in between school-delivery and school-collection. It seems that John did most of his own work, writing or editing, at night. He was self-funding, self-starting, a guerrilla documentarist in the great tradition: green anorak, ruined left knee, camera in pocket.

As soon as we fell into step, my role changed. John was the guide. His book, *This Other London: Adventures in the Overlooked City*, dressed this section of my walk in affectionate anecdotes. Bifurcating suburban avenues under plunging skies, access routes to cemeteries, were not *overlooked*. Nothing was beneath John's notice. But I was well aware that Leytonstone was an interlude, there would very soon be a parting of the ways. After Wanstead Flats, I would revert to the status of an *under*looker, pavement snoop. Locked into fantasies and involuntary flashbacks.

Hitchcock, Graham Gooch, Jonathan Ross: John conjured familiar faces from these streets, pubs, schools. He put in a call to the artist Patrick Brill (aka Bob and Roberta Smith) with whom he collaborated on films and other projects. Patrick was not at home. Bob and Roberta were not picking up. John explained that Leytonstone *really* was, for a few years, and for the usual economic reasons, an authentic culture quarter. After openings at the Whitechapel Gallery, all the artists came here to party. The influential filmmaker John Smith operated out of *this* house. His *Black Tower* was right *there*. And look up: a blue plaque for Stuart Freeborn, the 'godfather of modern make-up design' and creator of Yoda and Chewbacca of *Star Wars* fame. Freeborn was referenced by an unfinished mural under the railway. Many of the arches, John was proud to demonstrate, were still oil-puddled concerns, storerooms, small businesses. There was a precise point where organic microbrewers and performance spaces confirmed the emerging railway-slipstream property boom.

Back on London Fields, on Helmsley Place, John screened *London Overground* in a pop-up cinema under a railway arch: a neat twist in the evolving story. When trains ran overhead, the sound jumped; so that the yarn about Kilburn pubs Chris Petit finally delivered, after miles of strategic silence, was shredded to nonsense.

We kneel in the road to locate the subterranean whisper of a lost rivulet, the Philly Brook, once regarded as a flood risk to the putative Olympic Park. I was staring the wrong way, at a giant Stars and Stripes flag, with a miniature eagle perched on supporting pole, loudly trumping from a redbrick terrace, above the only Krypto Security alarm in the street. A satirical *1984* poster of David Cameron with WAR IS PEACE, FREEDOM IS SLAVERY, IGNORANCE IS STRENGTH, is more potent in tatters. The capitalised phrases could be copied straight from Trump's prompt card.

John turns back at the edge of Wanstead Flats. He identifies a broad avenue of sweet chestnuts, one of the radials of Wanstead House, originally planted by another John, Evelyn, on the instructions of Sir Josiah Child. The avenue is now a ride for local hackers, heading northeast, coming away from a twinned pair of tower blocks with unimpeded views of grasslands, ponds and traffic. An old woman on the seventh floor whistles up foxes. John told me how much he relished these wide-open spaces. And he advised on my best route: shadow the railway, down Dames Road to Wanstead Park.

Evelyn's prophetic words came back, reverberated: 'London was, and is no more.'

The push was on. A chain gang in orange Trumpsuits and hardhats were labouring, behind mesh barriers, to bring the decrepit railway bridge on-stream. I stopped for a coffee, left my unopened umbrella hooked behind my chair, and had to double back to collect it. I was well out of my knowledge and granular London light was going fast.

Forest Gate, previously little more than a rumour to me, a place where several of the Chobham Farm migrant workers lodged, was now resurrected as an established arboreal tributary. Hampton Road, flirting against the railway, and sandwiched by cemeteries, had a certain period grandeur. Detached villas and double-fronted houses were not downgraded into flats. Neat plantings kept quiet pavements apart from decorative porches and purple splashes of stained glass. When the Forest Gate developer Archibald Cameron Corbett laid out the Woodgrange Estate in 1892, he was giving away family units for £530 leasehold. With the opening of the Ginger Line service from Gospel Oak to Barking, the better Hampton Road properties will be trading at close to a million.

I stuck with the railway as far as I could; the streets were empty, shops were putting up their shutters, and I could hear in the distance the menacing roar of the elevated road. I knew that a major barrier was coming and I had no idea how to cross it. There is a buffer of municipal grass, dog-compost meadowland, playing fields on which nobody plays, before you are thrown against the unavoidable fact of the motorway. And, beyond that, the river: the Roding. I had hit a wall of sound – the A406, South Woodford to Barking Relief Road, becoming the North Circular – as unforgiving as Berlin or some other city divided against itself. I was more comfortable here, and less myself, the supposed narrator, than anywhere I had passed through that day.

Geography solicited the bite of the collaged *samizdat* pamphlets put out by the artist Laura Oldfield Ford. The ones that I found, from time to time, on ledges in concrete pillboxes, among empty bottles under broken benches, in some opportunist breezeblock café serving bean soup. A late-romanticism of ruins delivered with punk-vortex energy, Ford's *Savage Messiah* echoed the title of HS Ede's biography of the farouche young sculptor Gaudier-Brzeska, killed at Neuville-Saint-Vaast in the First War.

'Ghosts, revenants, memories haunting the fabric. London gripped in security cordons. A day out looking for projects on a recently evacuated and bombed out suburb,' Ford wrote in her chapbook for

2015. Long solitary walks, looping, shaping their own logic, brought grunge traces of vanished communities to the surface.

We found ourselves, in the immediate aftermath of the 2012 circus, 'debating' the Olympic legacy with a decorated oarsman, who was considering which major charity he would front, and a broadsheet sports scribe (with obvious investment in the continuing show). The audience in Cheltenham, patriotic to a fault, turned – audibly, visibly – into a pack of ravening wolves, a lynch mob. Ford, who had lived and worked for years on the ground under discussion, came close to being assaulted.

Only bicycles are permitted under the railway bridge. On the far side, terraces are threatened by road and railway. Along the impenetrable mesh fence, suspect cars, with boots open, are parked up for obvious deals between hooded men. There is no attempt at disguising what is going on. It's as blatant as the character on the train from Hackney Downs to Ponders End, a few months back, unwrapping a gun for sale.

I know it won't work but I follow a footpath under the motorway, through an open gate into an abandoned mushroom farm. The lights from tower-block windows of estates on the ragged fringe of Barking are a teasing illusion.

Watson Avenue should lead onto a footbridge to the better place, the solution to London's housing problems. THE PROTECTOR GROUP. MONITORED CCTV. PRIORITY POLICE RESPONSE. A panoramic edgeland vista: pylon, gasholder, single white goalpost, coarse grass the colour of pissed undergarments. Those too. Shredded on razorwire. Sky pressing like black insurance-scam smoke. An unexplained grey box that bleeps and flashes. Six lanes of traffic. Failed barriers to prevent the dumping of industrial waste. *I love it*. And there *is* a bridge over the road. I should make Barking before they put the lights out. For good.

I lean on the rail and look north to where the future Overground line will cross the North Circular. A theoretical circle within a circle, a ritual enclosure like a gentile *eruv*, overrides the inclinations of rivers, marshes, swamps.

'Fresh wilderness! Resurrected from the raw-broken concrete at the airfield's edge,' sang the poet Harry Fainlight at the Albert Hall on 11th June 1965.

A police car, the first I have spotted on a long day's tramp across London, is parked on Watson Avenue, some distance from the nearest fastfood outlet. It must be serious. A visible presence symbolically guarding the crossing point between worlds.

Martin Stone departs. Or perhaps my ability to hold firm to the spirit he represents fails? He is not, by inclination, a rambler of territories without shops and windows and bars and sounds, action. He scuttles. He sniffs. He belongs on trains. Getting a hit on the breeze of oil refineries and the estuary, the spectral guitar hero of Savoy Brown – Mighty Baby ('Britain's answer to the Grateful Dead'), Chilli Willli and the Red Hot Peppers ('Bongos over Balham'), the Pink Fairies – takes off, fast, for Canvey Island, to gig, one last time, with Wilko Johnson among the neat bungalows and squatted railway carriages. To tease out books the old rockers don't know they have: inscriptions, bloodstains. Secret histories. And to wait for a killer wave.

The phantom train on which Martin rides is illuminated by the soft glow of whale oil. Skinny saints are holding phone-torches under their chins. The carriages are lined with books. The ghost train is also a moveable library, in which the volumes required, the wrappered detective novels from the Golden Age, the unwritten Simenons, the second novels by Edgar Allan Poe and Emily Brontë, deliver themselves to your hand, station by station, into the night. Every halt has its special literature. The tip of Martin's glowing cigarette is like a tracer bullet exiting his cheek.

Barking resisted, but I made the transit. A retail park, bristling with photovoltaic scanners and booster masts, offered: VEHICLE GRAPHICS, BRAND CONSULTATION. Traffic circled a serious roundabout like pilgrims at a hajj. A strange ecumenical chimney dominated the island in the middle of all this action. Estranged traces of the abbey town on the Roding did their honest best to under-write potential development: electro-convulsive resurrection not regeneration. Barking was a settlement proud enough of its past to boast of a centre. From where, as soon as I achieved it, I took a train out.

I was tempted by the joint across the road from the station: BARKING HOTEL. Angry orange capitals against midnight-blue windows. Did I want to spend the night in somewhere that sounded as if it had been deleted from the second draft of a Thomas Pynchon novel? Pynchon's paranoid comedies looked much less funny, and not at all grotesque, on the day when Donald Trump bagged the presidency. Even Trump's name was off-form Pynchon. In *The Crying of Lot 49*, published in 1965, the elusive author has a flash-forward vision of Barking. 'Less an identifiable city than a group of concepts – census tracts, special purpose bond-issue districts, shopping nuclei, all overlaid with access roads to its own freeway.' To, in this case, the A13. Barking was a conceptual A13 pit stop that nobody wanted to take. A bypass to be bypassed.

The *London Evening Standard*, in pre-binned mounds at the station entrance, featured the man with the golden hair-hat giving his signature thumbs-up. TRUMP TRIUMPH SHOCKS WORLD. BILLIONAIRE PULLS OFF HUGE UPSET TO BECOME PRESIDENT. PUTIN AND MAY SEND MESSAGES OF CONGRATULATION.

Chris Currell, understandably keen to promote the area's pedigree, offered me a ticket to a talk on 'The First Golden Age of Barking'. Implying, of course, that a second, brighter age, brighter than a thousand stars, was about to happen. The lecture, by Professor George Garnett, Medievalist and 'expert in early modern history', would take place at Eastbury Manor House, a surviving Elizabethan property now in the charge of the National Trust. With drinks reception and tour of the house.

To avoid another trudge over the North Circular, I hopped on the District Line at Mile End. I arrived two hours early, to give myself time to appreciate the ordinary life of the place – and to find Eastbury Manor House, hidden away among redundant shopping centres, feeder roads and terminal suburbs, on the approach to the A13.

It was a night of multiplying existential dread. To emerge from the station is to volunteer as a CCTV suspect. I couldn't help making a connection with recent footage of the gay 'date rape drug killer', Stephen Port, who was captured, strolling side by side with one of the prospects he snared from the Grindr social media site. They were heading off down the shopping precinct towards his Barking flat. Port, a chef in a bus garage canteen, admitted a 'propensity for sex with unconscious men'. Post-coitus, he killed four of them.

A woman appeared on the local news, walking her interrogator through the tidy graves of St Margaret's Church in Abbey Park. I couldn't believe what she was saying in such a moderately alarmed way. Being on television meant holding emotions in check. She kept finding these dead men, eyes open, stacked against a wall. As if they had just shrugged free of earth's clammy embrace. Port liked to arrange the corpses and to place drugs in their pockets.

The Barking police took the bait: special interest groups doing their thing. Lowlife. Leave well alone. Go through the motions. The killer was finally prosecuted through the persistent efforts of one of the victims' sisters. Three of the dead men were planted with the sedative GHB. No mobile phones were found. I wasn't aware of it at the time, but the locations where the bodies were discovered pretty much duplicated my walk from the station. And this was the only map of the immediate area on which, thanks to the ever-vigilant *Telegraph*, I could draw. Neither the station papershop, nor any other place I tried, could offer a local directory. They'd never heard of such a thing. And thought I was mad to ask, a time-waster.

I navigated the night by blind instinct. An outsider, a Salvationist who drove into Barking every day – what a journey, worse than Bunyan – was able to point me in the general direction of the National Trust property. I tried to write down her complicated advice, but it was raining so hard the words were blots and smears.

There was a flyover to be negotiated, an underpass, roads named after English counties or Shakespearean dukes. Not appreciating the right moves or body language gives a tunnel or a path between high fences a definite frisson. The nocturnal kebab houses and convenience stores knew nothing of Elizabethan manor houses, even when they were right opposite one of them.

But I made it on time. The gates were padlocked. I circled sodden gardens. And desolate places where car met car, window to window, for furtive exchanges. The estate was purchased by a wealthy merchant after the dissolution of Barking Abbey. Tall chimneys were a symbol of that wealth. The grand house had family affiliations with the Gunpowder Plot.

Drenched, excluded and delusional, I rang Chris Currell. Yes, I had the right place, but I'd turned up a week too soon.

NIGHT HOSPITAL

'how these tracks ran on into others, others, knowing they laced,
deepened, authenticated the great night…'
Thomas Pynchon

The city slept like the hogs of god. London night called to our
wounds, psychic and physical, the hot pints of Andrew Kötting's
blood donated to the tarmac of Old Kent Road, the scars he proudly
showed, the healed gouges and tracks of the surgery that saved him,
up there in the night hospital on Denmark Hill, the one we photographed and inspected on our one-day pedestrian circuit of the
Ginger Line – and the hours, days, lost to the black sump of consciousness that is a single unbroken rope of words curling both ways
in time, an electro-magnetic anomaly, a pit in which we drink and
drown, remembering other walks, the prick, the goad, the flaw lifting
us from our desks, away from our tables, books, beds, families. So we
are in movement again, dissolving the halo of the original clockwise
journey, begun in daylight, for a counter-clockwise, widdershins,
nocturnal drift, Haggerston to Haggerston, through the long hours
of darkness, back into the light – and, this time, free of the burden of
keeping notes and photographs, forging a report.

This would be a walk, pure, begun around 7pm on 23rd February
2016, and also an erasure, a rubbing out of the original, as Robert
Rauschenberg rubbed out the drawing by Willem de Kooning that
he loved, solicited, in order to validate it. We are swallowed by ra-
don yellows and frosted whites, headlight beams, phones that are
torches, and we recall the framed artwork, which appeared to be a
blank piece of paper, and was actually inscribed, at the invitation of

Rauschenberg, by his friend Jasper Johns. I couldn't be sure who was doing the erasing of which memories and who was taking credit, but we set out in good heart, Andrew in costume, disciplined in his eccentricities, as worn for the first walk, the felt hat with ear flaps that I saw as Andean, a llama herder, in respect of my great-grandfather who ventured in those lands, and Andrew referenced to the Faroe Islands and his own paternal grandfather, who got a second family up there in wartime, connections undiscovered until Kötting made his *Deadad* film and travelled the world, Germany, Hollywood, Mexico, with giant inflatables of father and grandfather, in a spectacular (and successful) exorcism of the shouts and slaps of childhood trauma and geography (South London suburbia, Chislehurst), stamping the voices down, exploiting the special magic of film as false memory, and looking for another foolish expedition beyond reason.

London can absorb all this. Night can absorb London. Hogs roll and snore. The purity of the notion of looping the city through the hours of darkness, following the necklace of railway stations and freeing them from the narrative laid down by the account offered in my book, *London Overground*, with no record kept, no tablet grabs fed into the Cloud, was undone, at once, by the presence of John Rogers and his camera. John was making his own film of yet another pedestrian circuit of the Ginger Line and he would trot beside us, under a gravid moon, as far as Hampstead Heath, or the point where his left knee gave out. And then there was the consideration that this unwritten, unpromoted, unnecessary jaunt was being recalled and revised for another book. And sampled, edited and shown at select locations in the film by John Rogers.

'The leg is in pretty steady pain but no problem. My left hand won't grip and it feels dead. It's been stitched back the wrong way round. I've got some serious frontal lobe damage,' Andrew said. 'Should be worth enough compensation to fund a couple of films.'

He projected expeditions to canine burial grounds in the Atacama Desert, troubadour marches from the grave of King Harold at Waltham Abbey to the site of the Battle of Hastings. Many years older, closer in age to his deadad, I was ready to step aside, to find a way to be done with the business of London. Despite the horror of the Old Kent Road motorbike accident – or, perhaps, because of it – Andrew spoke of his returns to Deptford, Hackney, Soho, Camden, as homecomings; a delighted reimmersion in the familiar stinks and sounds, the breakfasts and banter, the chlorine laps of lidos, the friends who gave him welcome and shelter, the community, as he called it, the collaborators who, despite everything, signed on for the next voyage.

Movement was talk. John darting ahead to frame his shot, before we were gone again in a windmilling of arms. The traffic of hipster Hackney, railway Hackney, bicycle Hackney, skunk Hackney, was clustering and dispersing at Overground stations, fizzing with snap-chat opinion and sliced monologues of compulsive banality. 'You stood up and walked out? That was going to be a good story.' Winter tables where confessions are shouted across the thick babble from inside and cigarettes stubbed out in gluten-free burger substitutes. The tribe. The hats. The noise.

Soft dusk of mirrors out of which something was about to walk. Pynchon paperbacks in novel Kingsland Road independent bookshops, franchises twice removed from other markets. Coffee, a bun and a poetry slam.

I grab Andrew's elbow. His eyes glaze over, tolerant of another landslide tumble of digression – I'm deep into my nocturnal anec-dotage – but this is more urgent, a whisper.

'On the bench!'

Rounded back set against the prevailing evening traffic, expelled from his sanctuary, snow-hooded, hunched into himself, ballasted with plastic bags, is the Vegetative Buddha of Haggerston Park. EVERY LITTLE HELPS. His wrappings and paddings are not so re-markable in the neon-splashed hipster dusk. Tortoise-neck retracted. Thick-legged with layers of trousers and pyjamas like the rings on an old, diseased elm. I looked under the bench for the sawdust trail.

Now there was no view, no sightline for us to trace. Jigsaw of paving slabs. Steel-shuttered convenience store. Sealed manhole. Clothing appropriate to getting through the night. Our park fixture had moved a few hundred yards down Whiston Road and around the corner. His protector, St Leonard, had not yet snapped his chains.

'The identities of all the city's inhabitants,' Matthew Beaumont said, 'are indelibly inscribed on their bodies.' I had joined Beaumont for a discussion of his book, *Nightwalking: A Nocturnal History of London, Chaucer to Dickens*, in the newly established Kingsland Road bookshop we were now passing, Burley Fisher. Small-press local publications basking, unloved, on a table. Chairs to the door, the street. Proprietor lurking to bar unruly elements, old Hackney. Hard now to distinguish, in this territory, the bookshops from the artisan coffee outlets, the barbers. Books as objects are so *retro*, they can dress a set or be available for purchase. This is a cruising strip, busy with transients and tablets, with fewer of the deranged and desperate, the self-medicating aliens who challenged your footsteps for a certain length of road before breaking away and sweeping back, always remaining within stalking distance of the sub-post office, where they jumped the queue to play the cash machines with the latest scavenged card or dived forward on a speculative raid into the Turkish grocer, to ogle and stroke bottles they didn't have the energy to lift.

The Vegetative Buddha in hooded winter parka was not a man of the crowd, the drifting pavement monad, the party to which no one required an invitation: he was a man *against* the crowd; disaffiliated, mute. Breathing, but barely so. By day fixed on wooden slats in a high-walled enclosure facing south. By night on a metal bench facing east, facing the elevated hiss of the Overground railway. He did not acknowledge the passing stream. The ones, with their balconies and bicycles, turned into twitching insomniacs by their never-sleeping, never-satisfied electronic devices.

Eventually, as I explained to Andrew, as we passed the bookshop window, those who try to write and publish are obliged to present themselves here for the entertainment of Hackney readers, or potential readers, who might be persuaded to carry away a book defaced with a signature. Matthew Beaumont, appearing out of darkness, seemed to have slipped, directly, from the pages of *Nightwalking*. He was condemned to intone certain passages, to embody them, before being allowed to step back outside and being absorbed once more into the restless monad.

On the smokers' patch of pavement at Burley Fisher, even before I had time to fashion my report on the nightwalk with Kötting, a man in winter headgear much like Andrew's, and fingerless gloves, much like mine, ready for the weather, stood talking to early arrivals for his own bookshop event: Jarett Kobek. The author of *i hate the internet* lived in Los Angeles and had just arrived in London from Berlin, where his book was riding high in the charts. Kobek, with whom I had been in correspondence for decades – he made contact after reading *White Chappell, Scarlet Tracings* – was resolutely lower case in the fashion of late-modernist poets. And he made it clear from the beginning that he was capable of firing up his own paranoid-critical conspiracy theories from a safe distance. A remote viewer of the London *noir* of politics and ritual murder.

In terms of that marketable commodity, books, Kobek announced that Ayn Rand had corrupted the American psyche beyond repair, with her superman philosophy, her Trumpish towers and speeches that never knew when to stop. The comic-book genius Alan Moore, Jarett asserted, was the antidote, or better than antidote: a bright star in a darkening sky. Kötting tended to agreed about Moore, having espoused his theory of Eternalism: all of cosmological time being set, hard as Brexit, into a four-dimension block, a town plan where living and dead are separated by a couple of terraced streets in Northampton. Andrew had never read *The Fountainhead, Atlas Shrugged* or heard of Ayn Rand. Kobek composed lower-case Tweets and subverted Wikipedia fictions, which he collaged for the alarmed delectation of the post-truth blogosphere.

We went for a quiet drink in the Fox, which was once an authentic villains' pub, but was now assimilated and rushed with friendly beards and confident young women. Tables had to be reserved. And there was a trick to ordering a drink. We had to shout to make ourselves heard across two yards of space. Jarett was from California and not a native shouter. He kept his knitted cap well down on his head. It was part of his internet persona. He really could not believe what had happened in Germany. He set aside the one drink, a clinking pint of vodka, that he allowed himself before a reading, to show me iPhone footage of the *miles* of red-spined copies of *i hate the internet* on display at the Frankfurt Book Fair. Images are anecdotes in bars where you can't hear yourself talk. Like monkeys on typewriters, arriving at the composition of *Hamlet*, the tablet-strokers of the Fox would eventually call up the clip Kobek was offering me. You could see the red of the shelved books ripple across the room like a spreading bloodstain.

Approaching Dalston Junction, where yellow jackets were surveying potential non-swiping Oyster defaulters, I snapped a photograph, while assuring Andrew and the panting John Rogers, who was shouldering his camera, how great it was, this time, to be making the reverse Overground circuit without the requirement of keeping a record.

'London,' I said, 'submits to nightwalkers as to drunks. You get the same blurring at the edges, recklessness in the stride that can leave you flat on your face.'

It had been announced that we could all sleep safer in our beds now: if we could sleep at all for worrying over the possible eviction of Ed Balls from *Strictly Come Dancing*, a reality programme in which a dumped political bruiser was rebranded as a charmingly incompetent dad-dancer. This was a fitting spectacle, so Tony Hall, Director-General of the BBC, instructed us, to 'bring the nation together': in disbelief. United by the shared vision of robotic Salsa hoofing, we were prepared for a massive security upgrade in the vicinity of railway stations.

'Today,' the senior copper in the big hat explained, without winking, 'you will notice dozens of officers in high-visibility clothing handing out leaflets. Tomorrow you might not find a single uniform on the station concourse – but I can assure you, we *will* be watching. It might be that man in the long black coat. It might be a group of – hem – attractive young women at the coffee stall. It might be a solitary dog. *When you don't see us, we are there.* Our men have been trained to identify unusual patterns of behaviour around certain buildings, suspicious characters with digital devices standing too long in one place. We are aware.'

***

Grand-project burrowing makes the approach to Highbury & Islington station a matter of blind rushes and fence-hugging. I posed against a promotional hoarding masking the hole, the portrait of a stern yellow-tabard construction worker like an old Soviet hero given boy-band gloss. I hold up a copy of the *Evening Standard*. ROYAL LINE: CROSSRAIL NAMED IN HONOUR OF THE QUEEN. I feel like a kidnap victim or Isis captive making an execution video.

Highbury is alert to a Catalan invasion, the presence of Barcelona, who are challenging Arsenal in a Champions League group tie. Trudging down Offord Road, in the direction of Pentonville Prison, and the drones delivering tonight's ration of chemical pick-me-ups, we hear live groans from the Emirates Stadium – and, at the same time, view segments of the game through consecutive Islington windows. We stand for a few moments to appreciate the intricate patterns woven by pinball-men on a brilliant green lozenge in the electric night.

Up the ramp at Caledonian Road & Barnsbury, Andrew tries to engage a nightworker in the ticket office with football banter, news of the Arsenal score. He has more success with the drinkers outside a pub on Agar Grove.

The Kentish Town moon is a bellying kite threatened by planes that might be meteors. John Rogers tells us that he worked this patch, walking the gap between stations, Kentish Town West and Gospel Oak. Through his special nightvision eyes, we witness properties and dens visited by Russell Brand, snailtrails of expeditions undertaken with Will Self and Nick Papadimitriou. Wasn't Grafton Road, John reminisced, where Will located the death of one of his serial characters, Dr Shiva Mukti? Or was that another quack, another book?

Hunger barks. No time for a full Indian, leisurely service, Cobra beers – and not enough material gathered to fuel retrospective conversation. Like poor Ruth Ellis, up the hill at the Magdala, but without the gun, Andrew sweeps on a convulsive charge through a public house where it's far too late to bag a cheese sandwich. John and his camera are about to abandon us. The night is too cold. He is interior-nocturnal: the resting Leytonstone house, the faces and voices to be shaped for tomorrow's blog.

Now that my duncephone is back on, the calls start coming through from David Erdos. Hard to make him out above the steam and clatter of the kebab house, but he is persistent, clinically so. I met Erdos at a poetry event celebrating another nightwalker, David Gascoyne. Another Londoner who put his amphetamine-fuelled neurosis to good account. Gascoyne, like all of us, recalibrated his memory script to place himself in the crowd, in Cable Street or wherever, at the significant moment: in the Blackheath room when the Mass Observation project was launched, or the Surrealist Exhibition with Dalí and Dylan Thomas. 'The city's lack and mine are much the same.' He spoke of 'vagrant hope'. And how all great cities, the ones he had seen, become one. 'Big densely built-up area for a man to wander in / Should he have ceased to find shelter.'

The Gascoyne poem commissioned by the BBC's Third Programme, for broadcast in December 1955, was called *Night*

Thoughts. And like the more popular *Under Milk Wood*, this was a dream play, a nocturnal reverie, an 'encounter with silence'. The poet recalls his own nights wandering beside the Thames, imagining power stations as temples of some 'sacrificial rite'. The impulse, as in the expedition described by Will Self as an Afterword to Matthew Beaumont's *Nightwalking*, is always centrifugal: a jittery trudge through coshed suburbs to shake free of habit, then the fields, 'an open hillside'. There has to be: 'A public park space from which one looks down / Upon the mighty Nocturne of the Capital.' At this point of vantage, the pilgrim is somehow redeemed.

My Hampstead burger was related to no animal that walked this earth, no substance beyond scrapings from the sole of a shoe. Chips as in wood: curled chippings, off-cuts from a sawmill, macerated in linseed oil. The ruined wing of some horribly tortured chicken-thing is like a bite of deep-fried umbrella. Better, after squirting all the sachets of rancid mayonnaise, the plasma bags of ersatz tomato, to eat the polystyrene carton. Our digestive tubes have accepted a challenge that will take many London miles to break down. But David Erdos is still there, still hot. Still talking.

What is lovely about this night kitchen, far beyond the incidental food substitutes, is the grace with which the plates are served. The proprietor has a genuine calling. He is a missionary of the Heath fringes, running a late-night soup-kitchen for Gascoyne vagrants and random derelicts of no fixed abode. He smiles his saintly smile. And gifts us with complimentary fizzy drinks, sugar rushes to carry us over the Hampstead massif, the cabins and colonies of psychiatrists and anti-psychiatrists.

The faithful penitents of the burger chapel are lovely people too. They come in with nods and salutes. Do they think I'm a surgeon or an escaped patient from the Royal Free Hospital? This is where exhausted nurses, prostitutes between shifts, rambling junkies, take a break. And drop the regulated behaviour patterns of their professions for a sociable exchange over hot sweet tea and buttered slabs. We are not the connections they are waiting for, but it doesn't signify. Unlike the football men outside the pub and the workers guarding holes in the road, they have absolutely no curiosity about what we are doing or where we are going. All that is left outside. Left with the hogs tossing in their beds.

David Erdos is a compact package, inky haired, close-cropped and fast-talking, spinning names: a child of the northwest suburbs. He is writing producing performing and emailing by the yard. A restless particle. Reading viewing visiting. He wants to walk by my side, it doesn't matter *where*, to gather up the sentences for an online piece that might become print in a revived underground newspaper. I try to explain that my walks are ordinary, solitary. And silent. He persists, he batters me with repeated expressions of his extreme sensitivity to the fate of being a professional nuisance. I like him. Of course there are other walks that are strategic, collaborative. Like this one. It might be to our mutual benefit. David could become a character in the night, yeast to a flagging paragraph. A bridge between the burger hospice and the wilds of Willesden.

'Right, David. If you *must* have a pedestrian interview, fine. Tonight. 10.30pm. Outside Finchley Road & Frognal Overground station.'

'Ah! Yes!' he said. 'I'm just coming down with a heavy cold. Boils on the fundament. A new play to see and critique. Another time?'

But the calls keep coming, one every fifteen minutes. David is conflicted, he can't let it go. And, sure enough, the man is there, waiting patiently, as we approach. A scholar-hitman of the shadows in long grey business coat, blue-grey turtleneck. He is mouthy like Mick in *The Caretaker*. But smart and sensitive too. And he falls, im-mediately, into lockstep, bouncing, alongside one and then the other; so that, descending towards West Hampstead, we can no longer see where we are. David directs us through repeated disclaimers. He is not worthy of the task. Andrew becomes Davies with his Sidcup routines. And I am the brain-burnt mute, Aston. Fiddling with a screwdriver. And waiting to deliver the killer monologue.

'I had worried about interrupting the rhythm and flow not only of the night long walk… but also of their friendship, but both men were welcoming and as generous as you would wish and want them to be,' Erdos wrote in his report, entitled *Kensal Rising*. Of course we were. David was fresh content. Voice of place.

In his nice, well-mothered, Jewish fashion, Erdos has gifts for both of us. For Andrew, the script of Fellini's *Juliet of the Spirits*. And for me, the darker fare of Ingmar Bergman's *Serpent's Egg*, his tax-exile German film. 'Paranoia runs dementedly and tediously out of control in this *Grand Guignol* recreation of 1923 Berlin as a studio set,' said Jan Dawson in the *Time Out Film Guide*. Spot on.

Kensal Rise and the avenues of cemetery suburbs loomed on the western horizon. David talked of the burial ground where 'Pinter's personal silence is held.'

Not wanting to be left out of this bookish chat, Andrew swooped on a box of discarded stock still on the pavement after the protests around the closure of Kensal Rise Library. He chose a ballet girl romance, defaced it liberally in the spirit of Joe Orton, and doubled back at a brisk jog to post it through the letterbox of a sleeping friend in Bathurst Gardens. David saw the gesture as 'a true and touching manly sentiment'.

Erdos was game. The boil at his trouserline had rubbed raw with the miles of unlit houses, the disappearance of all other walkers, visible café life, pub life and football hysteria. The qualitative difference in the two Overground circuits, night to day, was palpable. When we set out towards the river on our clockwise circuit, we were coming fresh from sleep, our sluggish bed-senses were beginning to fire. The optimism of a new day was an extension of that body-to-body cycle of half-waking reverie, shared with a partner who stayed just where she was, before rolling across to settle in the warm, vacated indentation. At night, heavy-footed, responses running down, we were already sliding towards sleep. Or the denial of sleep. We were dreaming ourselves into London. 'Wilting areas of opaque obscurity,' David Gascoyne wrote. Brondesbury Park to Willesden Junction.

Matthew Beaumont told me that he was considering Gascoyne for a sequel to *Nightwalking*, provisionally titled *Midnight Sun*. The nightwalker is an insomniac whose blind wanderings are a 'metaphor for the crisis of Reason'. Gascoyne, hepped on Benzedrine, is a precursor to the thumb-twitchers of Olympicopolis; the addicted screensavers who doze in a pulsing ring of electronic devices, knowing that the world will not wait. It is bleeping its insect chorus as you snore. It is devouring its own resources. Somatic phantoms ripple across the railway map of London; dream-spectres jump from sleeper to sleeper, dragging trains of association and metaphor. District to district, infection is transmitted. The panic, the dread. The existential horror. The ghosts are talking back.

'Many's the night when I witness the hoi gloriously polloi-ing while I seek comfort in my singular tread,' David Erdos said. 'Listen to the future, now. Its bass notes are there in the past.'

A bitter future is encroaching on Willesden Junction and the hinterlands between railway and canal. Huge new development schemes for the west. In scratchy woods on the perimeter of the wilds of Wormwood Scrubs, we halt for lukewarm coffee from the thermos and a gargle of Spanish airport brandy. David does not partake. But he accepts a single communion square of Kendal Mint Cake. 'It tasted, not of victory, but of rejuvenation, not only of my small spirit, but of general possibility.'

Before we reach the Westway, we register our first cop car, parked and avoiding surveillance. The stilted highway is obedient to the accepted Ballard vision, but the planners have got it all wrong. Like commentators who employ the adjective – Ballardian – without reading the books.

A university campus slap on the road. Rolling screens of videos with sculpted faces looking vaguely like dead movie stars to divert motorists. A part-demolished media centre where art projections from North Africa illuminate the ruins: like the wrecked teeth of an Aleppo atrocity supervised by guerrilla film students.

Ballard hymned the Westway – speed now limited to 40 mph – as archaeology from a past that never was, Angkor Wat. 'A stone dream that will never awaken.' With no surveillance cameras. A fragment riding high, for three miles, above 'crowded nineteenth-century squares and grim stucco terraces'. Those squares, as we now observe, are deserted. Occupied terraces are coming down to make way for another culture quarter. A pseudo suburb. Where only construction workers are in residence.

We've had no talk with any such workers or figures of the night since Hampstead Heath. And they were indoors, smelling faintly of the street, of smoke and bodies. David has reached the limit of his self-allocated permissions. He will jump a night bus to Uxbridge. 'It was a rite of passage I hope I passed, if not at the time then in reflection… We peered over a railway bridge to gaze at the stabled mastodons of iron and rust. I felt the flame of happiness. I had bettered the darkness and my spirit has started to rise.'

Andrew crashes the Westfield mall at Shepherd's Bush. Lights are blazing in the sterile night, but there is nobody at home. If this retail labyrinth were a true city, it would never shut. The roofed and rainless avenue of street food from every culture would be available at all times. And to all cultures. Now there are only tired Balkan hygiene operatives on cherrypickers polishing the glass, scrubbing at *faux*-marble. Barging his way inside the vaulted atrium, Kötting shouts: 'You've missed a bit.'

David, who has been good company, is still apologising for his intrusion, as the bus, peopled by vacancies, pulls away. Maintenance crews with their heavy plant clog up the detours around the supermall. In their yellow overskins and hard hats, they are uninterested in conversation, or banter, ashamed to be found labouring in the still dead hours.

Now, all company dispersed. Streets of achieved silence. Now synchronised footfall. Now light sours and puddles around our swollen feet. Now we are carrying invisible corpse candles towards Brompton Cemetery. We are no longer talking, performing, sharing anecdotes. The stucco terraces, spurned by Ballard as a diseased pathology, are hollow, bereft of the communal ripple of swinish dream that followed us through North London. Frosted cliffs in multiple occupation by absentees.

The cemetery gates are locked. We find ourselves adrift, losing the railway thread, doubling back, risking useless circuits of echoing gulches between extinguished investments. There is nobody to put us right. My blisters, modest on the daylight circuit, now crop like mushrooms anticipating a new day. An Asian convenience store, backed against the cemetery, supplies cheap sticking-plasters and a necessary hit of Red Bull for Andrew. He drains a couple of cans and the light in his eyes comes back on like a transformed superhero.

Squatting on the kerb, I struggle to pull my boots off, to make an attempt at padding the worst of the damage. Out of nowhere, perhaps from the padlocked cemetery, a tall elegant black woman, a lamia from a superior class of sepulchre, appears at my shoulder. She gestures with an open hand. She sways towards the solidity of the wall, but does not touch it. She smiles. And passes through. I can hear her high heels ringing on the pavement, but she is not there.

The broad dark river. The moment on Battersea Bridge when we halt, shoulder to shoulder, to appreciate the ripples of reflected lights. The sense of a city willing itself into existence for another day.

We sat on a bench by St Mary's church, emptied the pink brandy flask, watched the Thames, and took the measure of what we had achieved and what lay ahead. In recent times, I had been reading nothing but Simenon. That was my nocturnal addiction. The formula worked so well: movement and stillness, punctuated by prodigious quantities of alcohol. Cool white country wines, beers, cognac – and disgusting liqueurs gulped down for strategic reasons. Maigret often walked the sleeping city. 'It's hard to believe he would have spent the night tramping around "just for the fun of it".' *Maigret's Dead Man*. Stalking and stopping, watching and waiting: centre to suburb, leftbank to right, river to zinc bar, and round again. Hour after tedious hour.

Andrew wanted to crap among the gravestones of the church where William Blake married Catherine Boucher, but thought better of it. He held on under a swollen moon. Staring at the Thames, he drifted into reverie, a vision from Hastings. Figures emerging from the water. 'I was sitting on a shelf, under the pier, in pouring rain, raging seas, when two utterly gorgeous naked nubiles braved the misbehaving waves with a bottle of brandy. They were knocked right over. Which sent them into fits of giggling hysteria. I could see myself blundering in to save them, when they crawled out, unaided, with just one small towel between them and the now empty bottle. I returned to the spot for three more nights, to no avail.'

This was Andrew's attempt to raise the temperature. And our spirits. But the very same thing had happened to me, years back, on one of my initial evenings on the coast. Close to the original St Leonard's pier, where pioneer showmen showed the first films in the town. I felt that my vision was a detached celluloid splinter, looping out there. My back fitted so comfortably to the seawall.

Two young women, one with notably red hair, walked with purpose down the left margin of the beach. They knew exactly what they were doing. They will never see this day again. The taller girl, the one I took for Russian or Polish, stripped, briskly. She marched into the sea. Her shorter, sturdier friend was already naked. Warning lights flashed on the western horizon. The tall one tumbled, lost her footing on the shingle. When they emerged, they rubbed each other down, dressed without talking, and passed where I was sitting in the shadows, and away along the promenade. Then other, hidden figures emerged, to come together, debating and discussing what they thought they had just seen. And how this place adapted so well to visitations.

I told Andrew about Matthew Beaumont's talk in the shop on Kingsland Road, a destination now more remote to us than Greenland. When Matthew was describing nightwalking as a resurrection, I thought he was saying: 'red erection'. Which conjured rushes of blood to counter the body's somatic slump into midnight hibernation. The first questioner from the bookshop audience said that he was frequently woken in the early hours, in the square where he lived, by birds imitating mobile phones.

We float through Brixton in a state of enchantment, avoiding the mistakes of the daylight circuit. Something substantial and mysterious is drawing us on. Approaching Denmark Hill, I trip over a twig, or black feather, and take a full–length fall: a weightless slowmotion dive into the paving slabs. Exhilaration. With no grazes, bruises, twists or collateral bumps. The ground is a rubber mat. And through the medium of this headlong plunge, the hospital appears.

Andrew recalls Marta, the Polish policewoman who saved his life on the Old Kent Road. They subsequently bonded. Bleeding out, traumatised, loaded with drugs, the accident victim was brought here in an ambulance to be reassembled from his constituent parts. And to begin the long slow road to recovery, the climb from the black hole.

On the first railway walk, we circled this building, musing on the way that King's College Hospital dominated the hill. Now, clammy with night and loaded with bulging rucksacks, we tipped straight through the automatic doors, so that Andrew could avail himself of the excellent toilet facilities. After which, massively eased, spruced, disinfected, we wander corridors like the battlements of Elsinore, swimming through CCTV footage of deserted halls and fretfully drowsing wards of drugged pain. And we went unchallenged for an exhaustive tour of the history of Andrew's rescue and his subsequent health reviews.

We had entered from the west, in the folds of the night. We exited, as Andrew said, 'lighter and vaguely refreshed', on the eastern side, in a daze of anticipation ahead of the rising sun. The hedges and houses were recovering their firm outlines. Andrew, clipping a GoPro camera to his forehead, became a recording Cyclops, resurrected and red-erectioned for the downhill surge towards his essential memory grounds.

My Nokia duncephone shrills its dawn chorus like a bird in the pocket. Anna is horrified to find we are *still* on the wrong side of the river, surfing Peckham Rye. Andrew speaks of his shotgun, a freshly dug grave somewhere in a forest in the Pyrenees. Bury me upright, he said, inside a tall tree.

I know that we're almost home when I see the latest notice in Bethnal Green: NO COFFEE STORED OVERNIGHT. Authentic East London artisans, in the days of build and bodge, were concerned about tool kits left in the van. Now ram-raiders have their predatory eyes on the barista game: coffee is the new gold. Anna told me, on the phone, that she was shocked by a radio report talking about bands of 'feral urchins' terrorising estates. Kids of the age she used to teach are hardened drug mules. 'Feral urchins' was lifted straight out of *Oliver Twist*. Dickens relocated his criminous rookeries from the heart of Whitechapel to Saffron Hill.

To my overstimulated senses, this home stretch is as hysterical as the slowburn high of a chunk of enriched cannabis--resin chocolate cake. Language has been terminally perverted. A series of 'designated smoking areas' leads to a corridor of capitalised oxymorons on the approach to Shoreditch station. FREE CASH... IMPERIAL EQUITY... CITY SHEEPSKINS... RESPONSIBLE GAMBLING... TAPAS REVOLUTION... PROPER HAMBURGER... SAINSBURY'S LOCAL: outside which, as ever, a square of pavement is warmed by a humble beggar. A fellow nightwalker, bristling of beard, dribbling with rage, exposed to the harshness of the new day, punches his companion as she tries to move away from him. 'I'm *doing* that, you fucking cow. I'm doing that. I'm fucking *doing* that.'

★★★

The ultimate detour is to Haggerston Park – where, as predicted, the Vegetative Buddha incubates a bench. We have rushed headlong at the city. He is slumped, retracted. Alone. He enjoys the benediction of virgin light playing across the slick green grass. He pulls his hood down over his eyes. Andrew, GoPro blinking, makes a pass. And both men, according to their means, are undone.

'Too frightful,' Andrew said. 'My mind was awash with bigoted misunderstanding. I became sadder than ever. I wandered past this human wreck, pondering his stench, the inflamed legs and ill-fitting shoes. A kind of sleeping sickness was holding him together. One last London exhalation of breath: 10.48am and time for bed.'

Rested, scoured, coffee-fired, I return to the park: our man has gone. *He is never seen again.* I was uneasy about his transubstantiation into film, into a written narrative. The Vegetative Buddha set me moving towards the stained-glass window of St Leonard, but these chains of poverty and mental distress were real. And they were not broken. The man was never a myth. His biography is untouched.

I admired the way that Will Self got his own nightwalk out of London, Stockwell to the North Downs, done and dusted – adventures, mishaps – in three pages. 'Dawn winkled us out of the woodland,' he wrote, 'and we found ourselves blinking by the lych-gate of St Leonard's Church, a little thirteenth-century gem tucked away on the outskirts of Warlingham.' Self had, inadvertently, identified the alignment between Haggerston Park and the coast. We had dropped the Buddha's desire line much too soon.

GUMMED EYES

'A lamp which is near its death-hour.'
EA Poe

Whenever I am asked about the *flâneuse*, I think of Effie Paleologou. In that tragic pause, questions being solicited at the end of a talk or reading, roving microphone manhandled like a dubious sex toy towards the woman with the upraised arm in the back row, I know just what is coming. Sometimes from a visiting American researcher, brandishing Rebecca Solnit or Lauren Elkin, sometimes from a native-born academic, a practitioner suddenly struck by the originality of her challenge: 'Why are there no women on your walks?' The tone might be forgiving, query put more in sorrow than in anger. Or it might be regally dismissive of everything that has gone before: no women, no validity to your report. Prejudiced, misogynist, inconsequential: *nailed*.

There is no defence. It's not worth trying, though I sometimes do, to list the women who have informed the journeys I describe. If you look hard enough, they are there; but, most of the time, I'm caught with the same crew of tramping males, painters, filmmakers, photographers and writers (not so many of them), taking time out. And then, from a certain perspective, it does look decadent. Indulgent. Colonialising the environment and the lives of others. The act is made for pleasure, the enrichment of the senses. And I don't see, even now, too much wrong with that. London walks do not aspire to the pan-European seriousness that Effie Paleologou, for example, brings to her stalking of the image: in cities, along the shore, through liminal places.

Many of my expeditions, over fifty years, have been made in company with my wife, with Anna. Courtship, companionship: seeing new things through her eyes. Gardens, people, clothes, our own past. A conversation achieved through comfortable silences.

When I talked about *Black Apples of Gower* in Cardiff, always an uneasy return for me, never knowing who might hold up a hand, the first question did take me by surprise. It was a good one. I had been banging on about carboniferous limestone pavements, the inhuman power of the rocks, and how, walking from Port Eynon to Rhossili, I abdicated all sense of self: there was no self to stand against the facts of geology. Hackney walks confirmed identity, I was recognised and tolerated by familiar markers. In Wales, I dissolved into the place through which I moved.

'I was interested in what you say. But can you tell me, this book is essentially a love letter to your wife?'

And it was. A letter which I had to write, but she didn't have to read. That's how it worked. There is no obligation to confirm the complete catalogue of those who walk beside you, or those who are you. The voices, the borrowed and subverted memories.

Effie came to London from Athens, Paris, New York, already fired by her reading of Walter Benjamin. She found her project in walking at night around the purlieus of railway stations and points of transit. There was a Sebaldian colour to the enterprise, well ahead of *Austerlitz* – a book that she, in some ways, attempted to illustrate before it existed. Her photographs, usually taken at a time when travellers are most vulnerable, most abandoned to the city, were in translation. Like Sebald's highly crafted prose. They were *of* England, but not English. They were London. Which is very different. London is multi-tongued, urgent. Cruel. London is everywhere, wide open: exploited and exploiting.

Liverpool Street station was the heart of Effie's pictorial essay: fugitive faces framed in window panels on Underground trains and late-night buses. Even those who live here, quite legitimately, look like paperless migrants. The waiting. The stretched hours. The achieved photographic capture is made in competition with a burgeoning net of high-angle surveillance cameras. And then the drifting away into the first places where immigrants would settle: blocks of austere flats viewed from a certain distance, the ring of sodium lights around an artificial football pitch.

Effie was securing her images and carrying them home for meticulous processing into prints that could be exhibited or catalogued. But she avoided direct confrontation. She kept her own identity, as photographer/recorder, out of the story. The anecdotes of misadventure, with discretion, were reserved for her friends. London values, but never rewards, anonymity. Effie explored the existential crisis in what she called 'the secret life of cities after dark'. She honed the neurotic rasp of concentration brought about by circumnavigating districts lit by the flare of imminent threat. She avoided the crowd, the monad, and waited for the sets to empty. Her sensibility was theatrical.

Benjamin, Baudelaire and Henry James were cited. Effie spoke about the *flâneur* as a person, a man, who discovered the city 'through desultory wandering and a trajectory which catches the transitoriness and ephemerality'. James would be the odd one out in that group, a confirmation of Paleologou's wide and informed reading among the classics, European and American. The meandering Jamesian sentence, with its internal logic and feline thrust, was an established part of the Greek photographer's practice: her nocturnal circuits. A feeling for the architecture of James only came to me when I strolled around his Lamb House garden: the pets' cemetery, the safe distance from a lit window, and the the high wall, the screen of trees separating him from the inquisitive toy-town of Rye. One breath taken. Sit on a bench. Wait. Sigh. Yawn. Compose. Revise.

I heard about Hastings at night, Effie's commission to produce the work published as *The Front* (2000). But this is not Martin Parr: no celebration of performative Englishness, candyfloss quiddity, arcade baroque, uncorseted excursionism, pre-Brexit breakfasts, amusing dogs, fun-fair tattoos. The melancholy mob at the shoreline are putting on time until they are allowed to go home. Significant moments, stopped motion. Effie *moves*. In such a small town, she is exposed and no longer invisible. They watch her, even as they drink around a fire. The lurkers on the beach ask about the expensive camera kit. They might have tracked her from the station. The mad old ladies with dolls in prams pass her in the narrow streets. She has to brave the subterranean facilities of night cafés. None of these incidents, the signs and scrawls and odours and chat, particular to this place, make it into her essential portfolio.

That is the purity of the *flâneuse*: yellow light leaks on a desert of pebbles. The infinitesimal pinprick of the lamp on a nightfishing boat, out in the bay. A stump of fallen tree looking like a hand broken from a giant statue. Real grass lurid as a pool table. Not one whisper in this drugged ghost town from a living, working, wandering human.

Or so I thought. Anna, examining a print that could have been a production still for Beckett's *Happy Days* – reddish gravel or atomic dust, a flattened dune, with broken ladder and bundle of rags – disagreed. She remembered a talk that Effie delivered when she processed a small group of art fanciers around the locations where she made her captures. Anna said that the bundle of rags, that shaggy black lump at the edge of the darkness, the drop edge of yonder, was Effie. Hooded, disguised, dug in. Shapeless and sexless within the rectangular frame.

Mysterious grey-white forms, like aerial photographs of a bombed city, or ruinously deformed eyeballs held against a sunless sky, appeared on huge hoardings in the development zone around London Bridge station. It was impossible to imagine what product they could be advertising. Except art. The universal fixative for the fallout from a brave project such as the Shard, with its satellite rail and retail parasites.

Until the area around the decommissioned Royal Docks in Silvertown, that sliver of land between the City Airport, the DLR tracks and open water, is confirmed as a Xerox Shanghai, Chinese investors are making do with views from the Shard; a riverscape of future enterprise more fantastic than the Olympic rebranding of

Beijing. Sax Rohmer's racist tales of opium dens in Limehouse and Fu-Manchu's global conspiracies are being revenged by London's cringing solicitation of Chinese wealth and energy. New cities within cities, deregulated, will test the metaphors buried within Sax Rohmer and other sensationalist railway shockers from the last days of the British Empire.

The vampire green of traffic lights washed the giant London Bridge hoardings with a gothic varnish, before being blooded again. Several pedestrians, manoeuvring to get the most effective iPhone steal from these enigmatic lunar advertisements, came close to being obliterated by a sneaky and ill-conceived cycle lane.

I was making my way towards a meeting with the photographer responsible for the hoardings, for those gummy eyeballs, the dead grey planets. Effie Paleologou was discussing her work in the chapel at Guy's Hospital. The old London teaching hospital was establishing a Science Gallery where art and science would 'collide': CONNECTING ART, SCIENCE & HEALTH INNOVATIONS IN THE HEART OF THE CITY. A small post-truth exaggeration, from the wrong side of the river, well beyond the City walls, plastered across fences.

It was the night of All Soul's Day, 3rd November, and we would follow a Requiem Mass into the chapel. *Agnus Dei, qui tollis peccata mundi, Miserere nobis. Agnus Dei, qui tollis peccata mundi, Miserere nobis. Agnus Dei, qui tollis peccata mundi, dona nobis pacem.*

Taking her son to school, venturing through Bethnal Green, going about her business, daily journeys, Old Street, Liverpool Street station, Effie walked with purpose. And she noticed how the places where she was forced to wait, put on time, were saturated with patterns of expelled chewing gum. She was no longer a stalker, she was a stopper. She logged the discriminations of gum with the rigour of a research scientist. She used macro-lenses to inflate the microcosm of splat, stiffened boils ridging the tarmac. Like bits of the inside of a cheek, chewed and expectorated. She bent to the fertile dirt. She was no longer anonymous. She had stopped moving, standing in the shadows, losing herself in the crowd. She was now the spectacle:

woman as police officer, council snoop or location hunter. An obstacle, something to be stepped around. While she stooped to her task. 'The aesthetics of the insignificant,' she called it.

The flat world of our city pavements, disregarded by most pedestrians, is revealed, under the obsessive scrutiny of Paleologou, as significant terrain. A carpet of ill-fitting stone slabs, decorated with fast-food detritus, becomes part of the curvature of the universe. The slightest scars – heel scratches, bicycle tracks, spilled blood, yesterday's vomit, sodden leaves embedded in cracks, ice damage – register a pathology that the qualified witness records and exposes.

One of Effie's defining gifts is the ability to work from wherever life chooses to locate her. Or wherever, on impulse, she chooses to locate her life. In the case of the chewing-gum series – *Microcosms, 2014* – the geographical limits the photographer decided to impose formed an occult triangle, lines of attraction and repulsion, between three stations: Bethnal Green, Old Street, Liverpool Street. Each of these active hubs had a freighted back-story. Bethnal Green: a wartime disaster with panicked crowds crushed on the stairs. Liverpool Street: a railway cathedral supported by carbonised columns like an iron forest, where involuntary exiles like Joseph Merrick, the Elephant Man, returned to London. Or where *Kindertransport* trains delivered so many future orphans. WG Sebald, arriving at Liverpool Street from Norwich, took to these streets in quest of postcards and memory-prompts that he could infiltrate into the crafted pages of his documentary fiction. The German poet used photographs to authenticate events that never quite happened. Paleologou speaks about uncovering an 'arbitrary cartography', points of arrival and departure. She is hunting for incidents or materials capable of sustaining her anonymity and, at the same time, confirming the only qualification that will permit her continued London residence: the accumulation of recorded detail making a new map of an old place.

The prints based on that humblest and most intimate metropolitan pestilence, chewing gum, forge a metaphorical connection, worthy of Bataille, between the bulging pregnancy of the glob on the pavement and the blood–veined eye of the observer. It was a brilliant notion: instead of cataloguing, in the traditional fashion of the dandified *flanêur*, shop windows, hats, shoes, advertisements, Effie kept her steady gaze on the unscrolled *mappa mundi* of the London pavement. A monochrome carpet of transience fouled by fossils of gum in patterns like an early star map. As above, so below. There was magic to this exercise. Repetition was part of its charm. From the black spots – in which so much could be read – we can imply a stupendous range of human intercourse.

There is a sexual tenderness in Effie's album of oral rejects. Dry mouths have been salved by the sugary-sweet coating around a capsule of rubber. The stain on the pavement is the DNA of a passing stranger who is now brought inside, into the domestic cell of the studio, by the intimate processes of the darkroom. Paleologou compares gum–chewing to eating and kissing. But here is an oral transaction with no nutritional value. Gum is anti–food. It mimics foreplay – nibble, suck, bite – but must not be swallowed. To swallow would be to choke. Gum is prophylactic, a shield against human breath, taste, life. Gum is a wartime US import, a gift of cultural imperialism, thrown from the invader's tank to the outstretched hands of children. Expanding pink balloons, puffed from lipsticked Lolita mouths, are unscripted speech bubbles from the Trumpist comic of the world.

What is beautiful is the poetry of reduction that Paleologou imposes on her quest. From her archaeological record of the density of gum sightings, the photographer conjures a narrative of spectral crowds 'forming random constellations as if in a parallel universe'. But the suspect act of photography is never enough. She kneels in the dirt, like a supplicant, a local historian making brass rubbings, to put paper over the sticky traces, to rub them with a pencil. This is an affectionate engagement with 'viral colonies of debris'. It makes no difference if we are seeing these pinpricks as glimmers of million–year–old light from deep space, printed from a telescope, or a pulsing cancer cell enlarged on a slide under a microscope. The fissures are geological.

Effie's images are contemporary in their desperation to reanimate the city by recording its most disposable but enduring detritus. And pre-modern, in the medieval philosophy of humours, in metamorphosis and alchemy. The prints defy category and date of origin. They are Victorian: hinting at the birth of photography, the death of fundamentalist Christianity, the beginnings of psychoanalysis.

It is not part of the official trajectory of the project, but Effie's image trail leads straight to the gravestone of William Blake in Bunhill Fields. Visitors, sitting on a bench under a drooping fig tree, contemplate the enormity of the poet's residual presence in London. And they spit out gum. The coins, placed every day in tribute on the lip of the gravestone, leave rusty traces. The stone is smoothed by exposure to sunlight and acid rain. Paleologou sees her retrievals as part of an established tradition. A tradition of accidental collaboration between attentive artist and the legions of ordinary citizens going about the business of survival. 'I question not my Corporeal or Vegetative Eye,' said Blake, 'any more than I would Question a Window concerning Sight. I look thro' it and not with it.'

After the event in the chapel, Effie walked me to the colonnade of the hospital, where a selection of her prints were displayed: moons, deserts, laboratory specimens. All derived from chewing gum. The photographer was eager to present her work as part of a triangulation with the oval tablet recording that short spell, 1941–42, when Ludwig Wittgenstein 'worked incognito at Guy's Hospital Pharmacy as Drugs Porter and Ointment Maker', and the unfortunate bronze effigy of John Keats, failed medical student, in one of the stone igloos rescued from old London Bridge.

Before catching a 149 bus at London Bridge station, I marvelled again at the way gum had been made into art, into advertisement, and how the subtlety of Effie's expanded images was barely noticed in the noise of the place. The night-smudged tower of the Shard broadcast its acoustic pulse into the fretful station concourse, where late travellers were talking to themselves, shouting at their hands.

SHE'S GOING TO BECOME A SPORTS MISTRESS. THAT'S THE ONLY FACT I KNOW ABOUT HER. IT'S NOT EXACTLY

ROCKET SURGERY. I SHOWED MY GIRLFRIEND THE
PICTURE OF YOU LYING NAKED ON THE FLOOR WITH
MONEY ALL OVER. YOU KNOW I DIDN'T SLEEP LAST
NIGHT. I REALLY HOPE SHE DOESN'T COME. SHE'S NOT
ON EMAIL. AND ALSO SHE CAME TO THE PASSING OUT,
DIDN'T SHE? SO I SAID TO JEFF ALL I KNOW ABOUT
EMAILS, RIGHT? REFUNDS NEXT YEAR? OH SHIT.
BLOODY HELL. I DO SO KNOW WHAT YOU MEAN. WITH
AN IRISH ACCENT? CAN YOU IMAGINE? I SHOWED MY
GIRLFRIEND THE PICTURE OF YOU. WHEN THINGS GOT
REALLY, *REALLY* BAD, ON THE ADVICE OF A FRIEND, I
WENT TO SEE A ZEN MASTER. I TRIED TO TALK, TO
TELL HIM WHAT WAS GOING ON, OUT IN THE WORLD,
UP IN MY HEAD. AND HE STOPPED ME. SIT PERFECTLY
STILL IN A ROOM FOR A LONG TIME AND ALL POSSIBLE
VERSIONS OF YOURSELF WILL ARISE. WHAT TIME DID
YOU GET YOUR HAIR CUT? THAT'S THREE BEDTIMES
TO GET YOUR HAIR CUT. YOU'RE JUST *LYING*, YOU
DIDN'T PUT MONEY IN MY BANK ACCOUNT. CAN YOU
ORDER SOME PIZZA? I'M ON MY WAY HOME. CAN YOU
BE NICE TO YOUR DAUGHTER FOR ONCE? DON'T TALK
TO ME LIKE THAT. I DON'T HAVE MONEY. YOU *HAVE* TO
PAY IT. I WANT A MEXICAN BARBECUE. SHE'S NOT ON
EMAIL. EVERYONE'S REALLY INTO THAT AESTHETIC
NOW. EVERYTHING YOU DID I'VE SCANNED FOR THE
CARPENTER. BUSINESSWISE, I WENT TO THE MEETING
AND I RAN THE MEETING. MY DAD IS HELPING ME
WITH IT, LIKE GIVING ME A LOAN. WE'RE BOTH IN THE
MONEY, SO WHY DO YOU WANT TO CHANGE THAT
FOR? I SHOWED MY GIRLFRIEND THE PICTURE OF YOU.
REFUNDS NEXT YEAR. NAKED ON THE FLOOR WITH
MONEY ALL OVER. YOU KNOW THAT THING WHERE
YOU GET ANGER MANAGEMENT? I'M GOING THIS
THURSDAY. HOW MUCH IS THE SOUNDBITE? CHECK
WITH AMAZON. KNOW WHAT, HARLOW? I SHOULD HAVE

KEPT MY MOUTH CLOSED IN REGARD TO MONEY. 180 DAYS, HALF A YEAR. I'LL KEEP MY MOUTH SHUT NOW. PEOPLE START THINKING. IT COMES TO A FEW QUID. THEY AIN'T MY MATES, KNOW WHAT I MEAN? IT'S NOT ROCKET SURGERY. BASICALLY THEN IN REGARD TO YOURSELF, YOU ARE THE ONLY PERSON I CAN COUNT ON ONE HAND. I'M DOING TRAVELODGE, PREMIER INN. TOTALLY GOOD MONEY. HE GRABBED MY SHOULDER, KICKED MY LEG. NANCY, MY BUM! PLUS THE FACT I'VE GOT MY HEADSET ON, YEAH? PEOPLE DON'T NOTICE IT. THEY LOOK AT YOU LIKE YOU'RE OFF YOUR HEAD. THE DOOR WON'T CLOSE PROPERLY. IT WAS SHITTY BUT NOT 100%. WITH AN IRISH ACCENT? CAN YOU IMAGINE? FUCKING AMAZING. IT'S NOT REALLY A TERRORIST MATCH. IT'S MINOR AND SERIOUS OFFENCES. ALISON WILL TELL YOU ABOUT IT. HE'S BEING REALLY CAUTIOUS, UNDERSTANDABLY, WHERE HE'S COMING FROM. WE'LL GET THERE. I'M GIVING YOU THE GREEN LIGHT. JENNY SENT THE INVOICE. SO IT'S ALL GOOD. ALL'S WELL THAT ENDS WELL, I GUESS. I WAS REALLY MAD AT ONE POINT. WE'RE ALL ON THIS JOURNEY TOGETHER. WE GET ANGER MANAGEMENT. HOW MUCH IS THE SOUNDBITE? COMPLEX ISSUES OF HUMANITY VERSUS DESIGNER IN HOXTON. IT'S NOT ROCKET SURGERY. ORDER SOME PIZZA. CHECK WITH AMAZON.

When I saw the drowned photograph, I knew that Effie was the only person to make a record of it: her cool eye, her passion. Her appreciation of the cruel madness of the city as revealed through found objects and captured images, scanned and printed until they lose all recognisable features. Paper returning to bark. Recovering those patterns and grains. The *detail* in slime and grunge and spill.

Underground streams, lost rivers, culverted brooks: they were making themselves known, bursting through roads, overflowing drains, overwhelming Victorian sewage pipes and water mains. LONDON FLOODING MAYHEM. The front-page spread of the railway freesheet gloried in a long-anticipated vision of a city of canals. *After London*. If Effie had been covering the story of the Islington disaster, she'd have fixated on the way sodium light flatters rippling sludge in Charlton Place, as evening settles over the shuttered galleries, antique shops and underwear pantries. I could see the site of my former bookstall, the tables where Martin Stone unwrapped his treasures, in the sweep of a new brown river. 'A disaster movie with torrents of water flowing into the upmarket shopping and dining district around Camden Passage.' Rare seventeenth-century Chinese vases, Japanese prints – 'many worth tens of thousands of pounds' – carried away in a rush of dirty water.

In sympathy with the great disaster, I enjoyed a minor, more absurd challenge of my own: a leak under the bath drained into the storeroom where books and papers were stacked to the ceiling, and where a Marc Atkins print from the era of *Downriver* hung above the desk where I used to work. Anna referred to it, unkindly, as 'your Hitchcock silhouette'. The Hitchcock of *Frenzy*, I suppose. The body washed up on the mud. The malign return of the fat Leytonstone boy from Hollywood.

We had come down to the foreshore in Wapping from the steps beside the Town of Ramsgate pub. I was suited, puffing a cigar, Tower Bridge behind me – with no intimation of the coming Shard or City Hall. I suffered from a persistent nostalgia for that moment, an author portrait for the handsomely produced US edition of my novel. The one that disappeared with the editor, vanished without a trace. Marc's portrait, classical, frozen, was all that remained of walks undertaken, with journalists or academics, in attempts to bring the excesses of my grunge-baroque London fiction to ground. 'This is where… and over, on the south bank…' But it never was. And it never will be. And now the photograph was up to its neck in thick black sludge. The expansive gesture of my cigar arm: waving *and* drowning. Goodbye analogue London. Goodbye to all that.

I never considered an insurance claim, for photograph, poster, or storage box of unsold market stock. A lifetime of remainders and unwanted multiples. A library of orphans. My attitude to insurance was Greek: forget it. Accept the blows of fate with a good grace. You probably deserve them. But I did think that the defaced image on the wall, vegetally smeared inside and outside its black frame, was a neat illustration for the book on which I was labouring: *The Last London*. And then, curatorial instincts kicking in, I emailed Effie. Her photograph of the ruined print would be an artwork equal to, if not surpassing, the original. The smoker on the beach was being slowly choked in sewage like some horrendous colonic-irrigation accident. To a person the size of Orson Welles in those late fallow years of compulsive dining around spiked scripts.

On a bitter November morning, wrapped against the wind, Effie arrived with bags and tripod. As I'd suspected, she was excited by the organic nature of the destruction. 'It's alive!' She clawed the photograph from the wall, raging against the deadness of the light. I swung a bulb. She pondered. This was almost as good as the chewing gum. After her experiences in the lab as Guy's, she was eager to give my print the full forensic analysis. She would carry it away to her threatened London Fields studio. A suitable project for the last days, before the bulldozers moved it.

'Iain, this is *wonderful!* Wonderful.'

The shadow on the wall, where the photograph had hung for so many years, was now an impression of tubercular lungs, thick with corrosion. 'A damp-stain map', Effie christened it. A set of bloated fingerprints. We looked and looked again: the dome of the mosque on the harbour at Khaniá in Crete emerged. Effie was beside herself. This spoiled Thames portrait, relic of a time that never was, was set aside, while she pondered the revelations of the accidental fresco. The prophetic writing on the wall.

'Don't let Anna touch it!'

We were forbidden, absolutely, from painting over the gangrenous mould. That would be an act of vandalism. We were accredited keepers of a holy relic. Effie emailed, at irregular intervals, to be sure that we were aware of our responsibilities: no swabs, no whitewash. She was in the process of revising her academic papers on: *Landscapes within Landscapes, Arbitrary Cartography, Archetypical Forms (Morphology/Archaeology). Pleasure and Disgust.* Especially the last. She had a new name for her photograph of a photograph, the phantom left by the removal of the destroyed Marc Atkins print: *greyfield*. I found a pertinent quote in a novel by the crime-poet James Sallis.

'Greyfields, he called them, for the sea-like acres of cement parking lots, harking back to the design of old industrial sites on brownfields.'

Eager to know how Effie's greyfield alchemy was progressing, I took my morning walk through Haggerston Park, in the direction of her terraced Bethnal Green house. Would I be trapped in a Dorian Gray scenario? The mud disappearing from the print and poulticing my eyes instead.

He was back. As a reflex gesture, every time I head south down what I now call 'the St Leonard line', I glance across at the bench where the Vegetative Buddha used to sit. For several months, no one encroached on his space, or the map of human stains (as yet unrecorded by Effie Paleologou). Arranged in his characteristic boneless slump, the hooded man, a stone or two lighter, with a reduced buffer of plastic bags, was staring south. He had wriggled a few yards further to the west, towards the spiral stairs to the upper deck, where rough sleepers in employment, Russians and Poles, often bunked down.

I strolled alongside to take a closer look, excited by the notion that the mischief of the Kötting GoPro capture was undone. London would accommodate, once more, this living statue. *Who was now black*. Shapeshifted. Younger. More alert. More engaged. Able to get up and move on.

When Anna saw Kötting's footage, she said, 'Are you sure it isn't a woman?' I wasn't sure of anything in our elasticated city, every morning the landscape was revised. It wasn't just the identity of the sitter, the man's position was a confirmation of the validity of place. When the latest Haggerston supplicant left after a month or so, a day-for-night casual took his warmed spot, a man in a red Arsenal sleeping bag.

Between the Academy's plastic football pitches and the sawdust trail to the woods, a man in a black T-shirt and baggy tracksuit bottoms stood rigid on the winter path: shoeless. His trainers were displayed, vertically, against the base of a thin tree. He was staring up at some unnameable thing in the sky, a shimmer in the leaves. His eyes were stonewhite. What does he see? *Nothing*. The void. This man has gone, hollowed out. Deprogrammed. Beyond him, where the trees begin, they have planted a voodoo mask like the one I found on the walk to Croydon with Stephen Watts. A few words are scrawled in black on the mask: 'Psalms his way of life.' When a loud leaf-blowing machine encroaches, spasms run down the visionary's spine. He is possessed. He will never move until the bark covers him.

There are too many disappearances to record. The old woman in the low-level flats on Goldsmith's Row. She called out to me, every morning, from her open window: 'Sorry, dear, which day is it?' Words exchanged, contact. She vanished when the scaffolding went up, the renovations, and she never came back.

Haggerston Baths, as we always knew, would not reopen. One of the activists, Josune Iriondo, reported: 'We have heard today the shocking news that Hackney Council's plan to save Haggerston Pool in collaboration with an independent business partner has collapsed in disarray, leaving three bids for the site from developers, none of which includes a pool.'

Coming through Broadway Market, and stopping to see if the latest Maigret had arrived, I heard that the independent bookshop, translated here from Notting Hill, now faced closure, eviction, rent hikes, more customised flats. More bench bars with brick walls. When the owner made a bid for a vacant property on the other side of the road, she thought she had clinched it. But, at the last moment, she was gazumped.

'Can you tell me who topped you?' I said.

'A barber.'

'A *barber*?'

'A barber for beards. Very upmarket beards.'

What would the old villains – vanished, on permanent call to parrot their senile confessions for heritage TV – have to say? The barber. The tailor. The panelled breakfast café on Bethnal Green Road. Charity boxing. Fit lads. Great prospects. The business. Celebrity funerals.

Yesterday's criminals are giving nostalgia a bad name in the Carpenters Arms, down in Hare Marsh. Myself among them, for balance, an overview. We are drawn back yet again, sunlight blinding interviewees, to the Kray Twins pub where we filmed the dying embers of the fugitive book trade in 1992. And where we listened to Tony Lambrianou rehearse the last ride of Jack the Hat. His brother Chris, who went away with him for fifteen years, is still around. Nicely mannered, a gent. Warm greeting for me. Veterans together. One of the Queensbridge Road boys. What a Proustian wake.

Maureen Flanagan, described as 'Britain's most photographed model', lent this heavy-shouldered macho mob, the memory men and their minders, a bit of fragrant style. She welcomed me like an old friend, and was sure that we'd bump into each other in Hackney one day soon.

   The film crew were young and bored. Single set-up. Fixed camera. Knock it off. The heaviest presence, I thought, was the Southwark publican and freelance funeral arranger (by appointment), Freddie Foreman. The man vulgarly known as 'Brown Bread Fred'. I'd like to have told him how impressed I'd been by some of the bits his son, the actor Jamie Foreman, turned in. That toadlike venom. The narrowing eye ahead of eruption. Bill Sikes for Polanski. But I thought better of it. Freddie glowered in his anecdotage and confessed (within safe limits). He kept his back to me.

   When he'd gone, and the car had taken him out of it, across the river, the director put me in the picture. 'Freddie thought you were Old Bill. Sweeney. Says he can smell them a mile off.'

   What has happened to our chartered Hackney streets? Artisan bakers, hip estate agents and beard-sculptors to Broadway Market frontiersmen with polished shoes. The old hairdressers to the under-world aristocracy, often immigrants, are long gone. The one Turkish barber left from the bad times has put up cuttings to boast of a location fee from David Cronenberg's Russian mafia piece, *Eastern Promises*. Times change. Maureen Flanagan met the Twins when she did the hair of Violet, their beloved mum. Now she is an established author, ghosting her serial memories.

BREXIT MEANS BREXIT

Just as my pedestrian circumnavigation of London, by way of the M25, the orbital motorway, began here, and just as I obeyed the impulse to celebrate the millennial eve in an Indian restaurant where the customers were putting it away fast in order to get down to the Thames for the fireworks, my end was my beginning: Waltham Abbey. One day's walk from my Hackney house. Almost out of it, but not quite. Close to the Eleanor cross marking the homecoming of a dead queen. Close to the park from which Wren's Temple Bar had been removed, stone by stone, and banished to Paternoster Square. One day's ride for King Harold and his battle-weary housecarls and conscripted peasants, victorious in the north: slaughtered Vikings, slaughtered brother, repelled invaders. Let's give those economic migrants from across the *English* Channel a bloody nose. No time or inclination to regroup and formulate a comprehensive battle campaign. The route, abbey to abbey, bone pit to bone pit, was a pilgrimage of disgrace. A footmarch of resistant populism (the populace had no choice). A crusade before the crusades in tribute to the last English king. Battle means Battle. A hill of skulls. The cropping of crows happy to peck at meat from anywhere.

If, during the May Bank Holiday of 2016, in the lull before the great Euro plebiscite – and banks are never on holiday now, money can't stop churning around and around, leaking from screen to screen – you were taking the enriched air of the Lea Valley, rambling close to the line of zero longitude, you might have noticed a strung-out procession of carnivalesque time-travellers: Salvationists, Levellers, Hunger Marchers or fugitive outpatients from Matthew Allen's High Beach asylum in Epping Forest. Limping and strutting and chanting, they advance on the distant rumour of London, city of towers. This is an established one-day yomp.

So – rat–a–tat–tat – the drum is beaten. They pick up their steps. And it is not, as they are frequently asked, for charity. The march is unsponsored oblivion. Revenge. Superstition. If our feet bleed, we are virtuous. If we cover the ground in Harold's hoofprints, we must surely win the day. Are we undoing an historic English defeat or confirming it? The excursion will be just as successful as the earlier attempt, by Kötting and Sinclair, to ridicule the pretensions of media-inflated triumphalism by pedalling a fibreglass swan from Hastings to Hackney, by way of the emerging Olympic Park: the chains and helicopters and armed response units. The swan was named Edith in honour of King Harold's mistress, Edith Swan-Neck. Mother of his children. The woman immortalised by way of an obscure but affecting sculpture, in which she is cradling the mutilated king. A life-in-death embrace. On a cement plinth, beside a bowling green, in West St Leonards.

The renegade troupe at the start of this five-day walk are stubbled, face-painted like border transgressors. They are the beaters of invisible bounds bedizened in outlandish fancy dress that is becoming noticeably less fancy with every mile endured. Phone-cameras are buzzing around a limited field of action. What's it all about? A shared midlife crisis or some grim last-punt geriatric spasm? They are resurrected battlefield droppings from a site of infamous carnage. There seems to be no agreement among them on a framing narrative or the spirits they are trying to invoke, beyond the base requirement to push on. They lurch between displays of public narcissism and masochistic ecstasy as blisters pop like seed pods and ill-advised footwear squelches on permitted slipways between the claustrophobic madness of the forest and soft heritage England.

The procession, if it had been reassembled from surveillance drones for post-atrocity TV coverage, would provide clinching evidence for the VOTE LEAVE lobby.

This is how the gang musters:

An alpha male in gypsum facepaint: Andrew Kötting, chief convener in absurdity. He is stocky and bristling in a reindeer herdsman's ear-flapped felt helmet. His chosen role is bodyguard-bouncer to the buried king. The planks of his upper body, honed by openwater swims between Hastings Pier and Bulverhythe, protest against the confinement of the potato-sack suit he has chosen to wear. Pale cloth defaced with felt-tipped Enochian symbols. An antique Sebaldian rucksack has been bulked with food bombs and reeking tidbits from earlier expeditions. When the weather turns, he will wear a kneelength raincape over the tight jacket and shrinking trousers. To the susceptible along our route, sensibilities heightened in the crisis of public debate, here is a terrible vision of Taliban fundamentalism. Unruly tribes coming down from the mountains.

At Kötting's elbow is a young woman decked out like a newly jilted Miss Havisham, stoic with no great expectations. Call her Claudia Barton. As she moves off, swinging gracefully into her long stride, she becomes a shrouded houri. An interior female escaped into the world. Or a brave creature running from her fate, a *Woman in White* fallen among gypsies. Taken to the road with savages.

Claudia is a Memlinc madonna with the voice of Audrey Hepburn. She lifts up her skirts and skips in black Doc Marten boots. She dances in daisy meadows, runs at hills. Sometimes she sings with Croatian buskers in tiled underpasses. She is painted with arrows and roses. Her headband is trophied with stiff feathers and roadkill pelts. She takes her siestas in hollow tree trunks, quiet cemeteries and on railway tracks. Her bridal train is a dragnet sweeping up nests of field mice, broken twigs, mole droppings, quantities of sand, chalk, animal blood and filthy footprints. You could hang this garment, unlaundered, on a white gallery wall. And recover the entirety of the walk to the coast. 'Never will I succumb to Norman rule,' Claudia says, channelling Edith. 'The heathens are back amongst us. The world's a wicked place. And evil days have started.'

Because they are all musicians and poets with wildly disparate voices, like a shotgun orchestra thrown together in a Chilean prison to make songs of protest, they have no sense of direction, no steady politics, and no purpose beyond forming the sum of their imperfections. They dream of evening pubs and soft beds. The 'rabbit-light' of Wallace Stevens, in which, so it seems, 'everything is meant for you, and nothing need be explained'.

Nothing *can* be explained until it's too late. Done and dusted. Recorded. Reassembled. And reforgotten. Didn't Stevens compose his 'Invective against Swans'?

When our landlocked ship's orchestra faltered, disputing maps or facing headlong traffic on narrow country roads, they were driven forward by the steady drumbeat of a man dressed in a Guantánamo bodysuit that he had borrowed from a French hunter, who believed that this virulent orange disguise would deflect the bullets of other forest assassins. The drummer's name was David Aylward. As a registered percussionist, David tested every obstacle he encountered: perimeter fences, cattle-grids, live oaks, log piles. He interpreted the score of territory by way of earthworks, ley lines, family histories and ancestral deposits.

He was only too well aware, as he took the DLR train from Deptford Bridge to Waltham Abbey, that his 'agent-orange wild boar hunter's twin-set' was casting a dangerous glow over the packed carriage of sweating Canary Wharf commuters, as they jabbered into their devices. Aylward, a card-carrying suspect, was inspired by an eclectic range of influences: Master Musicians of Jajouka, Mississippi Swamp-style trance shamen, Lamberg drummers of Ulster and the Bronze Age battle-horns of Ireland.

David takes a well-deserved herbal hit from the deep bowl of his Sherlock Holmes briar. The drumming, as a summons to war, or recruitment in time of civil conflict, blocks out the drowsing VOTE LEAVE suburbs and estates. 'Playing the landscape,' Aylward says, 'while it plays me.'

The man beside him never stops smiling at the wonderful weirdness of it all: Jem Finer. He is said to operate in the interstices between pataphysics and mathematics. A slender gold ear-piercing, like a perversely planted wedding ring, refines folk melodies rescued from torched cornfields, where a very occasional Southern Rail train hums in transit. Finer is operating his 'sonic salvage system' by dragging a spiked rotating drum like an Essex golf cart or shopping trolley dressed with bent forks and flattened beer cans.

'*Fitzcarraldo* Ocado,' he calls it. The device is a recording instrument, a sound catcher, and an affectionately mocking reference to local leisure activities. 'An audiotronic aggregator of the flotsam offered up by the road.' The squeaking cart, in its resistance, reminds me of the splashy machine I used to drag across Hackney Marshes, to paint white lines on eighty-two football pitches.

At the end of the day's walk, while the other pilgrims are spread across the verge picking at their sores and tabletting non-essential emails, Jem is surveying the acoustic properties of the latest car park. In short black coat and beret, he's a Basque bomber measuring the height of curbstones against Euro regulations. The man's main task, it appears, is to stream the Beefheart song, *Ice Cream for Crow*, for a Joseph Beuys impressionist in a many-pocketed fisherman's waistcoat.

The photographer tasked with keeping a record of the expedition, by digital film and pinhole capture, goes by the name of Anonymous Bosch. He stalks the edge of the frame in a hat made from the lining of Kötting's felt helmet. Bosch is infinitely obliging, a person who is already halfway to becoming a camera. The technology is redundant. Hundreds of images impose a blurred dignity on the excesses of a Dadaist retreat in the general direction of France. An impotent gesture of homage to threatened cultural links.

Bosch, who came into the world as Anthony O'Donnell, limps in the wake of the action. He is invaluable, a confessor who is always on hand, to find spiritual truth in a portrait. When he lines up the road brigands, he looks like a friendly executioner, a potman from Preston, assisting his publican-employer, through a paying sideline in rope-based extermination. He is Bosch and Breughel. But his butchered feet force him to travel in the van, reading the country ahead and waiting for the walkers to drag themselves over the horizon.

Left to himself, Anthony catalogues those notices pinned to saplings and lampposts, advertising lost pets. And people. He gathers up scrumpled shopping lists in supermarkets. He keeps an album of seaside eccentrics: thereby measuring the range and speed of social exclusion from London, the failure of 'care in the community'. In earlier times, he lived in a tent, fell down a motorway manhole into a sewer, stiched a finger back on. He stays young and gluten-free. It is always his birthday tomorrow. And he is too modest to mention it.

As the scribe to the expedition, I am the person in the Joseph Beuys waistcoat, flapping trousers and funny hat. I have never had much interest in fat or felt. But I am inclined, in this company, to deliver sermons based on jackdaw readings and misremembered histories.

The familiar I have adopted for the journey is a crow called Odo, formerly Bishop of Bayeux (sponsor of the celebrated comic-strip tapestry) and half-brother to William the Bastard. Odo, after the Conquest, became Earl of Kent.

On the first day of our walk, the bird perched on King Harold's grave at Waltham Abbey, dowsing for rotten meat. Arriving at the

Olympic Park in twilight, his clawed feet dropped into the Lea and sunk without trace. Legless (in all senses), the ex-bishop thrusts his beak out of a black rucksack, Poe-cawing rubbish prophecies on the fate of England. The crow was shamed to be keeping company with such rowdy wheel-tappers, jongleurs and heretics. His thirst for Italian ice cream could never be satisfied. He scorned any connection with the apocalyptic cartoon talked up by Ted Hughes. 'Words came with Life Insurance policies,' the poet said. 'Crow feigned dead.'

It was a great thing, now, to find six people, Londoners and former Londoners pushed to the coast, prepared to walk for five hard days, bonded as a group, in a fugue of drumming, reminiscing, engaging with towpath cyclists, accompanying buskers in tunnels, debating with Polish policewomen, explaining the pilgrimage to kitchen workers outside Indian restaurants in railway towns, crossing Elizabethan parks, at a time when the soul of the city was in dispute. When London, in adapting itself to incomers, refugees, economic migrants (billionaires and impoverished), was breaking away, painfully, from the rest of the island. The capital had become an illuminated cruise ship, a floating casino for oligarchs, oil sheiks and multinational money-launderers; a vessel, holed at the waterline, staffed by invisibles on zero-hour contracts, collateral damage of war and famine and prurient news reports, huddled in lifeboats. 'Crow's toes gripped the wet pebbles.'

This walk, Waltham Abbey to Battle Abbey, was also a homecoming, a return to the marble effigy of slaughtered Harold and his eternal consort, Edith Swan-Neck, in West Marina Park, St Leonards-on-Sea. The forgotten artificer of this haunting relic, Charles Augustus William Wilkie, was, like Kötting, our own felt-capped Führer, an Anglo-German.

Here was the pitch: to process from the stone slab at Waltham Abbey that marked the location of the original high altar and, perhaps, the resting place of King Harold II's divided carcass, as gathered up, lovingly, ritualistically, by Edith Swan-Neck (in one of many versions of the story confabulated by winners and losers after the battle in 1066). To carry the touch of that stone, as directly as possible, to the alternative memorial slab in Battle Abbey (set down by order of the victor: William, Duke of Normandy). And then, in twilight's last gleaming, to the sculptural tableau: the entwined necrophile lovers in the sea-facing public park at the western edge of St Leonards. Across the road from the Chinese restaurant.

To what purpose? A short ramble, over stretches of the same ground, a hundred miles or so, to attain some pale afterglow of what was invested in the Saxon army's forced march to York and Stamford Bridge – and back, almost at once, to Waltham Abbey, Westminster Abbey, so they say, Rochester, Maidstone, Bodiam and along the ridge to Battle. To lock shields, brother to brother. Living and dead. To fight through the long day. To achieve a necessary defeat: corpse-stripping, crow feasts. 'Everything took the blame,' Ted Hughes said.

Our coast walkers, ahead and behind the event, were drunk with loss, severance. The release that comes with the conviction that the bad thing has happened. Will happen again. With worse to follow. So strike out, step up, beat the drum. England was made, not by its victories, its colonial plunder, slave wealth, chemical weapons, broken treaties, oil, wool, battleships, but by heroic defeats. Catastrophes, from the battles of Catraeth and Maldon to the Light Brigade, make for better poetry. In recent times, the writer and artist Kirsten Norrie, in the persona of MacGillivray, honours this tradition, the heady plunge into 'nutrient slaughter', with *The Nine of Diamonds*, a savage repost to Culloden, conjured from tarot cards. 'I stand behind a frozen waterfall,' MacGillivray said, 'comprised of universal blood.'

When Edith the swan pedalo was hurled back by raging October seas in Hastings, MacGillivray's keening stilled the waves. Later, she took to the English roads in the black velvet of John Clare's burnt muse, Mary Joyce. 'Blood makes me the ghost.' The colophon of her publisher, Bloodaxe Books, shows a helmeted Viking warrior, shield, axe and apron-skirt, rushing to annihilation.

VOTE STAY. Those Normans were not for turning. We launch our pilgrimage from a motorway zone occupied by retail-park adventurism and banishment estates, after the French fashion, *banlieus* for those who are no longer welcome in the centre, in the themed quarters and pseudo-villages of a hustling, digital economy. This benefit-trimmed demographic finds itself embedded alongside the tidy, working-class white folk who moved out to the forest fringes to escape their original inner-city incursions in the 1960s.

Claudia challenges the status of Edith as mistress. The woman is a queen. She is the mother of a brood of Harold's children. She is the *anima* validating a masculine legend. In the marble effigy on the concrete, wedding-cake anvil in St Leonards, the royal couple are a single entity. A serpentine, self-consuming *memento mori* riding a whitewashed carnival float in a never-ending Day of the Dead.

Edith, Claudia asserts, was Danish. Julian Rathbone, in his romance, *The Last English King*, has her coming out of Ireland. The brigand Harold, one of the Godwinson gang, after a bit of bother with Edward the Confessor, is exiled to his raider connections, the Danish settlement in Wexford, where Edith is the wife of a thegn. 'She remained what she had always been – Harold's mistress, his concubine.' This is harsh. Claudia repudiates such casually applied misogyny. It is Edith who holds the story together, just as she collects and reassembles the scattered body parts. The bits she recognises by certain private marks.

In the necessary purification of blood, Claudia sings. And covers the ground. 'Travelling only with men has its drawbacks,' she says, 'though they are good and brave and have also seen their fair share of blood, from the tales they have been telling me along route. After childbirth, little can shock me when it comes to blood and liquids that surge like oceans within us. Though I would rather take my chances amongst the first warriors in a doomed battle than find myself giving birth again.'

Facts, slippery at the start of the walk, are completely unhinged by the time the troop invade Battle Abbey. The momentum is with Edith, shroud wife, stitcher of body parts. Claudia Barton, who improvises song as the spirit takes her, is possessed by the mystery of ritual. She picks up the folds of her bridal gown and steps forth. The brute males roll and lumber in her slipstream.

'Shortly after the Battle of Hastings Eadgifu Swanneshais known as Edith Swan-Neck was brought to the field at Senlac by two priests of Waltham Abbey,' claimed the author Carol McGrath.

'It must be true. It's in the Domesday Book,' whispers Claudia. Her trump card. As if she had read it. Or written it.

This is her fairy story: an heiress with dowry of land, Edith the Rich. A wife hand-fasted according to Danish custom. Mother of six: Edith the Fair, bloodless, marble-white. Victim, after the bloody battle, of a burning house, as depicted in the Bayeux Tapestry. Perhaps, as they say, Edith did return to Ireland. Reverse immigration. VOTE LEAVE. Muzzled cloister-swan. Disobedient daughter of Christ. Pilgrimage-provoking saint: Lady of Walsingham.

It begins: a pedestrian expedition to tap out the Brexit boundaries of Nigel Farage's fag-puffing mead-hall England, before the fleet of benefit-scrounging cross-channel winos comes sailing into Pevensey Bay. As gangs of Albanian drug-trafficking white slavers are now reputed to be sneaking ashore on Romney Marsh, at Deal and Camber Sands, on their RIBs, kayaks and leaking air mattresses.

David, who has been drumming on the rims of barges and the concrete pillars of underpasses, on tyres and cylinders abandoned beneath the M25, turns his attention to bicycles. Out here alongside the reservoirs, where pylons stand proud, cyclists are not such a *tsunami* of self-righteous entitlement. They are spiky individualists with schemes of their own, affection for territory, and they are prepared to engage with Andrew's banter. Taking his violin bow from the huntsman's tote bag, David asks permission to play the spokes of bicycle wheels, to sound the tension. A melancholy drone solo to which Barton sometimes adds her plaintive voice in lament for the dead Harold.

One cyclist, Sean Sexton, who handed me a card announcing himself as a dealer in 'Early Cameras & Photographs', pulled up his red T-shirt to show off the scars of major surgery. The towpath was his lifeline, he said, as he upped his daily quota of miles, returning to health and strength and Pickett's Lock.

Within the stretches of the Lea Valley from which the Travellers, camped under flyovers and diving for scrap metal, have been expelled, along with the broken bivouacs of rough-sleepers, our ragged troubadour procession passed without comment – beyond the occasional herbal wave of acknowledgement from a pirate narrowboat. As we approached the spectacular unreality of the Queen Elizabeth Olympic Park, mirage structures appearing and disappearing before we could reach them, the peloton of commuting cyclists thickened. They were silent assassins, sweeping from behind, often with growls of resentment that mere pedestrians were body-blocking their favoured highway.

Olympicopolis, now that the barriers were down and the military returned to barracks, was a 'park' only in the sense of retail park or car park. Or theme park still to identify its theme and waiting on input from a content provider. With no great stretch of imagination, they christened the water margin: *Canalside*. Bars and burger warehouses and bright new hangars so adaptable that they seem to have slipped, unimpeded, from the CGI versions that used to be plastered across hostile blue fences. The Olympic Park was provisional, like a promised Eden that might be withdrawn in an instant and returned to mounds of landfill.

'Canalside is the place to be on Queen Elizabeth Olympic Park. Set among green spaces and wild flowers on Here East's stretch of the Lea River, Canalside offers an eclectic mix of independent restaurants and retailers.' As, for example: MOTHER (a place where you can hang out, feel good and eat well… as all our ingredients are sourced locally). THE BICYCLE MAN (everything for the urban rider). RANDY'S WING BAR (established as a pop-up in a pub in Hackney). GOTTO (a slice of the Italian Riviera on Canalside Hackney Wick).

Everything is pop-up. Nothing is true. The fables are authorless and generic, finessed by computer programmes. Boasted green spaces are the conceptual green of plastic football carpets. Wild flowers are currently unavailable. A patch of scorched earth has been fenced off: 'Sorry, we are closed right now. We are busy growing new plants ready for you to enjoy.' Locally sourced fish and edible beasts are keeping well out of it.

Meanwhile, private security guards on electrified buggies, observing our antics through binoculars, can't decide which offences we are committing. They let us continue, unmolested.

Our disorientation was confirmed, shortly after my return from the walk, by a report from the London Ambulance Service on the shameful incident when a 60-year-old recreational cyclist at the Velodrome suffered cardiac arrest and died before paramedics could reach him. Two emergency ambulances and a rapid-response vehicle were hopelessly confused when their sat-navs failed.

'The access to E20 Olympic Park (in particular the Velodrome) is difficult, especially for crew not used to the area,' said the report. There was something of a history here. Hours after Sir Bradley Wiggins, with his history of perfectly legal drug exemption certificates, thrilled the nation by winning another gold medal at the time trial in 2012, Dan Harris, a 28-year-old internet consultant on a racing bike, was killed after being dragged under an Olympic bus within the shadow of the Velodrome.

When we came alongside the illuminated hulk of the former Olympic Stadium, the hollow bowl we must learn to call 'London Stadium', it was evident that the expensive (to us) rebrand had not taken: we were in the presence of the Death Star. An alien invader capable of destroying life as we know it. The karma of the transfer of West Ham United, a club founded by ironworkers at the mouth of the Lea, to this soulless and unsuitable environment, came with a catastrophic loss of form, crowd troubles and an overspill of resentment when thirsty and aggrieved football crowds crashed the locally-sourced artisan breweries and smoke-houses of Canalside, Hackney Wick. London Stadium means London Stadium – until a lucrative naming rights deal can be achieved by Karen Brady, the sorceror's apprentice. The new club crest has to incorporate the word *London*.

Olympicopolis is the new capital: a city divided into two hemispheres, two Westfield supermalls. A city of pop-ups, naming rights, committee-bodged artworks, cash-cow academies, post-truth blogs and charity runs. And government pay-offs to the right sort of private enterprise. The bill for this disastrous stadium conversion stands at £323 million. And rising. Without the fix, waved through by Boris Johnson, the original cost of £752 million would never have been agreed.

'So it has come at last – the Distinguished Thing,' I said. Meaning the shadow of death in the room for Henry James. Fallen to the floor, James heard a voice that was not his own. Olympicopolis was my own distinguished thing: the latest and last London. Beyond this point, there is nothing left but naming rights for ghost towns. A railway city divided against itself: Stratford in the east and White City to Willesden in the west. Brownfield wilderness to conflicted Eden. We were not marching like Harold and his troops *into* London, we were leaving it behind, the emerging digital conceit on the Viking bank of the River Lea. There were no abbeys, palaces, hospitals or madhouses. Olympicopolis was a curtain of fog on which anything could be projected. When our coastal walk was completed, I vowed to return for a tour of inspection. I had avoided the area in the years after the 2012 Olympics; it was time for another circuit.

My hunch was that the Queen Elizabeth Olympic Park was the checkmate in a long game initiated by Margaret Thatcher's tyranny of the suburbs: the unmaking of local governance, the emasculating of councils, the deregulating of financial markets and the scrapping of planning controls. The old centre was hollow, occupied by remote profit harvesters. The river was prostituted to tourists, implanted with vanity towers and helicopter obstacles.

Olympicopolis has been constructed in a style they call 'New London Vernacular': biscuit-coloured brickwork for airport-sliproad blocks admitting to no confirmed function. The most revealing shift in status is the promotion from Zone 3 to Zone 2 in the transport map. Property values soar. Established art brands – Victoria & Albert Museum, Sadler's Wells, the Smithsonian Institute – are parachuted in, or courted with sweetheart deals. Property speculators butter the map with bucolic claims and riparian associations: Manhattan Loft

Gardens, Stratford Riverside, Glasshouse Gardens, Neptune Wharf. Get in early. Get in often. 'Prices start at £615,000.' And finish in meltdown.

The former Olympic media centre, now known as Here East, is the cornerstone for the translation of a mixed economy of small businesses, grubby trades, warehouse artists and squatters, allotment gardeners to an aspirational park glorying in display and disguise. The view from a 'Manhattan' loft. A post-industrial grid calling itself the 'East Village': 'an emergent hub, an eco-friendly and sustainable neighbourhood'. With no visible neighbours. 'A green haven in the middle of one of the world's largest cities, with an emphasis on nurturing the natural environment.'

Cafés, eateries, gyms, cycle shops, teeth-whitening salons, beard barbers and mailbox services. A prestige address in a place where ambulances will never find you. Should you want to navigate the mysteries of Here East's terminal architecture, you are issued with an orange booklet; hip design features offering instruction in 'Atrium Wayfaring'. And counter-intuitive journeying. The maps are based on electrical circuit language and they work perfectly: they look beautiful and they are inscrutable. Every element of the building is a metaphor. The toilets, if you find them, are capicitators capable of temporary storage for electricity. 'They charge to a pre-determined level and then 'flush' themselves when full.' Visitors are still required to provide the content around which the device will operate.

It was a dream landscape when I made a slow circuit of the Olympic Park in the aftermath of our walk, a posthumous dream. I couldn't convince myself that I was really here. The panoramic sweep, that Sunday morning, was a single sentence, outside time and beyond place. I put it down to fatigue, boredom, frustration: a flash forward to a future that could manage very well without me.

The entrance, by way of Hackney Wick, came through sentimental corridors of squalor I no longer trusted; protest copywriting and spray-can obscenities approved by counter-narrative committees charged with dressing a small zone of the right sort of opposition, in order to make East Village and Canalside edgier and more authentic. The borderland bushes and concrete vaults under flyovers showed the usual signs of occupation, flattened shrubs, tunnels into the thorn, cans and blue bags rammed into mesh fences. Among the devils' heads and wolf-serpent nightmares, the Aitch Group have a loud pitch to make: MORE LAND REQUIRED.

The Lord Napier pub is an anarchist artwork: SHITHOUSE TO PENTHOUSE. MEANWHILE IN EAST LONDON, LUNATICS DECORATE THE BUILDING. The walls are sticky Rauschenberg composites: overlays, tattered advertisements, household paint, lumps, growths, found objects. The neighbouring building, offering household products, has a punt at blue-plaque heritage: ZAMO HAS BEEN IN THE WICK SINCE 1960, A THIRD GENERATION FIRM. BUSINESS NAMED AFTER THE FAMILY'S PRIZEWINNING GREYHOUND.

I step back to allow a focused jogger in a TALK WITH YOUR FEET vest free passage. On the wall behind him, it says: 9/11 FIFTEEN YEARS OF LIES.

The Olympic Park is a game reserve, lacking beasts as yet, but awe-inspiring in its privileged emptiness. Miles of unoccupied concrete floor at Here East, enough for regiments of rough-sleepers. Helicopters overhead. Flight path tourism. Downward-staring surveillance cameras are postmodern design features, black and corvine, on the rim of generic hangars. Beyond some lazy, golf-cart security, there is nobody about. On a pre-rusted steel overpass, two young Chinese women in Santa Claus outfits are arguing over the coolest backdrop for a selfie. The borders of the park are trimmed in orange. CONSTRUCTION IS A CAREER LIKE NO OTHER. Rectangular tubs of spidery grasses are reflected deep into the darkness of blandly sinister buildings.

Cycle lanes are cancelled for upgrades. Pedestrians are ordered to stand back to allow the morning's Dame Kelly Holmes charity half-marathon to thread through interweaving levels of road, pedestrian paths, canal. Flagging runners are encouraged by men dressed as bears, turning up the sound for Eartha Kitt's *Santa Baby*. Yuletide favourites boom over bitumen meadows: the stream of cars heading to Westfield, the emerging crop of investment flats, the red cranes, the anvil-dunes of remediated soil, the shuttered concession stalls and the scarlet ArcelorMittal Orbit with its viewing platform and screaming silver tubes.

The vision — blighted Eden, radiant hub — was awe-inspiring in the style of a cross-section diagram in an improving boys' comic from my childhood in the 1950s: canal with cyclists and joggers, scattered statement buildings too new to be used, polished roads, retail village, casino, breakfast bars, residential towers, muckheaps, public art, perpetual construction, helicopters, drones, shuttling trains, huge skies. But the sight that had me laughing out loud was the rank of pristine swan pedalos parked on a stretch of river staring straight at Westfield. Poor Edith! It seems that our absurdist voyage, crashing a Hastings pedalo against the chains of the emerging park, had been neatly subverted, in the four years between the Stratford and Rio Olympics, from provocation to inspiration for the latest promotional gimmick. The entire working model for the regeneration project — ArcelorMittal helter-skelter, swan pedalo ride — was a straight steal from the Flamingo Amusement Park in Hastings. Our liberated swan, consorting with vagrants, river rats, Alan Moore and Stewart Lee, was now available as one of the park's main visitor attractions.

I ran. I barged through ribbons of red-and-blue tape, shrugging off patronising hugs reserved for the charitable athletes who made it to the line: I escaped. And found myself catching up with earlier identities, adventures on the Northern Sewage Outflow, the improved cycle-friendly Greenway. Heading towards Victoria Park — which more than ever now felt like a proper park, an oasis, a green lung — I finished exactly where I had found myself, forty-two years ago, at the start of my theoretical London project, when I 'ran the oracle' for a self-published book called *Lud Heat*.

'No word other than the need for it.' I came up against a war-time relic, a six-sided concrete pillbox. A pissy shrine guarding the River Lea close to the point where the old Roman Road made its original ford. All those intervening years had brought me was a better class of confusion, obfuscation, error. A misreading of signs and symbols.

I stopped. The pillbox was intact and unimproved. It survived between blocks of exposed flats and the London Stadium, the Death Star. On the wall beside the bridge, someone had sprayed a naked plea: HELP ME. I looked through one of the machine-gun slats. On the pillar at the concrete core of the bunker was the outline of a ghostly figure drawn in chalk, King Lud as Green Man. A phallic stake had been driven through his cheating heart.

Pushing into early evening on the first day of our Harold tramp, we found that familiar markers had vanished. Novelty towers in striking colours rose above the remnants of dirty industries. The old detour that once carried walkers across the tricky vortex of the Bow flyover had been replaced by a shivering pontoon walkway, on the fence of which somebody had sprayed the obvious response: EVER CHANGING WORLD. All too soon, permitted paths ran out and we were trudging down the diesel-ditch of the A102 towards the Blackwall Tunnel, tapping curbstones in the choking fug.

Odo the crow, ex-bishop, registered his disapproval of the feminising of his name by some heretical development quango: ODA (Olympic Delivery Authority) was an insult he addressed by squirting a white splat on to the saddle of a red Santander bicycle, whose spokes a kneeling David Aylward was stroking with his violin bow. The other walkers stepped aside from the path, as and when required, to leave samples of their DNA, in liquid or compost form, in bushes, under flyovers, in buckets, bins, forests. A wolf trail of steamingly pungent traces. Trousers down, skirts spread.

The long march came to an end in the Greenwich Foot Tunnel with Aylward sawing away at more bicycle wheels and Claudia busking along with a blue-chinned, floppy-haired guitarist of Spanish gypsy appearance, who claimed to be Italian but who struggled with the rudiments of the language. Together, they made lovely, tile-bounced music.

Returning next morning to pick up the walk at Greenwich, I became aware that most of my fellow passengers, waiting for the DLR
connection at Shadwell, were mutants. They looked like regular
Docklands *colons* – shiny shoes, decisive hair – but there was always
one element out of place. The girl in the pristine white raincoat
had sprouted a pair of crow's wings. The programmer with the pep-
pery red eyes was carrying an expensive leather satchel and a plastic
lightsaber. Morning-after party girls with rescued maquillage had
spiders' webs across their faces and goats' horns poking from freshly
airfixed heads. Yesterday, it felt like a natural extension of the terrain
when I noticed a chunky young woman in a rubber Superwoman
outfit on the platform at Turkey Street. But now every Canary Wharf
commuter was morphing into a comic-book character, a second-life
spook with no terrestrial identity. The mutants were making their
own pilgrimage, striking east to the boosted Chinese-owned badlands around ExCel London for a giant comic convention.

'Hi – Lucinda? How's Max? Still watching it?'

'No worries. No worries then.'

'My sister's friend has made 25k this year. She hasn't *physically* got
it, because the house is in Croydon.'

'There's that help to buy. I know you didn't know. Nobody knows.
That's mad. That's *insane*.'

'Dad was a retired priest. Grandma was a retired dentist. She loves
grass with lots of space. And I don't love any of that, obviously.'

I waited for the Kötting troop in Greenwich in the place where, a
short while later, I met a procession of refugees and their supporters
in bright blue T-shirts coming down the Thames path, on their way
from Canterbury to Westminster. David Herd, poet and Professor
of Modern Literature at the School of English, University of Kent,
organised two of these summer walks, 'staged in solidarity with refugees, asylum seekers and immigrant detainees'. In June 2015, they
followed the old Pilgrims' Way. 'The principal aim,' Herd said, 'was
to counter the silence surrounding indefinite immigration detention
and in the process to call for the practice to be stopped.'

In silence I waited in a pub on the Pilgrims' Way for the first arrivals on that original cross-country walk. They were headed from
Canterbury, along the North Downs to Crawley, near Gatwick
Airport, to the centre where many of them had been detained,
without explanation or any hope of resolution for their claims.
More walkers, from villages on the route, after engaging with the
stories told by the refugees and the writers who travelled with
them, joined the march, which was unreported in the mainstream
media. In silence I tried to gather my thoughts for the moment
when, after they had eaten and rested, the refugees would suffer a
talk from a stranger, who was not going on with them. A talk to
be endured by innocent locals sitting outside with their pints and
travellers who had broken their journey, tempted by an heraldic
pub sign and decent car park.

Fired by the accounts I heard, the laws that changed with every
shift in public opinion, the years of court appearances, delays, depri-
vations, I launched into something, trying to respect Herd's conceit
of the Chaucerian tale shared with a random company covering the
ground between the city (and their old lives) and the cathedral. As
I spoke, I felt myself splitting: the words sounded sincere, heartfelt,
but they were faint echoes of what I had heard and what I would
not hear, never hear, by stepping away to return to London and the
book on which I was working. One self – better or more deceived?
– headed for the Downs, the track the refugees had already covered:
to walk, alone, to Canterbury. This was the self that had already taken
the decision to break off the attempt to write about the condition
of London. This was a borrowed identity, a self I have called 'Norton'
in various fictions: a prisoner of London's gravity, free to venture
through time.

Now, waiting again in Greenwich for the second refugee expedition – I am always early, always nosing about – the fantasy of escape,
as I had recently confirmed on the Kötting march to the south
coast, was undone. I would be carried to Deptford, Bermondsey,
Southwark, the centre of things, by this mass of blue T-shirted pilgrims and their bright-eyed, foot-foundered sympathisers.

All these walks intersected, east to west, north to south, at Greenwich. David Aylward drummed incessantly. Claudia sang her melancholy songs of defeat and love-beyond-the-grave. Jem Finer, who dealt in recordings intended to run for a thousand years, gathered up acoustic footsteps to process on his computer. The refugees did not drum or sing, but their walk, by the hard miles achieved, the nights sleeping on schoolroom floors, became much more than a worthy concept. I was a tourist among them, covering ground where my fictional self, Norton, began his career, by eavesdropping on the murder of Christopher Marlowe.

'Norton wants to be out on the river. Wants to be free of London, all the trash of history. Voices, whispers, busking ghosts, comic-strip chimeras.' Ground over which the Canterbury pilgrims walk and re-walk their stories.

We were heading for St Mary's Church in Deptford, the grave of the Pacific islander, Prince Lee Boo, brought to London as an exotic import, left to die. David Herd's brochure said: 'Reports on Detention and prison work. Eyewitness accounts of Greece and the Calais jungle. Free vegetarian lunch.' I fell into conversation with a man from Ghana who said that he had never learned to type, but that he was applying for a job as a computer programmer at the University of Greenwich. There are around eighty walkers, one for every mile they have covered. Herd, with a smile, tells me that yesterday's march from Gravesend felt like being transported into 'a post-Brexit *Downriver*'. There are new Silbury Hill mounds on our path, bad public art, viewing platforms to showcase Canary Wharf and a willed destruction of the old ley lines, sightlines, paths of desire.

Before I perform again, in a small park, I listen to a Tamil deportee, trapped for sixteen years in legal process, held in limbo on £35 a week, which is restricted to a card that can only be used in certain approved stores. But he is calm, resigned, and he will not give up the ghost. They bring out a birthday cake for a man brave enough to blow the whistle on a gang of people traffickers.

★★★

Those future memories are with me, as much as the stories I am telling Claudia about gardening days in Limehouse, as we climb towards the statue of General Wolfe on Greenwich Hill. David pointed out areas where ancient trees had been lost in preparing the ground for the equestrian events of the London Olympics. He claimed distant blood kinship with Wolfe, the man who introduced freemasonry into North America. And he told us to experience, at this notable viewpoint, the surge of energy from the ley line running down the broad avenue from Blackheath.

We detoured to take in a set of rough mounds that our guide glossed as Iron Age earthworks, set beside an established trackway. When he struck up on the drum, security moved in. The two officers, one male, one female, were sufficiently impressed by David's antiquarianism to allow the troop free passage; to play on, with muffled discretion, while the park guardians lockstepped out of earshot. We celebrated by positioning Claudia, in her wedding weeds, in the sunken bath reserved for queens of England. The red rose tattoo on the inside of her right wrist, swollen with resting blood, came to life and sprouted in a bangle of thorns.

We had crossed the river, come far enough from Harold's Essex tomb for the battlefield dead, down by the coast, to decide how they would channel our marchers. The warrior king insinuated his cussed stubbornness of purpose – always moving, always plotting – beneath Andrew's felt helmet. Claudia was the lament of Edith Swan-Neck, ensuring that councils of itinerant males respected her status and her saintly afterlife: 'All this, a medewe wete with dropes celestyall.' David's lineage went back much further than Wolfe, to the minstrel Taillefer, the juggling swordsman who rode out in front of the Norman army to spill his *Chanson* and mock the enemy.

Brief acknowledgement having been made, as we passed over Blackheath, to Wat Tyler and the Peasants' Revolt (war taxes, inequitable governance), we picked up the pace, and reversed the journey of the disaffected 1381 rebels by marching towards Kent. Saturday morning coffee sippers, alfresco on the narrow pavements of Blackheath Village, looked askance at this unmannerly intervention of freakishly dressed individuals grouped around a deserted bride, without proper charitable accreditation, robotically following the drumbeat of the man in the orange jumpsuit.

Suburbs unspooled into ribbon-development respectability. Parks and proud oases around persistent rivers like the Quaggy broke the tedium of our advance on Chislehurst. Somewhere in the neurasthenic tranquillity of Bromley, a French woman, with whom Andrew engaged in rapid-fire Franglais banter, was holding a garage sale in her front garden. I came away with a bag of three-legged cows and genetically modified sheep, pigs, bears, elephants and albino tigers, to populate the abandoned garages and unoccupied Euro-funded farms I'd already scavenged from the Hackney streets for my grandchildren. And for myself, I couldn't resist a toy that might have charmed André Breton: the severed head of a fox, to which had been grafted a pair of binoculars. By tweaking the beast's right ear, it was possible to view a carousel of surrealist images. A generic Alpine scene of transhumance. A *Judex* figure in a catacomb much like the Greenwich Foot Tunnel. The post-apocalyptic North Downs as barren as the Sahara. A dog with floppy ears against a night sky. A farm hut surrounded by sinister canisters. Three figures gathered around a grave. I — of course — interpreted the sequence as a pre-vision of our walk. Andrew reckoned it was a marketing spin-off from Roald Dahl's *Fantastic Mr Fox*. Closer inspection revealed that the merchandise had been produced in China for the McDonald's burger franchise.

The walk became personal, an exercise in edited autobiography for our captain. The past, which he can butt against but not improve, makes him melancholy. 'One can imagine everything, predict most things,' Andrew said, 'save how low we can all sink. My outward movement is indeed a return to the now with potent hindsight.' He reminisced about family and a runaway brother who slept rough in the holly bushes beside a pond — while we feasted on preserved beetroot balls and miniature pork pies, and dribbled over Co-op cheeses and tubs of messy coleslaw.

Here was the school in which the sturdy infant Kötting pulled himself up to the window to gaze on his first love, the Mary Joyce of his immortal longings: a never-aging sprite called Philippa Wells. Here were his primitive initials gouged in redbrick in a prescient gesture of artistic vandalism. Here was the sturdy oak where he buried the placenta of his beloved daughter. 'In the years since I have come back to it,' Andrew said, 'the tree has grown to become part of me. It is held together by memories, even as I am falling apart.' He shed a single tear. Lost, for a breath or two, in former times, he clutched a reproduction whalebone box containing a model of the embracing Harold and Edith from the Bulverhythe plinth. A trickle of blood ran down Kötting's self-wounded cheek, as if he had been scratched by the painted thorn on Claudia's wrist.

The second day's tramp ended at a busy roundabout at Green Street Green, on the edge of Orpington, with a hallucinatory lurch into a tease of country lanes that carried us back, after thirty minutes' slog, to a point twenty yards from where we'd started. Already I could hear the hissing derision of the M25 as it subverted the Pilgrim's Way.

The only VOTE REMAIN placard I'd registered in this phoney-war period was back in Hackney, propped against the head of Buddha in the basement window of a Victorian villa. The only BRITAIN STRONGER IN EUROPE sticker was pasted on a green recycling bin at the end of my road.

Leaving the peaceful village church at Chevening behind, a necessary detour to pay our respects to the memorial stones for Andrew's father (subject of his *Deadad* project), and his paternal grandparents, we ran up against the first major white-on-red VOTE LEAVE board. It was propped against a rustic fence like a border warning. When we processed over the multiple lanes of unseeing M25 traffic, we were committing ourselves to another country. Jem's cart bleeped a warning as it bounced over the uneven surface. There were hard uphill miles ahead to the Sackville park at Knole. Anonymous Bosch found a shop selling gluten-free cakes with which to celebrate his birthday. Andrew encouraged children in the care of a distinctly Europhile young woman in a grey Jean-Luc Godard *Masculin Féminin* sweat-shirt to make felt-tip additions to the primitive art on his baggy suit.

With the dappled acres of Knole, deer lying in the cool shadows of oak avenues blatantly tarting for heritage TV serials, long straight paths, and the descent by tangled hollow way to Samuel Palmer's visionary Underriver, we became fugitive figures in a particular kind of English pastoral. Footpaths opened up without the blessing of our various and contradictory maps. We meandered by quiet fields, groves of flopping gunnera, remnants of haunted woodland, into the outskirts of Tonbridge.

In the golden hour, we emerged alongside Tonbridge School, where the privileges of private education were demonstrated by immaculate cricket pitches that rivalled anything in the professional game. Delivering a talk at this school, back in 2015, I was astonished not only by the well-equipped theatre and the boutique studio in which an interview was filmed, but by the precocious intelligence of 15-year-old pupils who had taken the trouble to read my books before the event.

Between Tonbridge and Tunbridge Wells, we cut across the devas-tation of deadline-abused road improvement schemes and through buttercup meadows in which Claudia might have been expected to break out with a life-enhancing aria from *The Sound of Music*. But, as the musty breath of Edith is cold on her neck, she sings of loss: husband, lord, land. 'We'll sing for your soul, these evil days.'

Our joshing, jaunty walk darkened beneath the rounded redbrick arches of the 1845 Southborough railway viaduct, where a legend in purple capitals had been sprayed: JACK DAVIS GOT RAPPED UNDER THIS BRIDGE. Had Jack been the subject of a boastful sexual assault? Or had he been rapped at by ravers, tortured with loops of disco banality familiar to Guantánamo detainees?

Soon afterwards our footpath disappeared into a deserted farm from which there was no obvious exit. Even the convex roadside mirror marking a dangerous bend had been stolen, leaving a dull pewter shield. NO LIVESTOCK WILL BE ACCEPTED DIRTY!!! The sheds and outhouses stank of slaughter. We found a pen of sheep crammed together, bleating helplessly, untended, in an open barn. We splashed through puddles of blue disinfectant and yellow shit. A point of absolute confusion: beyond the city and far from the shore. 'London was, but is no more.'

Royal Tunbridge Wells is taken as the exemplar of a certain strand of spa-town respectability. We felt its undisguised hostility. Our access road trenched through a yawn of car showrooms and fore-courts in which gleaming vehicles were penned as close as the sheep. MOTORLINE: BUSINESS AS USUAL. Waxed Skodas come with a self-satisfied number plate: APPROVED.

The uphill miles of colonised estates to be negotiated before we struck out for Wadhurst, with David in the vanguard, drumming for his life on blind corners, had been freshly planted with bungalows struggling for air like those shrublings in tubes beside new bypass schemes: a cardinal procession of VOTE LEAVE signs. A rally for the not-so-silent majority. When I paused to photograph our knackered troop, on their dumb crocodile ascent, with one of the scarlet signs in the foreground, a large lady shot from her house to warn me off. Her discreet advertisement, the size of the widest pub-screen TV, was not intended for unapproved consumption. It stood on private property. How she and her shaven-headed partner, hovering with menace in the doorway, intended to vote was their own affair. I had misunderstood the sign's function. It was an order: *fuck off*.

At the summit of the slope, more signs loomed over brutally bar-bered privet. They twinkled like the boasts of estate agents out of picture-book English gardens. *Peter and Jane Explain Brexit*.

David's drumming never faltered, the bride never missed her step, but the road into Wadhurst was the longest mile and a half I have ever encountered. We were encouraged by the friendly interest taken in our expedition, and especially Claudia's part in it, by the cooks and waiters who congregated outside an Indian restaurant. They were quite prepared to follow in our wake with trays of takeaway curry. More than any of the disgruntled – and, so they felt, disenfranchised – native villagers (retirees from city and colonies), the tandoori chefs recognised our ritual intent, a last-ditch celebration of eccentricity; the wedding procession to the battlefield, before a divorce from reality.

There were more adventures ahead, and many more red hoardings of uniform dispensation in the tidy hamlets of Kent and East Sussex. This election would be a close-run affair, with Scots and metropolitans slanting one way and the rest, stirred by tabloid-inspired visions of unlicensed immigrant hordes, Magna Carta liberties lost to faceless European bureaucrats, opting out. This time the Normans were going to lose: Brexit meant Brexit. Nobody, apart perhaps from Odo the crow, knew where we were going or how long it would take to get there. But we all smelt meat on the smoke. Our throats were red with dust. Whichever way the plebiscite falls for plebs, peasants, drones, rentiers, bishops and bottlemen, *we can't leave this place*. We can't revise the human contract. There is no small print. 'The croaking of ravens at their feast,' Claudia sang. 'In thousands they lay, corpses mangled and torn. One of them yours.'

The site of Harold's fatal battlefield was still in dispute. Andrew tried to muster enthusiasm for a group portrait on a busy roundabout that flattered some recent advocacy for Senlac Hill. Now we understood how wrecked those shield-locking warriors must have been, after a forced march to York and back. The military commanders, the piratical Godwinson siblings and their allies, rode between engagements, and then parked the horses.

We were welcomed into the single-street tourist town by a yellow AA sign offering: BOWS, ARROWS & BATTLE TACTICS. After protracted mobile-phone negotiations, we were given permission to round off our expedition with a photograph at Harold's other monument, inside the grounds at Battle Abbey. Escaping from a lavishly stocked giftshop, we were confronted by a flustered female official who immediately withdrew the original offer. The commemorative slab was covered in tarpaulin, scaffolding was in evidence. English

Heritage do not permit images of scaffolding. Many of the other buildings were also forbidden, while restoration work took place.

Odo cackled. Odo preened. 'And Crow yawned – long ago / He had picked that skull empty.' I wedged him on a stick and he bestrode the hill of slaughter like the triumphant symbol of a Roman legion. The crow was the Geiger counter for the ionized radiation of this bloody shambles. He could sniff out a succulent eyelid at fifty paces. He preached merciless annihilation in his best dog Latin.

The black negation of the crow. The distressed white of the bereaved bride tasked with assembling the scattered limbs of her husband and lover. The silenced troubadours.

Hopelessly lost, challenged in our communal identity and purpose by acceptance of the coming horror, we straggled over the battlefield, where no physical evidence of battle was ever found. Harold, I concluded, was an Anglo-Saxon Osiris, his body parts distributed across the country. Some said he was buried under a cairn of stones at the shoreline. A mound on which, Viking fashion, Duke William climbed to assert his sovereignty. Bosham laid claim to assorted limbs and Waltham Abbey took the head: a peeled autopsy skull-lantern with lidless eyes. Later legends had the king surviving the battle and living out the rest of his days as an anchorite in Chester.

According to the *Dr Who Annual* for 1985, Harold was healed of his wounds. He took on the convenient identity of Hereward the Wake in order to fight a guerrilla campaign against paperless invaders. According to Alan Moore, in a speculative essay called 'Wake the Dead', published for Arts Lab Northampton, Harold is 'a barebones signifier of resistance'. The sacrificed hero tried on many masks. 'He can be everyone.' Including a Fenland Straw Bear. A felt-capped performance artist. Boris Johnson. Nigel Farage. Or a carved lump of weathered marble in the corner of a municipal park, between the toilets and the bowling green.

A Siberian wind nips as we circle the sculpture of Harold and Edith Swan-Neck in St Leonards, before laying out our battered tributes: the whalebone box, the roadside chaplets of native weeds

and fox bones. I notice, as I push against the breeze on the promenade, that the laminated map of Normandy, which stood for
years decorating a car park and tempting us across the Channel,
has been removed in a gesture of intent, leaving nothing but two
bare posts.

A few days later we heard that three Iranian men had been rescued
by the border force vessel HMC *Seeker* just off Hastings. 'The group
will now be processed,' a spokesman said.

But this is just the beginning of our understanding of what we are
giving up. We are moving into an era of strategic postponements,
professional obfuscations and six-figure-salaried providers of coun-
ter-narratives. Politicians are falling on their rubber swords. David
Cameron, who believed in setting policy by the whims of public
opinion, has been undone by that public's perversity. He's gone,
Cotswolded into a premature afterlife of well-rewarded speechmak-
ing. Boris Johnson, who believes in himself, and nothing but himself
(VOTE LEAVE), and who championed Brexit to see if he could, is
now Foreign Secretary. Teresa May (or May Not), whose rise was as
subtle as John Major in drag, is giving nothing away: as slowly as she
can. A Schrödinger cat, simultaneously living and dead, May is the
form mistress of equivocation. She staggers into a booby-trapped
future on unsuitable heels, trying to keep the political agenda to serious topics: expensive leather trousers (her own) versus the designer
handbags (of her critics). The real story, we now know, votes being
counted and recriminations begun, is called THE SIX PROUD
WALKERS.

There were six of us on the road. But the road doesn't stop in
Hastings. And it doesn't vanish into the sea.

In the teeth of the Brexit news, we were travelling on, by crawling
backwards down what Alan Moore locates as a psychic trench between
Northampton and London. It was agreed among us, journey done,
that we should bring the bones of our story to the Northampton cave
in which Moore produced all those books that became films that put
legions of protesters and occupiers on the streets of the world's cities

in *V for Vendetta* masks. Unmoving, steady in purpose, Alan was a growling, chuckling analogue oracle. 'I believe politics must always be driven by culture, not the other way round,' he said.

Just as the Vegetative Buddha of Haggerston Park locks the gravity of London by staying still on his bench through the hours of daylight, so Alan Moore appears to anchor England's centre, and the centre of that centre, with the steadiness of purpose of the sculptural West Marina Harold staring up at the Pleiades. The myth of the 1066 walk therefore begins at its ostensible point of dissolution: a dripping Northampton garden, with Claudia Barton's Edith poised between two men making smoky linguistic loops around the vanishing subject.

That night, 22nd June 2016, in the darkness before the dull, numbed morning of the referendum, the London sky tore and split with lightning strokes and running fire. 'Man's nature cannot carry the affliction nor the fear.'

Alan Moore builds a thousand-page novel, *Jerusalem*, from the matter of Britain. Men, afflicted by angels, hang on chimney pots and women give birth on the cobbles. King Harold can be butchered and scattered, or buried under pebbles beside the sea. Or he can continue in a parallel universe, resurrected as Hereward the Wake. In which character he burns witches in their towers and fights a giant bear. The creature returns, on the end of a rope, attached to the mad poet John Clare. And now the Fen monster, this sticky heap of mud and twigs, the Straw Bear of Whittlesey, must be put to the torch. Reborn to suffer again. To dance with blackface mummers in boots and skirts.

Hereward's wake is also Finnegans: his name on grey stone along-side the grave of James Joyce's daughter Lucia in the Northampton cemetery where we stood in the rain.

Alan Moore sees Hereward as another mad old ranter on the streets shouting at cars. And Joyce agrees. His own undead Harold from *Finnegans Wake* raves about how he is condemned to be part of an eternal cycle of Williams killing Harolds and Harolds firing their arrows into the eyes of royalty in private forests.

In the dripping Northampton garden, we sit in line to contemplate Moore's conceit of the doughnut of time. A magician's circle burnt in smouldering butts in the carpet around his chair. He scratches his beard and introduces the notion of Six Proud Walkers from the timeless folk song, *Green Grow the Rushes, O*. 'Much corrupted and often obscure… An unusual mixture of Christian catechesis, astro-nomical mnemonics, and what may be pagan cosmology.' *Six for six proud walkers*. The prophet Ezekiel speaks of six men with swords come to slaughter the people, whose leaders have filled the land with violence.

'Following the witch, the princess and the monstrous bear,' Moore writes, 'he disappears down urchin-tunnels in the undergrowth

311

and ducks into the English dreamtime; becomes one with the re-membered landscape, fuses with its chalk giants and its swerving, street-drinking Tom Cobley songlines, joins the nine bright shiners and the six proud walkers.'

It took this digression to Northampton to identify our troop as nothing more than one verse from an English folk song. As David drummed and the tired but elated pilgrims circled the marble ef-figies in the municipal garden, those six proud walkers – Kötting, Barton, Finer, Bosch, Aylward, Sinclair – fused into a communal ring, a dance feeding back into the fading memory of itself. Before cold Belgian beers on the damp stone, opposite a white hotel, where the triumphant Duke William first dined. Our particle exchange is accomplished, the trench dug. 'One is one and all alone / And ever-more shall be so.'

I watched the remorseless waves for three days. I couldn't bring my-self to return to London, which was now a city abolished, set against the rest of the land. The stained-glass window of St Leonard, with red bus, Shoreditch Church and chained sinner, to which I had been led by the damaged man on the bench in Haggerston Park, had ex-tended a line of desire to this speculative coastal resort; to a building like a concrete boat, to St Leonards-on-Sea. The right place to be in receipt of bad news, to process the unthinkable.

Seeing no way out, after discussions with Andrew Kötting, who was keeping his own demons in check, and massaging wounds from earlier skirmishes, I decided on a walk with no halts, no respite, St Leonards-on-Sea to Canterbury: dawn to dusk, day through night, through day again. This pilgrimage had been hovering for a long time. Canterbury, where I had a connection at the university, prided itself on its outward vision, its lively Parisian campus. Would that now be lost?

Slumped against the concrete of the sea wall, I let my fatalistic reverie wind back to the start, the decision to follow wherever the Vegetative Buddha's eyes would have carried him, if he had been capable of lifting his burdened head. The nunnery. Then Hackney Road. I tracked the brash retail signage of this local border, realising that our future had been in plain sight all along, going east from the trader offering FRIENDSHIP VEGAN SHOES. With the suggestion that, if we became peckish on our coastal tramp, we could always eat our footwear.

The shops of Hackney Road underwrote the present debate: PURE WHITE ACCESSORIES (WHOLESALE). EURO CATERING. DECENT INTERNATIONAL LIMITED (JUST BAGS). GREEDY COW (INDIAN). *RICH*DEMOLITION UK. They dominated established immigrants like Litvinoff & Fawcett, dealers in pine cupboards and chests, bespoke beds and artisan tables.

By choice, we had picked the worst of days to launch our final excursion: cold and wet, with the promise of worse to follow. We took the slippery coast path, sweating up and down numerous muddy steps, blocked by fallen trees, before dropping to rocks where, in season, leathery nudists basked like seals. Then on, through scattered settlements losing their gardens to the sea, past salt-glazed, picture-windowed hideaways for weekend celebrities, until we reached that triumph of paranoid engineering, the military canal excavated from the marshes to keep out Napoleon. Proud Rye squatted on its cobbled toy-town hillock like a fat hen on a nest of pebbles. Traders celebrated the withdrawal of the English Channel. And did their best to exploit, with antiques and tea rooms, the grudging Cinque Port status granted when New Romney silted up.

We would draw in the beads on the necklace of the Cinque Ports – Hastings, New Romney, Hythe – before coming across country, by moonlight, or the luminescence of the battlefield dead, to Canterbury. Andrew had his bone to pick with the cathedral city after another headlong stumble. To keep our non-stop, Trappist walk interesting, he had twisted an ankle, and repeated it, while wrestling with disobedient planks of wood, before falling into his area at home. And this on his already ruined leg: the one ripped, shinbone to groin, in the motorcycle accident on Old Kent Road.

'I folded the ankle in half,' he said. He was reduced, without complaint, to hopping, hobbling, and occasionally crawling, like Beckett's

Unnamable, through bogs, across shingle, nettles, tarmac, bullock-patrolled fields and caravan parks. He never repined. He gloried in the pain. 'I had better exist.'

It was too late for the ossuary. But we had visited it before, testing the legend that bones gathered up from the field of battle, after the slaughter of Harold and his army, had been deposited in a Norman church at Hythe. Like trophies of a cannibal lord. Or worse. Skulls shelved in arched bays, a thousand or so, stamped with black numbers; trepanned, spade-damaged, lacking mandibles. Biting wood. The immense coins of their hollow black sockets confronting our future gaze.

The charnel house was established, an attraction on the Canterbury pilgrim route, from defleshed, separated bones rescued from cemeteries, plague pits, or sites of massacre, according to speculative theory. More females than males, a small proportion having died from blows to the head. The collection, it is now thought, began in the thirteenth century.

My first visit, accompanied by Anna, was a detour from a drive to Folkestone, a lunch on the harbour: so all those chattering diners, happy families, hopeful couples, business associates, were badged by mortality. Every mouthful taken dropped from a missing lower jaw. It was impossible to dissociate the theatre of the skulls, so tactfully laid out by size and shape on their church shelves, with living images from recent conflicts.

When a study was conducted in 1908, to determine the cephalic index, the ratio of maximum breadth to maximum length, in order to discover the origin of these mute relics, it was found that a 'significant number' were of Italian origin; from the Roman port at Lympne or other sites of trade with mainland Europe.

The Hythe church was a halt on the way to the grave of Saint Thomas à Becket, for pilgrims from *beyond our shores*. As another Beckett, Sam, endured a few weeks at the Hotel Bristol in Folkestone, so that he could establish English residence before his marriage to Suzanne Déchevaux-Dumesnil, his companion in those bitter years of war. The tramping and the turnips. In a postcard sent to his friend Avigdor Arikha in Paris, Beckett reported that '*Sang coule plus calme dans la ville de Harvey.*' Blood, he joked, did its duty, circulating in the fashion prescribed by William Harvey – years after the medical pioneer left Folkestone for London.

Beckett circulated too: Hastings, Rye, Canterbury. He road-tested our pedestrian tramp in his *Deux Chevaux*. The Irish playwright tinkered with *Happy Days* and lusted after the state of invisibility achieved, in speculative fiction, by HG Wells. Wells, curiously enough, relocated to the Folkestone area in 1896, taking a small furnished property in Sandgate, before finding Spade House, with its commanding view and proximity to a water-powered lift to the Leas: the precise site of the now demolished hotel where Beckett propped up the bar. And counted out his small cigars. *The Invisible Man* was serialised in *Pearson's Weekly* in 1897 and published as a novel the same year.

The world tilted. And we clung on by our fingernails. Climbing, we needed crampons. The older Hythe of period houses and narrow twisting lanes had us leaning back, supported by cushions of hot air. The charnel house was closed for the night, but the waxy glow of the skulls seeped under the heavy door. I registered the name of the church: *St Leonard's*. Our occulted triangle was now complete: Haggerston, Hastings (West), Hythe.

In the church porch, where we dragged ourselves for shelter, was a stained-glass window, blooded in the light of Andrew's elevated phone app. A pamphlet I picked up spelled it out: 'There was a new spirit across the whole of Europe. Many had expected the world to end in the year 1000. Men had been holding their breath, especially after a comet was seen in 989 (it was Halley's), but God stayed his hand.' Edmund Halley, Astronomer Royal, was another lost Haggerston man. His manor house, obliterated now, was close to Haggerston Park.

The *iconic* St Leonard, left arm raised in benediction, lacks a hand. His eyes are closed in inward meditation. He does not strike off the chains of the kneeling penitent. Instead, he passes him a thick, upside-down book.

Hackney, 1975–2016.

ACKNOWLEDGEMENTS

My thanks to the pilgrims, nightwalkers and witnesses who kept these journeys alive and alarming: David Aylward, Claudia Barton, David Erdos, Jem Finer, Bradley L Garrett, Stephen Gill, David Herd, Andrew Kötting, Rachel Lichtenstein, Anthony O'Donnell (Anonymous Bosch), Chris Petit, John Rogers, Anna Sinclair, Martin Stone, Stephen Watts. And Patrick Wright in the last days of Dalston Lane. And to Effie Paleologou for her brilliant forensic analysis of my drowned portrait.

For their company, editorial insights and acts of generosity towards the project, I would like to express my gratitude to Chiara Ambrosio, Adolfo Barberá, Matthew Beaumont, Renchi Bicknell, William Bock, Peter Bush, Jorge Carríon, Sam Carter, Brian Catling, Chris and Anne Currell, Alberto Duman, Gareth Evans, Jürgen Ghebrezgiabiher, Benedetto Lo Giudice, Simon Inglis, Jeff Johnson, Jarett Kobek, Sven Koch, Laura Longrigg, Jock McFadyen, Robert Macfarlane, Stephen McNeilly, Sophie Mason, Mark Morgan, Alan Moore, Tim Noble, Bill Parry-Davies, Simon Prosser, JH Prynne, Karen Russo, Stanley Schtinter, Paul Smith, Susan Stenger, Jessica Treen, Diana Tyler, Sue Webster, Adjoa Wiredu, James Wilson, Ken Worpole.

'Digging for Victory', 'Free Breakfast for Bikes', 'Two Swimming Pools' and 'Downriver' were originally published, in very different forms, under different titles, in *The London Review of Books*. My thanks to the editor and commissioner of these pieces, Jean McNicol.

Some of the WG Sebald material, in an earlier version, was published as a limited edition, '*Austerlitz* & After: Tracking Sebald', by Test Centre in 2013. My thanks to Jess Chandler and Will Shutes.

Elements of 'Pigeon Fishing', in earlier form, were published in

2014, as part of the collection *Park Notes*, edited by Sarah Pickstone.

An earlier account of the 'Brexit Means Brexit' march to the coast was produced in 2016 by Andrew Kötting as part of *Edith (The Chronicles)*, a collaboration by the six walkers and others. This illustrated record, with pinhole portraits, maps and recordings, was published by Badbloodandsibyl.

My thanks to the authors who have allowed me to quote from the following works: *The Great Fire of London* (Hamish Hamilton, 1982) by Peter Ackroyd, *Nightwalking: A Nocturnal History of London, Chaucer to Dickens* (Verso, 2015) by Matthew Beaumont, *Savage Messiah* (Verso, 2011) by Laura Oldfield Ford, *i hate the internet* (Serpent's Tale, 2016) by Jarett Kobek, the *Edith* 'Songs' by Claudia Barton and Andrew Kötting (2016), *On Brick Lane* (Hamish Hamilton, 2007) and *Estuary* (Hamish Hamilton, 2016) by Rachel Lichtenstein, *The Nine of Diamonds* (Bloodaxe Books, 2016) by MacGillivray, *Heligoland* (Jonathan Cape, 2003) by Shena Mackay, *Jerusalem* (Knockabout, 2016) and 'Wake the Dead' by Alan Moore, *Austerlitz* (Hamish Hamilton, 2001) by WG Sebald, *Ancient Sunlight* (Enitharmon, 2014) and *Republic of Dogs / Republic of Birds* (Test Centre, 2016) by Stephen Watts, *A Journey through Ruins* (Radius, 1991) by Patrick Wright. And thanks also for permission to quote scattered sentences from B. Catling, David Erdos, the estate of David Gascoyne, James Sallis and Will Self. And to Effie Paleologou and Anonymous Bosch for permission to use their photographs.

INDEX